THAMES VALLEY PAPISTS

from
Reformation
to
Emancipation

Tony Hadland

Contents

Foreword

This book is one that many have considered writing but were daunted by the task, so it is a great triumph for Tony Hadland that he has drawn together the recusant history of the Thames Valley.

It is a story about people and the sacrifices that they were prepared to make. Today it is interesting to reflect on just how many of us would be willing to make a similar stand. This is the age of protest and demonstration, when rights are regarded as all important, but the story of those difficult times illustrates that loyalty and acceptance of hardships are courageous qualities, worthy of our admiration.

In future, local history will be incomplete without some reference to, or understanding of, the basic facts that Tony Hadland has brought together for the first time in this book. It is interesting too to realise that, due to the need for secrecy, it was impossible to record much of the early history in writing. Indeed, what was recorded was usually the high drama of discovery, which leads us to imagine how much similar activity was never detected.

I was very pleased to be asked to write this foreword and I have been fascinated by the wealth of information that has been collected and so well presented in this book. Although I was familiar with much of the detail, I have learnt the answer to other queries that have puzzled me in the past. I feel sure that the book will intrigue many in the Thames Valley, including of course those who live in the houses and villages that are featured.

Those to whom this is a new and strange tale will surely be struck by the tolerance that was shown throughout by good neighbours - no matter on which side fate decreed that the participants found themselves.

John Eyston
Mapledurham House
May 1991

Introduction

This book tells the story of the Catholics of the Thames Valley from Henry VIII's break with Rome until Catholic Emancipation nearly three hundred years later.

The area covered consists of pre-1974 Berkshire, southern Oxfordshire and part of south Buckinghamshire. It includes the valleys of Thames tributaries such as the Kennet, Pang, Loddon and Thame, the former great forests of Windsor and Bernwood, the southern Chiltern Hills, the Berkshire Downs, the Vale of White Horse and Ot Moor.

Before the Reformation virtually all English people were Catholics. Although most eventually abandoned Catholicism, a tiny minority remained loyal to the old faith, despite social pressures and the attempts of the authorities to make them conform to Anglicanism. In the Thames Valley the proportion that remained Catholic eventually dropped to about one in a hundred. However, among the gentry the proportion was very much higher. Indeed, it is said that in the south Oxfordshire Chilterns almost one in three of the gentry remained Catholic.

After the Reformation the Thames Valley was neither one of the strongest nor weakest areas of Catholic survival. There were generally too few Catholics to have much influence on their Protestant neighbours. But in some locations there were enough Catholics with good leadership to constitute effective communities. That leadership was usually provided by a Catholic squire, from whose manor house a Catholic priest could exercise his ministry, sometimes at great personal risk.

In Tudor times, just as today, the Thames Valley straddled the great routes from London to the West. It was already becoming a commuter area. Merchants and professionals from London and other parts of the country found the many small estates ideal as country residences, within easy reach of the capital. But the Thames Valley was also home to families who had lived there for centuries.

The people who remained loyal to Catholicism were drawn from both groups. Their little-known story is full of interest and often closely mirrors events of national significance. Many of the places they knew still exist.

The first three chapters of this book set the scene by explaining how Christianity came to the Thames Valley, by briefly examining the Lollard legacy, and by describing the importance of the Thames as a transport route. The remainder of the book tells the story of the Thames Valley Catholics chronologically from 1534 to 1829.

The book is based primarily on published sources, a full list being provided in Appendix B. The research began in earnest in June 1988 and the final draft was completed in July 1991.

The principal libraries used were the Guildhall Library in the City of London, the Local Studies Section of Reading Central Library, and the monastic library of Douai Abbey at Upper Woolhampton, Berkshire. Many of the houses and sites referred to in the book were visited, including a number not normally open to the public.

All the illustrations are by the author. Most show the buildings as they are today, but those of Shiplake Court, Swyncombe House, Hendred House, Greys Court and Shirburn Castle are based on old engravings. The author also researched and drew the location maps.

Although the author is a Catholic much of the impetus for the book came from his wife Rosemary Hadland, a member of the Church of England. The book is therefore dedicated to her in gratitude for her support.

The author also wishes to thank the many people acknowledged in Appendix A, who aided his research in ways great and small.

Conventions Adopted

England did not adopt the modern calendar until 1 January 1752. Until then the new year began on Lady Day, 25 March. Hence what we would call 13 February 1690 was known to the people of the time as 13 February 1689. That date can therefore be described as 13 February 1689/90, or 13 February 1689 Old Style, or 13 February 1690 New Style. For the sake of simplicity all dates quoted in this book are New Style.

The county boundaries observed are those that existed at the time. Hence Wantage is referred to as a Berkshire town, Caversham as an Oxfordshire village.

All spellings have been modernised. Different spellings of the same surname have been standardised where this avoids confusion. For example, Hildesley is the standard form adopted for the many 16th century variants of that name.

Where the same Christian name was used by successive generations of a family, a suffix has sometimes been added, e.g. William Wollascott IV. Such suffixes are merely devices used by historians for the sake of clarity and were not used by the individuals themselves.

Approximate present-day equivalents have been quoted for all monetary values referred to in this book. These equivalents are derived from 1989 data supplied by the Bank of England.

Distances quoted are approximate and 'as the crow flies', unless otherwise indicated.

The dates in parentheses under chapter titles identify the principal periods covered. Therefore, for example, the dates under the heading 'Charles I' do not cover his whole reign, his latter years being covered by the next chapter.

The expression 'parish church', when describing a building after 1558, refers to a church used for Anglican worship. The term 'Catholic' is used in its commonly understood sense of Roman Catholic.

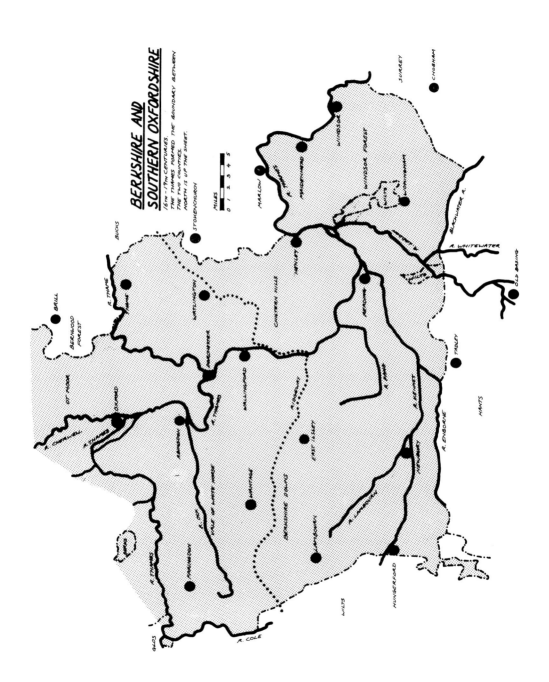

BERKSHIRE AND
SOUTHERN OXFORDSHIRE

16TH - 17TH CENTURIES
THE THAMES FORMED THE BOUNDARY BETWEEN
THE TWO COUNTIES.
NORTH IS UP THE SHEET.

MILES
0 1 2 3 4 5

BRILL
BERNWOOD FOREST
BUCKS
R. THAME
Thame
OT MOOR
R. CHERWELL
OXFORD
R. THAMES
ABINGDON
R. OCK
VALE OF WHITE HORSE
FARINGDON
R. COLE
GLOS
WILTS
BERKSHIRE DOWNS
LAMBOURN
R. LAMBOURN
HUNGERFORD
NEWBURY
R. KENNET
R. ENBORNE
EAST ILSLEY
WALLINGFORD
R. THAME
WATLINGTON
CHILTERN HILLS
HENLEY
R. LODDON
READING
THATCHAM
THE KENNET
TADLEY
HANTS
STOKENCHURCH
MARLOW
R. THAMES
MAIDENHEAD
WINDSOR
WINDSOR FOREST
BLACKWATER R.
R. WHITEWATER
OLD BASING
SURREY
CHOBHAM

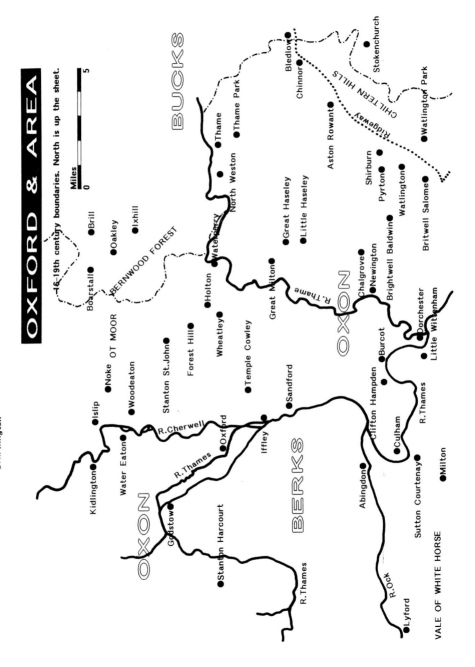

OXON

R.Thames

●Buscot

Buckland●

Faringdon●

VALE OF WHITE HORSE

Abingdon●

Gt.Coxwell●

●Little Coxwell

Lyford●

R.Ock

R.Thames

R.Cole

West Hanney●

Sutton Courtenay●

Denchworth●

Steventon●

●Milton

Sparsholt●

Wantage●

West Hendred●

●East Hendred

Compton Beauchamp●

Letcombe Regis●

Lockinge●

●Ashbury

Letcombe Bassett●

Ridgeway

BERKSHIRE DOWNS

●West Ilsley

WILTS

South Fawley●

East Ilsley●

Lambourn●

●Whatcombe

●Catmore

●Brightwalton

●East Garston

●Maidencourt

Peasemore●

●Leigh Farm

●Great Shefford

R.Lambourn

Hermitage●

●Donnington

Hungerford●

Speen●

●Thatcham

Newbury●

WEST BERKSHIRE

R.Kennet

16-19th century boundaries. North is up the sheet.

KENNET VALLEY

●Enborne

Miles

0   5

R.Enborne

HANTS

R.Thame
Dorchester● ●Overy
R.Thames

Watlington●
Britwell Salome●
Ewelme● Watlington Park●
Swyncombe●

BUCKS

Fingest●

Didcot●
Wallingford● ●Crowmarsh Gifford
South Moreton●

Stonor●

Ridgeway
North Stoke●

BERKS

Bix●
Henley Park●
Ipsden● Stoke Row●
Littlestoke● Badgemore●
Moulsford● South Stoke● Greys Court●
Checkendon● Rotherfield Greys●
Woodcote● Rotherfield Peppard●
Harpsden●
Streatley● ●Goring Blount's Court●

R.Thames

●Henley

OXON

Shiplake●

BERKSHIRE DOWNS

Basildon●

Whitchurch
Hampstead Norreys● Pangbourne● Mapledurham● Dunsden●
Purley● Caversham● Sonning●
Bere Court● Purley Hall● R.Thames
Yattendon● Tidmarsh● Reading●

R.Loddon
Wilts

Wellhouse● Tilehurst● Bulmershe●
Marlston● Englefield● Coley● Whiteknights●
Bucklebury● Calcot●
R.Pang

Wilts

R.Kennet
Sindlesham●
Beenham● Sulhamstead● Burghfield●
Upper Shinfield●
●Thatcham Woolhampton● Ufton Court●
Woolhampton● Padworth●

BERKS

Aldermaston● Wokefield●
Brimpton● Wasing● Wilts●
Hyde End
R.Enborne Silchester● Finchampstead●
Tadley● Blackwater R.
Stratfield Saye●

READING & AREA

HANTS

16-19th century boundaries. North is up the sheet.

Miles
0   5

R.Loddon

R.Whitewater

Old Basing●

Lyde R.

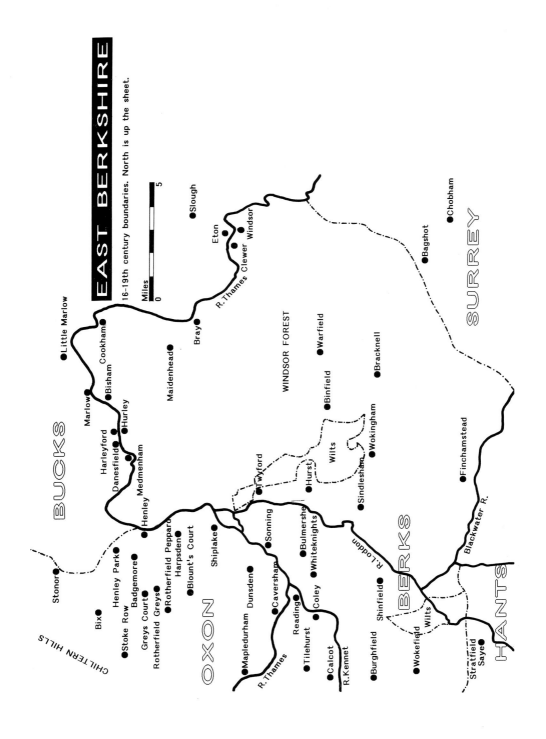

EAST BERKSHIRE

16-19th century boundaries. North is up the sheet.

Miles
0 — 5

BUCKS

OXON

SURREY

HANTS

CHILTERN HILLS

WINDSOR FOREST

BERKS

Wilts
Wilts
Wilts

R. Thames
R. Thames
R. Kennet
R. Loddon
Blackwater R.

Little Marlow
Cookham
Bisham
Marlow
Hurley
Harleyford
Danesfield
Medmenham
Henley
Stonor
Bix
Henley Park
Badgemore
Greys Court
Rotherfield Greys
Rotherfield Peppard
Harpsden
Blount's Court
Shiplake
Mapledurham
Dunsden
Caversham
Reading
Tilehurst
Calcot
Coley
Whiteknights
Bulmershe
Sonning
Twyford
Hurst
Sindlesham
Wokingham
Binfield
Warfield
Bracknell
Finchamstead
Shinfield
Burghfield
Wokefield
Stratfield Saye

Maidenhead
Bray
Eton
Clewer
Windsor
Slough
Bagshot
Chobham

R.Thames

How Christianity Came
To The Thames Valley

(3rd - 7th centuries)

Nobody knows when Christianity first reached England. According to a medieval legend, Joseph of Arimathea, who was given custody of Christ's body, built a church at Glastonbury in Somerset. Another legend tells of a British king called Lucius, who is said to have written to the Pope in the year 156 to obtain a conversion to Christianity.

Although there is little or no evidence to support these stories, it is quite possible that Christianity reached England not long after Christ's execution. At that time Britain and Judaea were both part of the Roman Empire. And the Empire's road and sea communications enabled new ideas to travel a long way fast.

By the middle of the third century Christianity had established a foothold here. This was noted by the African church father Tertullian and the Middle Eastern theologian Origen. According to the seventh century historian Bede, the Britons preserved the Christian faith until the Great Persecution instigated by the Emperor Diocletian in 303.

Ten years later the Edict of Milan gave full freedom of worship to Christians throughout the Roman Empire. This enabled three British bishops to attend a church council at Arles in France. Forty-five years later British bishops attended another council at Rimini in Italy.

The remains of what may have been a Christian basilica, built about the time of the Council of Rimini, were found at the ruined Roman city of Calleva Atrebatum, about ten miles south-west of Reading. Further evidence of early Christianity was provided in 1890, when the skeleton of a Romano-British priest, holding a pewter chalice, was discovered under London Road, Reading. And in 1988 a lead baptismal font dated to about 360 was found at Dean's Farm near Lower Caversham (formerly in Sonning parish). This font bears the chi-rho symbol which consists of the first two letters of the Greek word for Christ. (It looks like a letter P superimposed on an X.) The font is now in Reading Museum.

With the breakdown of the Roman Empire came a collapse of Church administration. The deacon Gildas, writing sometime about 540, described the chaos: 'Britain has kings, but they are tyrants ... Britain has priests, but they are madmen ...'

Sixty years later the pagan kingdom of Kent, based at Canterbury, dominated most of southern England. When the Kentish king married a Christian, the Pope saw an opportunity to reorganise the remnants of the Church in Britain. In 597 he sent a company of monks to England under the leadership of St Augustine. King Ethelbert of Kent was baptised and subsequently many of the Kentish people converted to Christianity. Canterbury, Ethelbert's base, and York, the former Roman military headquarters, became the two senior bishoprics of the Church in England.

Another generation was to pass before a papal missionary had a lasting impact on the Thames Valley. He was a Roman monk called Berin, better known by the Latin version of his name, Birinus. On the orders of the Pope, Birinus was consecrated bishop by the Archbishop of Milan. But instead of being given an existing diocese, Birinus was instructed to establish his own in a mission territory.

He therefore travelled to England in 634 and eventually reached Dorchester-on-Thames. This town, in the heart of the Thames Valley, had been an important walled settlement during the Roman occupation. It was protected by the Thames on two sides and by its tributary the Thame on another. On the banks of the Thame in 635 Birinus baptised Cynegils, king of Wessex. Every king of Wessex thereafter was a Christian, the last being Alfred the Great, the first king of England. And every English monarch after Alfred was also a Christian.

King Cynegils gave Dorchester to Birinus as his see, the base for his huge diocese which stretched from Hampshire to Yorkshire. A cathedral was built where Dorchester Abbey now stands.

Birinus died in 650 and about twenty years later the see transferred to Winchester. But in the ninth century Dorchester became a cathedral town again. This second see of Dorchester was later transferred to Lincoln. Hence the present Anglican dioceses of Winchester and Lincoln both derive from the church established by Birinus at Dorchester-on-Thames.

In the Middle Ages the body of St Birinus was widely believed to be at Winchester, where a shrine to him had long since stood. However, in the 1400s the monks of Dorchester argued that the saint's remains were at Dorchester and got the Pope's permission to open the original tomb. Claiming to have found Birinus's body, the monks built a shrine of their own in a new Lady chapel on the south side of the abbey church.

At the dissolution of the abbey in 1536 the shrine was destroyed. Many of the fragments were used to block up a Norman doorway. In the nineteenth century these pieces were rediscovered. For nearly half a century they were exhibited in the Lady chapel. Finally, in 1964 they were incorporated into a new shrine of St Birinus, designed by Russell Cox. It should be noted that this does not contain the saint's relics.

The name of Birinus or Berin lives on in the Thames Valley in a number of ways. There is Berinsfield, the modern village a mile and a half north of Dorchester, and Berinshill, the steep climb up the Chiltern Hills six miles south-east of the town. The nineteenth century Catholic church opposite Dorchester Abbey, and the twentieth century Anglican church at Calcot, near Reading are both named after him. And the local National Health Service institutions for the mentally ill comprise the St Birinus Group of Hospitals.

Perhaps his name lives on most meaningfully in the St Birinus Pilgrimage. This takes place every year on the first Sunday in July. Hundreds of people of different Christian traditions assemble at Churn Knob, a hill where Birinus is said to have preached, some seven miles south-west of Dorchester. From there they walk cross-country to the abbey for a packed and joyful united service in which local leaders of the Anglican, Catholic and Nonconformist churches take an active part.

It is somehow fitting that the saint who, 1,300 years ago, brought the Gospel from Rome to the Thames Valley, should once again be the focus for Christian unity. And it is interesting that, despite tremendous difficulties, a small group of Christians in and around Dorchester remained loyal to Rome even after the Church of England rejected the authority of the Pope.

L o l l a r d   I n f l u e n c e

(1382 onwards)

From the time of St Birinus the Church in the Thames Valley had been free from serious religious dissent for more than 700 years. This situation was changed by an Oxford scholar and priest, John Wycliffe, who was born in the year 1330.

Wycliffe questioned almost every aspect of Catholic doctrine and practice. Most significantly, he argued that the Bible is the sole authority for the doctrine and practice of the Church. This contrasted with the Catholic position that the Bible should be interpreted in the light of Church tradition stretching back unbroken to the time of the Apostles.

By 1382 Wycliffe's ideas had been condemned by the Church. But he was not excommunicated and was allowed to spend his last years as parish priest of Lutterworth in Leicestershire.

Wycliffe was a man of ideas rather than of actions. However, he attracted supporters of a more practical bent, particularly among the increasing numbers of literate, self-employed craftsmen and traders. He also drew discreet support from some of the gentry and nobility.

The Wycliffites formed a secret underground church and circulated handwritten copies of an unauthorised translation of the New Testament into English. Because of their need for secrecy they were said to whisper to each other. Hence they became known as Lollards, from an Old Dutch word for mumblers.

In 1389, about five years after Wycliffe's death, three Lollards were brought from Leicester to Dorchester-on-Thames to make their submission to the Church authorities. Two of them were alleged to have burned a statue of St Catherine. All three recanted.

A dozen years later the Lollards were seen as such a threat that Parliament passed anti-heresy legislation. The Act 'De Haeretico Comburendo' of 1401 introduced death by burning as the penalty for heretics who refused to recant. A period of up to forty days was allowed for recantation, and most of the Wycliffite leaders were persuaded to conform to Catholicism. Some Lollards, however, continued to operate underground in a loosely organised but often deep-rooted way. This they did for well over a century until the Reformation.

As Wycliffe had been based at Oxford it is not surprising that his ideas made some headway in the Thames Valley. One district where the Lollards became particularly well established was the Buckinghamshire Chilterns around High Wycombe, in places such as Little Missenden, Marlow, Chesham, Denham, Hughenden, Chenies and Drayton Beauchamp. In Amersham a Lollard named Richard Sanders was so influential that neighbours who informed on him were deprived of their livelihoods.

Another area where Wycliffite ideas took hold was the lower Cherwell valley north-north-west of Oxford. In the early fifteenth century William Brown, a glover from Woodstock, organised Lollards in Bladon, Hanborough, Kidlington, Kirtlington and Upper Heyford. They included a fuller, a tailor, a cooper, a carpenter, a miller and a mason.

The strength of Lollardy in these areas left two legacies after the Reformation. The first was that Catholicism tended to be particularly weak in these places. The second was a tendency on the part of the inhabitants to adopt the 'general' form of the Baptist faith, which rejected predestination, rather than the more Calvinistic 'particular' form. The underlying persistence of Lollard ideas in these communities probably owes much to their secret espousal by influential families, who outwardly conformed to Catholicism, and after the Reformation, to Anglicanism.

The legacy of a third Thames Valley Wycliffite stronghold was rather different. In the Vale of White Horse Lollards are known to have been active in Buscot, Faringdon, Abingdon, Hanney, Wantage, Steventon, East Ginge and the Hendreds. But it was in the Vale that the last Lollard rebellion was crushed in 1431. (Another rising had been suppressed seventeen years earlier.)

The rebels mustered at East Hendred and were defeated at Abingdon. This seems to have eradicated Lollardy from the Vale of White Horse. Indeed, in that area there was a relatively strong Catholic survival after the Reformation, especially in East Hendred. The influence of leading local families was certainly crucial to this survival, just as it seems to have been for the Lollards and their descendants.

The Thames Highway

(16th - 19th centuries)

During the main period covered by this book (1534-1829) the river was the principal highway of the Thames Valley area. Road transport was much less reliable, and could be from three to twelve times as expensive.

As many as 300 flat-bottomed 'Western' barges plied the river. The largest of these were four times as long as a London bus and more than twice as wide. They could carry up to 200 tons of cargo. Yet when fully laden they could operate in water little more than four feet deep.

The construction of the Western barge changed little over the centuries. The flat bottom was usually built of elm planks, three inches wide. These ran along the length of the vessel and were grooved together, the joints sealed with pitch and old rope fibres. There was a planked floor to prevent the cargo damaging the bottom of the barge.

The vessel's sides were formed of oak planks coated with pitch, and the upper edge of the hull was protected by a substantial timber rail called the gunwale. The stern was square cut and strongly constructed to support a huge rudder. Crew quarters were situated at the stern and consisted of little more than a space covered by a canvass awning. The rest of the vessel was devoted to cargo.

Whenever possible a sail was used to help propel the boat. The mast stood amidships. It was usually from the top of this that the barge would be towed.

Until the mid eighteenth century it was unusual for horses to be used for towing. Instead teams of hauliers were recruited from the dregs of society along the river valley. A heavy barge might need as many as sixty men to pull it, and the haulier gangs were feared by the more respectable Thameside residents. Only in times of drought would animals be used to augment the efforts of the hauliers. When the water level was low barges could be stranded in mud for weeks, and horses or oxen would therefore be borrowed from local farmers to try to free the vessels.

When the use of horse teams eventually became commonplace, as many as a dozen horses were used to pull a large vessel against the current. The massive tow ropes could be over 200 yards long and might weigh more than six hundredweight. They needed frequent replacement and cost the equivalent of about £500 each in today's money.

The old bridge at Henley-on-Thames posed an obstacle to navigation, being impassable by larger craft during the drier half of the year. This necessitated transferring cargoes, either to other craft, or to road transport. Wagons carrying relatively light cargoes destined for Wallingford, or further upstream, could take a short cut across the Chilterns, avoiding the long loop in the river between Wallingford and Henley. Further upstream large barges were prevented from reaching Oxford by the rocky river bed at Clifton Hampden. Their cargoes would therefore be transferred to smaller craft at Burcot, a mile or so downstream of the rocky shallows.

From 1624 onwards navigational improvements were made by the installation of more and better locks, by the digging of new channels to bypass difficult sections of river, and by the introduction of regulations to control toll charges and the operation of locks. The canalisation of one of the Thames's major tributaries, the Kennet, began in 1719. But the problems at Henley remained until the old bridge was demolished to make way for the present structure, completed in 1786.

By the early nineteenth century the river journey from Oxford to London could be completed in three and a half days. It was also possible to travel by barge from the Thames Valley to the West Country and the Midlands.

However, three years after Catholic Emancipation a committee was formed to investigate the possibility of a railway to link London and Bristol. The result was the Great Western, which operated its first public service between Reading and London in March 1840. It was the beginning of the end for the Thames as a commercial highway.

The Early Catholic Martyrs

(1534 - 1539)

Henry VIII's break with Rome produced few objectors at first. Kings had quarrelled with popes before and few of Henry's subjects were prepared to take issue with him, whatever their personal opinions. At the time most English people were broadly Catholic in outlook and, apart from the important issue of papal authority, there was little doctrinal disagreement between the King and Rome.

The two most famous men publicly to oppose the King were the Bishop of Rochester, Cardinal John Fisher, and the former Chancellor, Sir Thomas More. Both were canonised by the Pope (that is, formally declared to be saints) in 1935. Relics of both are in Hendred House at East Hendred in the Vale of White Horse.

This house, built in the late Middle Ages, is mentioned many times in this book. It is the home of the Eyston family who have always been Catholic. They are the keepers of Cardinal Fisher's ebony walking stick and Sir Thomas More's timber and silver tankard.

Henry VIII's break with Rome arose from his unsuccessful attempts to persuade the Pope to annul his marriage to Catherine of Aragon. Cardinal John Fisher was her confessor and a fierce critic of the King. He was beheaded on Tower Hill, London in June 1535 because he had refused to take the Oath of Succession. To take it meant recognising the right of succession to the throne of any children the King might have by Anne Boleyn. It also meant acknowledging the King's supremacy in matters of Church authority. Cardinal Fisher would do neither.

Cardinal Fisher's successor was a Dominican friar called John Hildesley. He belonged to the Beenham branch of the Hildesley family of East Ilsley on the Berkshire Downs. The name Hildesley is an old version of Ilsley.

The main line of the Hildesley family remained Catholic after the Reformation. Bishop Hildesley, however, was an enthusiastic supporter of the King's religious policy. It had been his job to ensure that the Dominican friars of England swore allegiance to the King as Head of the Church in England.

Having been a friar, Bishop Hildesley was not wealthy. Five days after he was consecrated he requested various possessions of his executed predecessor, including a walking staff. The

---

evidence suggests that his wish was granted, and that after his death the staff passed to his Catholic relatives.

One of the last Catholic Hildesleys, Mary, married Robert Eyston. She died in 1709 at the age of thirty and was buried in the Eyston aisle in the parish church of East Hendred. The first record of the Cardinal's staff being at Hendred House is nine years later, at about the time that the Hildesley's last interest in East Ilsley was being sold. It was then that the former Mary Hildesley's brother-in-law Charles Eyston, known as the Antiquary, bequeathed the Cardinal's staff to his son Charles. It has been at Hendred House ever since.

Sir Thomas More, the subject of the play and film 'A Man for All Seasons', was executed on Tower Hill a fortnight after Cardinal Fisher and on the same pretext. He was a graduate of Oriel College, Oxford and had an international reputation as an intellectual. His most famous book 'Utopia' described an imaginary place with an ideal social and political system, and gave a new word to the English language.

Sir Thomas More favoured religious reform, but within the framework of the Catholic Church. His friends included fellow Catholic reformers such as the Dutch theologian Desiderius Erasmus and Dean John Colet of St Paul's Cathedral, London.

In 1814 Maria Teresa Metcalfe, a descendant of Sir Thomas More, married Charles Eyston, a great grandson of the Antiquary. Through this marriage the martyr's tankard came to Hendred House. The present owner of Hendred House, Thomas More Eyston, is a great great grandson of Charles and Maria Teresa Eyston.

East Ilsley, once the home of the Catholic Hildesleys, is only five miles south-south-east of East Hendred. In the north wall of the north aisle of the parish church of St Mary is a group of three early Victorian stained glass windows. The window on the right depicts Erasmus, that on the left Dean Colet. Given pride of place in the middle is their friend Thomas More, honored by the Church of England as a reformer who died for the unity of the Church.

Although Sir Thomas More had been an Oxford scholar, neither he nor Cardinal Fisher was closely associated with Berkshire or southern Oxfordshire. The two most prominent local men to be executed for opposing the King were Sir Adrian Fortescue of Brightwell Baldwin and Abbot Hugh Faringdon of Bere Court, Pangbourne.

Sir Adrian Fortescue was a first cousin of Anne Boleyn. His house at Brightwell Baldwin probably stood in Brightwell Park (2 miles WNW of Watlington). His first wife was Anne Stonor who inherited Stonor Park (5 miles SE of Watlington). This estate is mentioned many times in this book and, unlike many of the others, is regularly open to the public.

The Fortescues moved into Stonor in 1499. This led to a long dispute with the Stonor family which was settled by Henry VIII about the time of his break with Rome. Under the terms of the settlement Sir Adrian had to surrender Stonor House but retained part of the estate. He also gained all the Stonor lands in Gloucestershire, Devon and Kent. These were much greater in size than Stonor Park itself.

Presumably Sir Adrian had let his house at Brightwell Baldwin because he moved from Stonor to the 14th century moated castle at Shirburn (1 mile NNE of Watlington). This belonged to the Chamberlain family and is referred to a number of times later in this book.

Shortly after the move to Shirburn Castle, Sir Adrian's second wife, Anne (nee Reade), gave birth to their second son. The child's Godparents included Thomas Reade, probably he of Barton, Abingdon whose daughter Catherine married Thomas Vachell, son of the commissioner who suppressed Reading Abbey.

Although he was Anne Boleyn's cousin, Sir Adrian Fortescue did not agree with the King's religious policies. The month after Anne's marriage he became a lay brother of the Oxford Dominicans. He had already joined the Order of St John of Jerusalem which led to his arrest and imprisonment for about six months in the Marshalsea Gaol at Southwark. His wife and two servants lived with him in prison. One of the servants was John Horseman, probably a member of the Oxfordshire Horseman family who remained Catholic into the seventeenth century.

In 1536 Sir Adrian inserted in his Missal (Mass book) a leaflet that had been issued by the King commanding certain prayers be said by all his subjects. Sir Adrian struck out a reference in the leaflet to the King being Supreme Head of the Church in England. Sir Adrian's Missal, complete with leaflet and deletion, is still in existence.

One of Sir Adrian's sons-in-law, Thomas Fitzgerald, Earl of Kildare, was hanged, drawn and quartered at Tyburn in 1537 for his part in a rebellion in Ireland. The following year Sir Adrian had to buy back his first wife's tomb and pay for its transfer from the suppressed Bisham Abbey to Brightwell Baldwin church.

He was arrested again in February 1539. This time he was imprisoned in the Tower of London and attainted by Parliament for treason, sedition and refusing allegiance to the King. It seems that there was no trial and no further details were given of his alleged crimes. In July 1539 he was beheaded on Tower Hill. The Pope beatified him (that is, awarded him the title 'Blessed') in 1895.

When Sir Adrian Fortescue was executed the suppression of the abbeys and priories had been proceeding for several years. The King's main aim was to replenish his treasury while reinforcing his claims of supremacy over the Church. First the smaller houses had been closed, including Studley Priory on the edge of Ot Moor and a string of establishments on the Thames: Rewley

BERE COURT, PANGBOURNE

Abbey in Oxford, Dorchester Abbey, Goring Priory, Medmenham Abbey, Hurley Priory, Bisham Priory (reinstated briefly as an abbey), Little Marlow Priory and Ankerwick Priory near Slough.

Then it was the turn of the larger establishments: Thame Abbey, the friary at Donnington near Newbury and a series of religious houses on or near the Thames - Godstow and Osney abbeys, the friaries and monastic colleges at Oxford, the great Abingdon Abbey and the friary at Reading.

The only head of a religious house in the Thames Valley to refuse to surrender to the King was Hugh Cook, Abbot of Reading. He is better known as Hugh Faringdon, because presumably he was born at Faringdon in north-west Berkshire.

Reading Abbey, though smaller and less ancient than Abingdon's, was one of the ten biggest Benedictine monasteries in England. Founded by Henry I, it stood by the River Kennet on the eastern outskirts of medieval Reading. It was the site of many notable events. Thomas Becket dedicated it. Henry I was buried there. The Patriarch of Jerusalem visited it to offer Henry II the crown of Jerusalem. In its huge church John of Gaunt married Blanche of Lancaster. Parliament assembled there three times. There too Britain's earliest surviving example of four-part harmony was written down, 'Sumer is Icumen In'.

Hugh Faringdon had been on good terms with the King and had even signed a petition to the Pope urging him to speed up the proceedings for Henry's annulment. He had also offered research facilities in the abbey library for those arguing the King's case. The abbot's support was appreciated by the King who, in 1532, sent him a New Year gift of a white leather purse containing £20 (= £4,700 today).

Hugh Faringdon became a royal chaplain and twice took the Oath of Supremacy acknowledging Henry as Supreme Head of the Church in England. He celebrated one of the Masses at the lying in state of the body of Henry's third queen, Jane Seymour, at Hampton Court. He was given a place of honour in the choir at her funeral in Windsor and was later made a justice of the peace.

After the act for the dissolution of the greater monasteries came into force, any abbot not surrendering his monastery to the Crown's agents was deemed guilty of treason. But Hugh Faringdon refused to surrender and is said to have been captured in a secret hiding place at his favourite summer residence, Bere Court (1½ miles SW of Pangbourne).

There has been a house on the site since at least the ninth century and it was owned by Abingdon Abbey before passing to Reading. In Hugh Faringdon's time the house was the centre of a much larger complex of buildings than today. These included a medieval chapel which, after the Reformation, was put to secular use and subsequently demolished.

Today Bere Court looks like an early Georgian house. However, some of the building fabric from Hugh Faringdon's time has survived, including the medieval cellars and the massive beams that span one of the bedrooms. Of particular interest is a grand carved and painted stone fireplace, decorated with the scallop shell motif of Reading Abbey. It was discovered fairly recently behind panelling. Its base was several feet lower than the present floor level in what was originally the upper gallery of the house. The owner is now carefully restoring the original painted decoration of the fireplace. It is virtually certain that this was Hugh Faringdon's fireplace.

Bere Court once had some good stained glass but this was sold in modern times. Some is held by Reading Museum but is not on display. It includes two roundels with Hugh Faringdon's initials surrounded by a border of hunting dogs. (The abbot was a keen huntsman and had hunted with Henry VIII.) It has been suggested that the similar stained glass roundel in the Catholic chapel at Hendred House also came originally from Bere Court.

Like Sir Adrian Fortescue, Hugh Faringdon was imprisoned in the Tower of London. He was indicted on a charge of treason. It was alleged that on three occasions he had spoken out against the Royal Supremacy. The verdict seems to have been predetermined as a surviving note states: 'The abbot of Reading to be sent down to be tried and executed at Reading with his accomplices.'

No defence was allowed and the abbot was found guilty, along with two priests, John Eynon and John Rugg.

Fr Eynon was the curate of St Giles's, Reading. During the suppression of the religious houses the biggest rebellion in English history took place, the Pilgrimage of Grace. It had many causes including opposition to the suppression of the monasteries. The uprising began in Lincolnshire and spread rapidly through most of Northern England. Fr Eynon had made a copy of a letter explaining the rebels' aims and consequently had been investigated by a Royal Commission.

Fr Rugg was a prebendary of Chichester Cathedral said to have hidden the alleged hand of St Anastasius when Reading Abbey's considerable collection of religious relics was seized. (St Anastasius, who died about the year 700, was abbot of a monastery on Mount Sinai.)

Certainly a human hand was hidden. It was placed in an iron chest and concealed in the base of a wall at the east end of the abbey church. There it lay, black, leathery and shrunken, for nearly two and a half centuries. It was found by workmen building Reading Gaol in 1786 and put on display in a small private museum.

In the nineteenth century the museum closed down and the hand was bought by a Catholic convert, Charles Robert Scott-Murray of Danesfield, Medmenham. He had been Member of Parliament for

Buckinghamshire and later became High Sheriff of the county. Scott-Murray and many others believed that the hand was Reading Abbey's principal focus of pilgrimage, the hand of St James the Apostle. This was a much more important relic than the hand of St Anastasius, and Fr Rugg may have been involved in a cunning switch to fool Henry VIII's agents.

From Charles Scott-Murray the hand passed to the Catholic church of St Peter in Marlow, where it is kept out of sight and under lock and key. The Church makes no claim whatsoever concerning its authenticity. However, it is of great interest, not least as one of the very few medieval religious relics to have survived the English Reformation. It also contributed to Fr Rugg's downfall.

He, Fr Eynon and Abbot Hugh Faringdon were sentenced to a traitor's death. Their fate may have been sealed by the friendship of the abbot and Fr Rugg with the family of the exiled Cardinal Pole who opposed Henry's religious policies and sought reunion with Rome.

On the 15 November 1539 the three were hanged, drawn (disembowelled) and cut into quarters. Their remains were then hung up in chains as a warning to others. According to local tradition this took place at the abbey's main gateway after the condemned men had been dragged through the streets of Reading on hurdles.

It is said that friends retrieved the remains and buried them at Bere Court. In the late seventeenth century the Breedon family bought the house and it is said that during their occupancy three lead-lined coffins were found under the floor and subsequently reburied elsewhere.

Like Sir Adrian Fortescue, Abbot Hugh Faringdon, Fr Rugg and Fr Eynon were beatified by the Pope in 1895. Reading's Catholic comprehensive school is named after the town's martyred abbot.

In the early nineteenth century interest in Reading Abbey's past increased. Through the efforts and financial support of a prominent local Catholic, James Wheble of Woodley Lodge, the ruins were excavated. In 1834 Wheble bought the land on which was subsequently built the Norman-style Catholic church of St James. This was designed by Augustus Welby Pugin and constructed mostly at Wheble's own expense, partly out of stones from the abbey ruins. By this means Catholic worship returned to the site of the abbey after an interval of some 300 years.

The abbey ruins belong to Reading Corporation and are open to the public. On the walls are three stone plaques, erected to commemorate the first and last abbots and the composition of 'Sumer is Icumen In'.

North of St Laurence's Church, which stood at the abbey's west gateway, is an intact flint-built remnant of the Hospitium of St John the Baptist. The Hospitium originally provided lodgings for pilgrims and other travellers. The oldest parts of the present building date from 1486 when it became a school.

The late thirteenth century inner gatehouse, known as the Abbey Gateway, was heavily restored by George Gilbert Scott in Victorian times. There is an useful plan of the abbey on the north wall of the Abbey Gateway, which helps to relate the former structures to present-day buildings.

Reading Museum has some twelth century column capitals from the abbey cloister. Others are in the Victoria & Albert Museum, London. The museum also has a model of the abbey before its suppression, which gives a good idea of its vast scale.

After its dissolution some of Reading Abbey's books passed into the secret possession of local people. For example, in the early twentieth century an antiphonal (a book of psalms or similar verses to be sung by a choir) was found hidden in the wall of a building in Broad Street, Reading.

In the sixteenth and seventeenth centuries a branch of the secretly Catholic Wollascott family lived at Shinfield House (now demolished). There in 1792, in what seems to have been a secret hiding place, was found what became known as the Fingall Cartulary. It is a notable collection of abbey records, and is now in the British Museum. Other finds at Shinfield House are believed to have included a twelfth century book now in Reading Museum and a fifteenth century book of hours, now at Downside Abbey near Bath. The evidence suggests that, in Elizabethan times, these and other books were kept at Shinfield for Thomas Thomson, who may have been a Catholic priest.

But how did books such as these escape the destruction of the abbey's library, and the suppression of Catholic books thereafter? The answer probably lies with the Vachell family of Coley Park.

Thomas Vachell, Member of Parliament for Reading, was the commissioner responsible for the suppression of Reading Abbey. The Vachells were a long-established local family. Two hundred years earlier a Vachell had given part of Tilehurst to Reading Abbey. Commissioner Vachell's eldest son, also Thomas, remained a Catholic and lived for more than seventy years after the dissolution of Reading Abbey. The younger Thomas's widowed sister-in-law Mary Martyn (nee Reade) spent her latter years living with her son-in-law William Wollascott at Shinfield. Thomas Vachell the younger was probably the link between his father who suppressed the abbey and his wife's niece, in whose final lodgings the abbey's books were found two and a half centuries after the dissolution.

The Religious Changes

(1534 - 1558)

In the twenty-four years following Henry VIII's break with Rome in 1534, the Church in England was like a religious pendulum. Under Henry it remained more or less 'Catholic without the Pope'. During the reign of the boy-king Edward VI, Henry's son by Jane Seymour, the Church veered strongly towards Continental Protestantism. Then under Mary, Henry's daughter by Catherine of Aragon, it was reunited with Rome. Finally under Elizabeth, Henry's daughter by Anne Boleyn, the Anglican compromise between Roman Catholicism and Continental Protestantism was evolved.

Not surprisingly, these were confusing times for the English people. Those with strongly held views had to learn when it was safe to express them. Many became neutral or indifferent to the the religious changes. Some adopted the attitude of Simon Aleyn, the Vicar of Bray near Maidenhead. During the reign of Henry VIII he witnessed the burning of a Windsor man who refused to accept the Six Articles: legislation introduced by the King to prevent the spread of Protestant teaching. Aleyn is said to have vowed never to risk his own life by standing up for his religious beliefs. He therefore kept his job right through to the reign of Elizabeth I.

During this period of religious change the Thames Valley families that were later to come into conflict with the authorities for remaining Catholic generally held on to public office. Few openly objected to the anti-Catholic aspects of the monarch's religious policy. And few had any scruples about acquiring real estate seized from the abbeys and priories.

Sir Walter Stonor, Sheriff of Oxfordshire and Berkshire, had held high office throughout the reign of Henry VIII. He attended the coronation of Anne Boleyn and the christening of Prince Edward (later Edward VI). Like Abbot Hugh Faringdon he took part in the funeral of Jane Seymour. But in the year that both the Abbot and Sir Adrian Fortescue were martyred, Sir Walter was criticised for being backward in matters of religion. The criticism came from Miles Coverdale, producer of the first complete English translation of the Bible. Coverdale was then based at Newbury, eliminating what he called 'the hindrance of superstition'.

Until this time English churches typically had what was called a rood beam above the boundary between the main public part of the church (the nave) and the chancel where the priest celebrated Mass. This beam supported three statues. In the middle was Christ on the Cross (the rood), with the Virgin Mary on the right, and St John on the left. Usually there was a screen below the beam. Instructions had been issued for the removal of all roods but that at St Mary's, Henley-on-Thames was still in place. Coverdale accused Sir Walter Stonor of being partly responsible. However, it seems that Sir Walter Stonor's record of loyalty to the King saved him from serious trouble.

Early in the reign of Edward VI came the second Chantries Act. It was intended to stamp out the celebration of Masses for the dead, something that Protestants regarded as a superstitious practice.

Chantries were chapels for the celebration of such Masses. Some chantries were associated with almshouses or schools. The almshouses and school at Ewelme are examples of this sort of institution. But there were many private chantries whose purpose was purely spiritual. Those that had not already closed voluntarily now had their revenues seized by the Crown. Consequently 300 acres of beechwood behind Stonor House, which for two centuries had supported the chaplain of the house's ancient chapel, were seized and passed to the dean and canons of St George's Chapel at Windsor.

Next came the smashing, dismantling or defacement of Catholic furnishings: altars, statues, stained glass, murals, holy-water basins (stoups) and any surviving rood screens. Service books were vandalised for their jewels, gold-leaf, and silver hinges and clasps. At Pyrton, a typical parish church a mile north of Watlington, 5s 8d (equivalent to about £54 today) was paid to obliterate the murals in the parish church. A year or so later the altar was smashed out and replaced by a Communion table.

Use of the first edition of the Book of Common Prayer was made compulsory from Whit Sunday 1549. Three days before the deadline the Western Rebellion broke out in Cornwall. In less than a week the uprising had spread to Oxfordshire. The rebels wanted the Latin Mass, prayers for the dead, restoration of the abbeys and priories, rejection of the Book of Common Prayer and removal of the Bible in English from the parish churches, because they thought it encouraged heresy.

German mercenaries brutally suppressed the uprising. More than a dozen executions took place in Oxfordshire at places such as Watlington, Islip and Oxford. The rebellion seems to have had no support from the gentry and little popular support in Berkshire.

Sir Francis Englefield's principal residence was Englefield House (6 miles W. of Reading). The family claimed to have settled at Englefield (which means the settlement of Angles among the Saxons) about 250 years before the Norman Conquest. Like most other people, Francis Englefield had acquiesced in Henry VIII's religious changes. He took the Oath of Supremacy and was given the manor of Tilehurst (now in western Reading) formerly held by Reading Abbey. He was subsequently appointed

ENGLEFIELD HOUSE

Sheriff of Oxfordshire and knighted at the coronation of Edward VI. But he became disillusioned with the direction of the English Reformation and joined the household of the Catholic Princess Mary.

In the summer of 1551 Sir Francis and two colleagues were summoned before the Privy Council at Hampton Court and accused of being 'the chief instruments and cause that kept the princess in the old religion'. The three were sent back to Mary with instructions to stop her chaplains from celebrating the Catholic Mass. The Princess refused to accept the instructions and sent Sir Francis and his friends back to the Council to tell them so. The Council merely reiterated the command, at which point the three refused to relay the message to Mary. They were therefore imprisoned in the Tower of London until the following spring.

A little more than a year later, in June 1553, Thomas Vachell of Coley, the Crown commissioner who had helped suppress Reading Abbey, began a new task. He joined with other Berkshire commissioners to begin stripping the county's churches of their valuables. Shortly afterwards, on the 6th July, the young King Edward died. Vachell did not long survive him. However, the stripping of the churches continued until February 1554, four months after the coronation of Edward's Catholic half-sister Mary. During the eight month pillage the Berkshire commissioners sent to London nearly 1500 ounces of silver, and silver and gold plate.

Across the Thames in Oxfordshire Lady Elizabeth Stonor had gone to All Saints, Rotherfield Peppard and reclaimed a great chalice worth £10 (= £1,900 today). Lady Elizabeth was Sir Walter Stonor's wife. Recently widowed she had gone to stay with her brother-in-law John Stonor and his wife Isabel at Blount's Court, Rotherfield Peppard (5 miles SSW of Stonor). Lady Elizabeth was no stranger to this house, having lived there with Sir Walter until they gained possession of Stonor House from Sir Adrian Fortescue. Today the much altered Blount's Court is the headquarters of Johnson Matthey Research.

On the death of Sir Walter Stonor in 1550, Stonor House was inherited by John and Isabel Stonor's son Francis. He was the godson of Sir Francis Knollys, an Oxfordshire commissioner for the seizure of church plate. Knollys, a great opponent of Catholicism, had his principal residence at Greys Court, the fortified manor house of Rotherfield Greys. This is now a National Trust property and is less than two miles across the fields from Blount's Court.

Francis Stonor married Cecily Chamberlain, daughter of Sir Leonard Chamberlain, another Oxfordshire commissioner for the seizure of church plate. Sir Leonard owned Shirburn Castle near Watlington, where Sir Adrian Fortescue lived after moving out of Stonor House. He was Henry VIII's keeper of Woodstock Park, had served as official land confiscator (Escheator) for

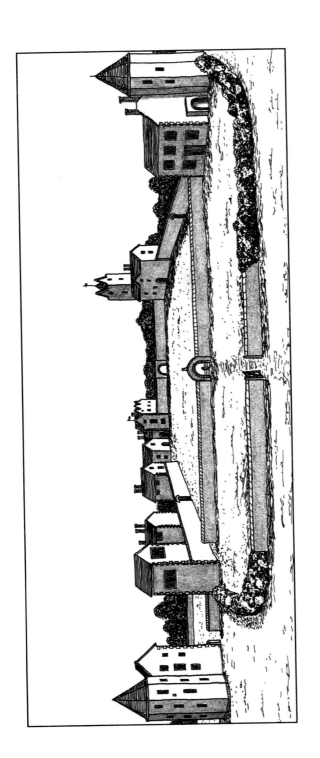

GREYS COURT IN ELIZABETHAN TIMES – from an old engraving

Oxfordshire and Berkshire, and was involved in large scale trading of former monastic properties. Like Sir Walter Stonor he was twice Sheriff of both counties and sometime Lieutenant of the Tower of London. He was also involved in suppressing the Western Rebellion in Oxfordshire.

On the death of Edward VI in 1553, Lady Jane Grey was proclaimed queen in a bid to stop Mary Tudor succeeding to the throne. Although the pro-Catholic Western Rebellion had attracted little support in Berkshire, the county's militia marched on London in support of Mary. And as soon as Mary was proclaimed Queen the Catholics of Oxford were observed to 'dig out as it were from their graves their vestments, chalices and portasses, and begin Mass with all speed.'

Mary Tudor was the first English queen to rule in her own right. At her coronation early in October 1553 Lady Fortescue, widow of the martyred Sir Adrian Fortescue of Brightwell Baldwin, was one of ten noble ladies who rode immediately behind the Queen's carriage. Sir Adrian's daughter, Lady Wentworth, sat with the Queen in the royal coach.

During the coronation festivities Francis Stonor of Stonor House was knighted and his mother Isabel was granted a pension by the Queen. His father-in-law Sir Leonard Chamberlain of Shirburn Castle was also knighted. By the end of the year he was Member of Parliament for Scarborough and Governor of Guernsey.

The Queen also rewarded Sir Francis Englefield for his loyalty and he became one of most prominent members of the Privy Council. He was appointed keeper of Reading Abbey and given a lease of the manor of Pangbourne. This included Bere Court, the former residence of the martyred abbot Hugh Faringdon, which was only two miles north of Englefield House. Together with lawyer John Yate of Buckland, Sir Francis Englefield was granted the manor of Faringdon. Yate's mother and wife, and Englefield's wife were all members of the Fettiplace family, which had many branches in western Berkshire and southern Oxfordshire. Sir Francis was also granted the manor and park of Fulbroke, Warwickshire and was Member of Parliament for Berkshire throughout Mary's reign.

Queen Mary's religious policy was moderate at first. She 'wished to force no one to go to Mass' but 'meant to see that those who wished to go should be free to do so'. She encouraged the minority of hard core Protestants to go into exile on the Continent. One of those who took this advice was Sir Francis Stonor's godfather, Sir Francis Knollys of Greys Court.

During Mary's reign James Brooks, rector of East Hendred and a 'zealous maintainer of the Catholic Religion', became Bishop of Gloucester. Meanwhile the parish churches of England began re-equipping themselves for Catholic services. The parish church at Pyrton near Watlington bought a chalice, Mass book, paschal and baptismal candles, and an altar stone. But Pyrton, like many other churches, could not afford to re-equip at one go. It was to be several years before all its Catholic furnishings were reinstated.

Formal reunion of the English Church with Rome necessitated the return of Reginald Pole, the exiled Cardinal who had been living on the Continent for the last twenty years. Two of Mary's ambassadors who negotiated for the Cardinal's return were from the Thames Valley, and both were related by marriage to the Stonors. Sir Philip Hoby, a Protestant who lived at Bisham Abbey, was Sir Walter Stonor's son-in-law. Thomas Chamberlain was Sir Leonard Chamberlain's son and therefore Sir Francis Stonor's brother-in-law.

The Cardinal's mother, brother and a cousin had all been executed during Henry VIII's reign. Henry, who according to one estimate was responsible for the deaths of 72,000 people or 2½ per cent of the population, was not easily forgiven by Cardinal Pole or Queen Mary. Sir Francis Englefield claimed to have been present at Windsor when the Queen and Cardinal had the former king's embalmed body disinterred and burned.

The Comptroller of the Cardinal's household was Sir Anthony Fortescue, a grandson of the martyred Sir Adrian of Brightwell Baldwin. Sir Anthony had married the Cardinal's niece. The Cardinal's gentleman usher was William Perkins of Brimpton.

In December 1554 Parliament revived the heresy laws which had been introduced in the early fifteenth century to combat the Lollards. Two months later the first burnings of Protestants in Mary's reign took place. The Queen and her Chancellor, Bishop Stephen Gardiner, had been accused of being soft on heresy. The Privy Council favoured inflicting the death penalty on those who, over the previous year and a half, had neither left the country, learned to keep their views to themselves nor conformed to Catholicism. Mary agreed to the Council's wishes in the hope that a short, sharp campaign would resolve the situation.

It was a forlorn hope. Mary's campaign saw the burning of some 300 Protestants in less than three years. About a third were clergy and a fifth were women. Most were ordinary people, two thirds of them from London or the Home Counties, where Protestant ideas had taken deepest root. Most were reported to the authorities by their neighbours. Many of the executed were Anabaptists, regarded as arch-heretics by Catholics, Lutherans and Calvinists alike.

Edmund Plowden, a Catholic lawyer and associate of Sir Francis Englefield, led thirty-eight MPs in a protest against Parliament's reintroduction of the heresy laws. The Attorney-General commenced proceedings for contempt against the protesters, but Plowden refused to submit and the case was eventually dropped.

Edmund Plowden was born at Plowden Hall, Shropshire and had been manager of Sir Francis Englefield's 400 acre estate at Rossall near Shrewsbury. He made his home in the Thames Valley, as did his half-brother William Wollascott. At various times during Mary's reign Edmund Plowden was Member of Parliament for Wallingford, Reading and Wootton Bassett, near Swindon, where Sir Francis Englefield's brother John lived.

There were relatively few burnings in the Thames Valley. However, Oxford was the scene of the execution of the three most notable Protestant martyrs, Thomas Cranmer, Hugh Latimer and Nicholas Ridley. The Ashmolean Museum at Oxford has a fragment of a stake believed to be that at which the Oxford Protestant martyrs died. The museum also has an iron band said to have been warn by Cranmer. In 1841 a 73 ft. high memorial to the three Protestant martyrs was erected at the south end of St Giles's Street. It was designed by Sir George Gilbert Scott, whose grandson Giles Gilbert Scott, a Catholic, designed the recently completed Anglican cathedral at Liverpool.

By 1557 things were going seriously wrong for Mary Tudor. The burning of heretics was proceeding at about a hundred times the rate to which the country had been accustomed for the last century and a half. This was creating a sense of unity among the opponents of Catholicism, even those who were far from united in matters of doctrine. Ironically, it had even got to the point where the bones of a burned Essex Protestant were being carried around the country and revered as relics.

The Queen's marriage to Philip of Spain was also proving unpopular, especially as there had been no offspring. Her supporters knew that, if she died without leaving a son or daughter to succeed her, the crown would pass to Elizabeth who could not be relied upon to keep England Catholic. Bad harvests and the loss of Calais only made matters worse for Mary's faltering administration.

Then came another major setback. Incredible though it may seem, in June 1557 the Pope summoned Cardinal Pole to Rome to face a charge of heresy. The Queen protested but to no avail. She therefore refused to let the Cardinal leave the country.

Exasperated by the difficulties they faced, the Queen and the Cardinal became increasingly ill. The Cardinal was faced by a massive overload of administrative matters. In addition to the formidable task of renewing the Catholic Church in England, there were also routine matters of church law to deal with. One of the last of these was a request from John Eyston of East Hendred for a dispensation to marry a relative, Joan Clifford. This the Cardinal granted on 8 November 1558.

Nine days later, at St James's Palace, London, just before dawn, Mary Tudor died whilst at Mass. The news was relayed across the Thames to Cardinal Pole at Lambeth Palace. The Queen's death was too much for him and he passed away early that evening. His gentleman usher, William Perkins of Brimpton, died a few days later, perhaps of the fever that killed so many that year.

Stonor, Fortescue, Chamberlain, Vachell, Englefield, Yate, Perkins, Plowden, Wollascott, Eyston; members of all these families were to remain loyal to the form of Christianity re-established under Mary Tudor.

The Elizabethan Settlement

(1558 - 1570)

At Mary Tudor's funeral the Bishop of Winchester lamented that 'the wolves be coming out of Geneva and other places of Germany and have sent their books before, full of pestilent doctrines, blasphemy and heresy to infect the people.' Indeed Sir Francis Knollys of Greys Court had already returned from Strasbourg to become a member of the new Queen's Privy Council. He and the other returning Protestant exiles put considerable pressure on Elizabeth to set up a national Protestant church, on the lines of the Reformed churches of Switzerland.

In April 1559 a new Act of Supremacy declared the Queen to be Supreme Governor of spiritual matters in England. An Oath of Supremacy could now be demanded of holders of public or church office, and anyone taking a degree. (From 1563 the oath was extended to schoolmasters.) Penalties were introduced for those who supported the Pope's jurisdiction in England. A first offence against the Act of Supremacy could mean loss of all goods and movable possessions. A second offence could result in life imprisonment and loss of all real estate. A third offence was regarded as high treason and could carry the death penalty.

A new Act of Uniformity, also passed in April 1559, declared the Queen to be Supreme Governor of spiritual matters in England. It introduced heavy penalties for those who refused to conform to Anglicanism. Failure to attend the new Sunday service could attract a fine of one shilling (= £6 today). This was two or three days pay for many of the Queen's lowlier subjects. An alternative punishment was excommunication from the Church of England and a consequent loss of civil rights.

Attending the Catholic Mass could attract colossal fines of 100 marks for the first offence (= £8,250 today). A second offence quadrupled the fine. Offending a third time could mean life imprisonment and the loss of all goods. The same punishments were threatened against those who criticised the Book of Common Prayer. Anyone assisting at Mass was liable to six months imprisonment for the first offence, a year for the second, and life for the third.

Sir Francis Englefield of Englefield House, having been one of Queen Mary's most loyal councillors, found it impossible to reconcile himself to the new religious situation established by the legislation of April 1559. Queen Elizabeth therefore promptly granted him a licence to live abroad for two years, provided that he did not reside in Rome. Leaving his wife Catherine in Berkshire, Sir Francis set out with eight servants, 600 ounces of plate and 100 marks (= £8,250 today).

He spent the summer in Louvain, Flanders, then travelled via Paris to Italy. He was never to see England again.

In 1563, four years after the introduction of the new Acts of Supremacy and Uniformity, the Convocation of Clergy issued the Thirty-Nine Articles, summarising the dogmas of the Anglican Church. These included declarations that the 'Bishop of Rome hath no jurisdiction in this Realm of England' and that Masses offered for the souls of the living and dead were 'blasphemous fables, and dangerous deceits.'

Now, once again, the parishes were put to the expense of modifying the interiors of their churches. At Pyrton in the year of the new Act of Uniformity a copy of the Book of Common Prayer was purchased and the altar was again demolished to make way for a Communion table. Within three years the rood loft had been pulled down. At Wantage's parish church the heavy altar stone was placed under the church steps where it stayed until found during nineteenth century renovations. Was it carefully hidden away for the day when Catholicism might return, or was it merely used as a piece of salvaged stonework to help support the church steps?

Shortly after the new religious legislation was passed, Archbishop Nicholas Heath, as acting head of the Catholic Church in England, stated that 'There is nothing to be done, but everything to endure, whatsoever God may will.' Archbishop Heath was not prepared to take any action against the national interest, but neither would he associate himself with the new state church. Nor would the other English Catholic bishops. Some had gone along with Protestantism in the past, but now the issues were clearer. They were no longer prepared to compromise.

Most were old men and were treated reasonably well by the authorities. Some were jailed for a while and almost all were placed under house arrest, or put in the custody of a new Anglican bishop. Before long several were dead, including Bishop James Brooks of Gloucester, the former rector of East Hendred, who died in jail. Three of the bishops eventually escaped to the Continent.

Archbishop Heath spent three years in the Tower of London but was then allowed to retire to his house in Surrey, just three miles from the Berkshire border. This was Chobham Park, bought from Queen Mary in the last summer of her reign for the huge sum of £3,000 (= £400,000 today).

Elizabeth's religious legislation of 1559 did not result in an immediate formal break with Rome. For another two years the Pope continued to send Papal ambassadors (nuncios) to Elizabeth's court, but she refused to receive them.

While Rome adopted a 'softly, softly' approach, and the Catholic bishops steadfastly refused to co-operate with the Anglican Church, the country's 8,000 parish clergy were placed in a difficult position. Most were poorly paid and not particularly well-educated. The new Act of Uniformity put them under immense pressure. If they refused to use the Book of Common Prayer they stood to lose a year's income and be jailed for six months. For a second offence they could lose their jobs and be jailed for a year. A third offence could mean life imprisonment. It seems that only about 300 clergy, less than 4 per cent of the total, were dismissed for refusing to conform. But many continued to celebrate the Catholic Mass in secret.

There was considerable resistance to the new religious legislation at Oxford University and a number of heads of colleges were dismissed for refusing to conform. It was said that fewer than one in twenty Oxford men would take the Oath of Supremacy in the early days of Elizabeth's reign. John Jewel, the Anglican Bishop of Salisbury, advised against sending any Protestant youth to Oxford, so strong was Catholic influence there. And the Mayor of Oxford reported that not three houses in the city were without papists.

However, by the mid 1560s the pressures on Oxford Catholics were considerable. It seems that some may have found the pressures too much to bear. John Hanington, a philosophy graduate, came from the Hampshire village of Tadley (9 miles ESE of Newbury). John Plunkeney, a law student, came from Forest Hill (4 miles ENE of Oxford). Both were Catholics and both were found drowned, Hanington in Italy, Plunkeney at Oxford.

Some Catholic scholars from Oxford, together with others from Cambridge, emigrated to Flanders. Their main base was Louvain, from where the Catholic case was argued by means of pamphlets and books smuggled into England.

Perhaps the most notable of those who emigrated from Oxford at this time was William Allen. A Lancastrian, Allen was Principal and Proctor of St Mary's Hall, Oxford. Shortly after the accession of Elizabeth I, he resigned rather than take the Oath of Supremacy. In 1561 he joined the exiles in Louvain. The following year he returned to England. Using Oxford as his base he spent two and a half years roaming the countryside arguing the Catholic case and boosting Catholic morale before returning to Flanders.

He was ordained priest and in September 1568 established an English College at Douai to train Catholic missionaries to work in England. The college was in a rented house and, for its first seven years, depended entirely on voluntary contributions.

Despite all the legal difficulties placed in their way, some Thames Valley Catholics still managed to achieve or retain high office under Queen Elizabeth. Sir Leonard Chamberlain of Shirburn Castle, himself a former Lieutenant of the Tower, retained his position as Governor of Guernsey. He died about two years into Elizabeth's reign and was succeeded by his eldest son Francis. At about the same time Sir Leonard's second son, George Chamberlain, was granted Alderney. George subsequently went into exile in Ghent, Flanders but his family were allowed to retain their rights over the island. In 1562 John Eyston of East Hendred, who had sought the dispensation to marry from Cardinal Pole, was appointed official land confiscator of Oxfordshire and Berkshire.

In many cases Catholics were able to hold high office because there simply were not enough suitably qualified Anglicans. In practice it was often possible to evade the Oath of Supremacy by feigning illness or arranging to be in another part of the country when the Oath was administered. There were also some Catholics who believed that an oath sworn on a Protestant Bible did not bind them.

During Elizabethan times many lawyers were Catholic. In those days landowners often trained as lawyers to gain estate management skills. The Middle Temple, one of the London Inns of Court, was said to be 'pestered with papists', a number of whom were Thames Valley Catholics. The most notable was Edmund Plowden, 'the greatest and most honest lawyer of his age', who was appointed Treasurer of the Inn, despite being a Catholic.

Edmund Plowden had many landed interests in the Thames Valley area and was involved in the running of a number of other people's estates. He was estate manager for his half-brother William Wollascott of Tidmarsh Grange (1½ miles NNE of Englefield House) who held the Shalford estate comprising much of the Kennet Valley between Newbury and Reading, including Brimpton, Midgham, Padworth and Woolhampton. Under Elizabeth, Plowden himself acquired the Wokefield estate between Burghfield and Stratfield Mortimer, and neighbouring land at Stratfield Mortimer, Sulhamstead Bannister and Burghfield.

But while Edmund Plowden continued to prosper, his exiled former employer Sir Francis Englefield was now in trouble with the authorities. Sir Francis had failed to return when his travel permit expired. This led to the loss of his lease on the manor of Pangbourne, including Bere Court. He also lost Whitley Park, Reading of which he had been master of game and keeper of the park and lodge. (A remnant of Whitley Park existed until the nineteenth century between the Basingstoke, Christchurch and Shinfield Roads.)

In the spring of 1565 Sir Francis Englefield was named as patron of the new Anglican Vicar of Shiplake (between Reading and Henley) where he held the rectory, Shiplake Court. But that autumn he was outlawed for high treason, allegedly committed by consorting with the Queen's enemies at Namur in the Spanish Netherlands. His vast estates were sequestrated and £300 a year (= £36,000 today) of their revenue diverted to the Treasury. The rest of the estate income was frozen. Sir Francis

SHIRBURN CASTLE – from an old engraving

Englefield subsequently entered the service of the Spanish as adviser to the Duke of Alva, Stadtholder of the Netherlands.

It is impossible to know how many of the population remained Catholic at this time. The majority of those who had reached their mid-thirties had been brought up as Catholics. But the religious changes of the previous quarter century had left many confused or indifferent about religion. It is certain that committed Catholics were by now a minority. However, there were many people who were sympathetic to Catholicism but deterred from actively supporting it by the threat of fines, imprisonment, confiscations, loss of livelihood and social rejection.

To add to the confusion, most Catholics were uncertain as to the nature of their relationship with the new state church. Many, while continuing as best they could to practise the old faith in private, regularly attended Anglican services, thus avoiding the penalties for non-attendance. Such Catholics were often referred to as 'church papists'. Catholic opinion was divided about attending Anglican services. Some thought it was permissible if done solely in obedience to the Queen. Others, including William Allen, invoked canon law, which stated that attendance was a grave sin.

And what were Catholics to make of the Anglican clergy? Most were the same men who had, until recently, been their Catholic parish priests. Such men were undoubtedly validly ordained in Catholic eyes. Many were to varying degrees reluctant members of the Church of England, and a significant number continued to celebrate the Catholic Mass in private. And there had still been no official papal condemnation of the Anglican Church.

The religious tensions of the time often divided families. For the ambitious it was a great temptation to conform to Anglicanism. The Fortescue family provides an example with local connections.

The eldest son of the martyred Sir Adrian Fortescue of Brightwell Baldwin, Sir John Fortescue, conformed to Anglicanism. On Elizabeth's accession he was appointed Master of the Great Wardrobe. In 1589 he became Chancellor of the Exchequer and Under Treasurer, and joined the Privy Council. He was further rewarded in 1601 when he was made Chancellor of the Duchy of Lancaster. Sir John's youngest brother Sir Anthony, who had been Comptroller of Cardinal Pole's household, remained a Catholic. Early in Elizabeth's reign he became involved in a ludicrous plot against her and consequently was imprisoned for seventeen years.

In the spring of 1568 Mary Stuart, Queen of Scots, fled from Scotland seeking refuge with her cousin Elizabeth, who had offered her asylum. Sir Francis Knollys of Greys Court was then Elizabeth's Vice-Chamberlain and was sent to Carlisle to take custody of Mary. Knollys described her as 'a notable woman' who 'thirsteth after victory'. She was considered too dangerous to set free in England.

In the autumn of the following year the Rising in the North broke out. The Catholic northern earls intended replacing Elizabeth with Mary Stuart. But even in areas of the North where the majority of people remained Catholic, only a small number actively supported the rebels.

In Oxford all the young men related to the rebels were ordered to be 'stayed'. The Sheriff and magistrates of Berkshire were ordered to meet at Abingdon and sign a document confirming their conformity to Anglicanism. A former justice of the peace, John Yate, failed to appear. Instead he sent a letter of excuse and his bond. This John Yate was probably the lawyer who jointly held Faringdon manor with Sir Francis Englefield, and who had been excommunicated by the Church of England. Five years earlier Bishop Jewel of Salisbury had complained that Yate had 'never yet received Holy Communion since the beginning of the Queen's reign'.

Edmund Plowden was the only one present at the Abingdon meeting who refused to sign the declaration of conformity to Anglicanism. He was given a week to think the matter over. At a second meeting, held at Reading, he declared that, although he had regularly attended Anglican services since they were introduced, he would not sign the document confirming his conformity to Anglicanism. He was therefore bound over to keep the peace for a year and put on notice that he must appear before the Privy Council when summoned.

Two months later the Pope received garbled, out-of-date reports that a large army had risen to support the Catholic cause and that English public opinion favoured rapid reunion with Rome. In February 1570 the Pope therefore issued the Bull 'Regnans in Excelsis'. This edict finally and formally acknowledged that Elizabeth had parted company with Rome. It described her as the 'Servant of Wickedness' and declared her to be a heretic. It excommunicated her and her followers. But most importantly it declared her to be 'deprived of her pretended Title' of Queen and absolved all her subjects from any allegiance to her, commanding them not to obey her or her laws. Any Catholic not obeying this instruction was to be considered excommunicated.

The content, timing and tone of the Bull came as a bombshell. Even Mary Tudor's widower, Philip II of Spain, described the Pope as allowing himself 'to be carried away by his zeal'. Philip forecast that 'this sudden and unexpected step will ... drive the Queen and her friends the more to oppress and persecute the few good Catholics still remaining in England.'

It was an accurate prediction.

The First Missionaries

(1570 - 1581)

In the aftermath of the papal bull of 1570 came a legislative backlash. A new act made it treasonable to call the Queen a heretic. Another act made it illegal to bring papal bulls into the country, or to bring in Catholic devotional aids, such as rosaries. The 1571 Act Against Fugitives Over The Sea forbade Catholics to leave the country or to be trained overseas for ordination. Those who had already gone were given six months to return repentant or forfeit their goods and estate incomes.

There was also an attempt to stamp out Catholicism within the legal profession. Members of the Inns of Court suspected of Catholic sympathies were asked formally whether they regularly attended Anglican services, whether they received Communion according to the Anglican rite at least three times a year, and whether they had attended Mass or any other Catholic ceremonies.

Those who did not make outright denials used their legal skills to give evasive answers. For example, John Greenwood of Oxford said he had been so overloaded with work that he had not been able to get to church. But not all were able to talk their way out of trouble. James Braybrooke of Sutton Courtenay (2 miles S. of Abingdon) was expelled from the Inner Temple and later spent fourteen months in the Fleet prison for his refusal to conform to Anglicanism.

In 1573 the Privy Council ordered that all pro-Catholic books in Oxfordshire should be seized. But in the Hundred of Pyrton and Binfield no resident justice could be appointed because all the local gentry were Catholic.

In the same year the first missionary priests from Dr William Allen's seminary at Douai landed in England. Within seven years a hundred Douai priests had been smuggled into the country.

By 1580 about a seventh of the members of the Inns of Court were still strongly Catholic. Among those listed as 'recusants' - people who refused to attend Anglican services - were Edmund Plowden of Shiplake Court, his nephew Humphrey Sandford (who acted as an international courier communicating with the outlawed exile Sir Francis Englefield) and Sir Walter Curson of Waterperry (7 miles E. of Oxford). Another recusant, John Yate, was listed as a fugitive at Louvain. There were several related John Yates alive at this time. This one was probably a son of the John Yate of Buckland previously mentioned.

The Yates of Buckland were actively supporting the underground Catholic clergy. At Candlemas 1577 Buckland Manor was raided by a priest-hunter named Hodgkins. Fr William Hopton, who lived with the Yates, hid in a priest-hole and only narrowly avoided capture. The priest-hunter found Fr Hopton's gown which was still warm under the armpits.

John Yate senior died less than a year later. He left five sons and seven daughters, whose images are etched in brass on his tombstone in the parish church at Buckland. His eldest son Edward inherited Buckland Manor and soon afterwards married Jane Giffard, sister of the Archbishop of Rheims. Edward Yate, like his father, had been a student at the Middle Temple and the authorities had noted his absence from Anglican services.

By now Catholicism had significant support from people in the book trade. In the summer of 1577, at the instigation of the University authorities, Roland Jenks, an Oxford stationer and bookbinder, was convicted of speaking against Anglicanism. His sentence included being nailed by the ears to the pillory.

At about the time the sentence was passed a strange illness spread through the court and beyond. It killed two judges, the clerk, coroner, sheriff, under-sheriff and most members of two juries. In all, several hundred people died and the court proceedings became known as the Black Assizes.

Strangely the epidemic had little effect on women, children, apothecaries or doctors. In the popular view it was either a judgement from God on Protestantism, or the result of a (literally) fiendish Catholic plot. Roland Jenks seems not to have contracted the illness and was still in jail the following year. The Black Assizes were soon the subject of popular jingles which were promptly banned, such as:

> Think you on the solemn 'Sizes past
>
> How suddenly in Oxfordshire,
>
> I came and made the Judges all aghast ...

The Anglican bishops were now concerned that 'The papists do marvellously increase, both in number and in obstinate withdrawing of themselves from church.' Archbishop Grindal of Canterbury wrote to the Chapter of Oxford saying that he was 'informed that the Diocese of Oxford is more replenished with such recusants ... than any other diocese of this realm.'

The Privy Council therefore ordered the bishops to send in lists of all taxable recusants, together with estimates of their revenues. The bishops were given just one week to compile the lists and hence only the most prominent Catholics were named.

The 1577 Oxfordshire list included three Stonor widows. At Stonor lived Dame Cecily, widow of Sir Francis Stonor, daughter of Sir Leonard Chamberlain of Shirburn Castle, niece of the Carthusian martyr Sebastian Newdigate and a cousin of Cardinal Pole's executed mother. Her income was assessed at £500 a year (= £540,000 today), the highest figure for any Catholic in the county. Dame Cecily's brother-in-law's widow, Marjorie Stonor, lived by the Thames at North Stoke (2 miles S. of Wallingford). Less than a mile downstream, at Littlestoke, lived Dame Cecily's sister-in-law, Margaret Hildesley, nee Stonor.

In the ninth century the Saxons defeated the Danes on the Berkshire Downs nine miles north of Newbury. The area became known by the Anglo-Saxon word for battlefield, Hildes-laeg. The name became transmuted into some eighteen different forms, including Hildesleigh, Hilsley and even Yelsley. Today the villages adjacent to the battlefield are known as East and West Ilsley.

The Hildesley family were probably early settlers in the area. By the time of Henry VIII their holdings included Ilsley Farm (later known as Manor Farm) which they retained until the early eighteenth century.

It was noted earlier in this book that the martyred Cardinal Fisher's successor as Bishop of Rochester was a Hildesley descended from the Beenham branch of the family. Another Beenham Hildesley, John, was Henry VIII's Yeoman of the Longbows. John Hildesley's elder brother Edward became head of the East Ilsley line, by which time their main residence was at Newnham Murren adjoining Crowmarsh Gifford on the Oxfordshire bank of the Thames facing Wallingford. This dwelling was probably on the site of the present Newnham Manor, on the south side of the Nettlebed to Wallingford road.

Edward Hildesley's son William married Margaret Stonor of North Stoke, a mile and a half downstream of Newnham Murren. William died in 1576, the year before the first recusant list was compiled. William and Margaret Hildesley produced thirteen children, of whom four sons and four daughters survived their father. A brass in the parish church at Crowmarsh Gifford shows William Hildesley with his four sons on one side of him and a space on the other where once were the four daughters. This family was to play an important role in the survival of Catholicism in western Berkshire and southern Oxfordshire.

One who avoided being listed as a recusant was William Wollascott II of Tidmarsh, a nephew of the Catholic lawyer Edmund Plowden. The year before the first recusant list was compiled a tell-tale note was written on the fly-leaf of a fifteenth century Book of Hours, once part of the great library of Reading Abbey. It asks for prayers for Thomas Thomson, probably an underground Catholic priest, 'that he swerve not from the faith nor renounce holy church, that he may avoid the sorrow of sin and dissimulation, that he may die with general repentance, and receive the real sacrament.' The writer, probably Thomson himself, goes on to add that these sentiments are also 'meant for the worshipful William and Susan Wollascott ...'. This Book of Hours is now at Downside Abbey near Bath and is thought to have been discovered with other books of Thomson's at Shinfield House in a secret hiding place in 1792. This was a Wollascott residence from about 1587 when William Wollascott II's son William married Anne Martyn, heiress of the manor of Shinfield.

It seems then that William Wollascott II was a church papist, practising Catholicism in private, while outwardly conforming to Anglicanism. So too was Arthur Pitts who held the rectory and manor of Iffley, two miles downstream of Oxford. His wife kept a Catholic priest hidden in the house but, although a convinced Catholic himself, Arthur Pitts outwardly conformed to Anglicanism. He died in 1579 while entering St Mary's, Oxford. Uncompromising Catholics saw it as a fitting judgement on a church papist to be deprived 'by sudden death, or other obstacles, of sacramental confession.'

But, like many church papists, Arthur Pitts left behind him a strongly Catholic family. His widow Margaret became a leading recusant and three of his sons became priests. The family estate was forfeited to the Crown when two of the sons went abroad without a licence, presumably to study for the priesthood.

Owen Oglethorpe, squire of Newington, on the River Thame (2½ miles NE of Dorchester) was also a church papist. His son Owen was a recusant but in 1585 became Sheriff of Oxfordshire. The Oglethorpes were of Yorkshire descent and were related to the only Catholic bishop to take part in the crowning of Queen Elizabeth.

The Jesuits were founded in 1534, the year Henry VIII broke with Rome. During their first forty-five years they did not operate in England, although a number of Englishmen joined them to work in foreign missions. One of these was John Yate of Lyford, a hamlet on the River Ock (4 miles N. of Wantage). The Yates of Lyford were related to the Yates of Buckland who lived only four miles away. John Yate became Fr John Vincent and went to Brazil to work as a missionary.

Dr William Allen, founder of the English College at Douai, felt that brave young Jesuits such as John Yate would be better employed in England. Therefore, about the time that Yate sailed for Brazil, Dr Allen travelled to Rome and obtained an agreement that the Jesuits would start sending priests into England from the newly established English College at Rome. The first to go would be Robert Persons and Edmund Campion.

Robert Persons was a Somerset man and had been a Fellow of Balliol College, Oxford. He had taken the Oath of Supremacy and become a tutor but was subsequently expelled. On his way to study medicine at Padua he visited Louvain and became a Catholic. He eventually abandoned his medical studies and joined the Jesuits in Rome.

Edmund Campion, a Londoner, was six years older than Robert Persons. He had studied at St John's College, Oxford, taking the Oath of Supremacy and becoming the University's proctor and public orator. After a short time as an Anglican deacon Campion converted to Catholicism. In 1578 he was ordained priest while professor of rhetoric at the Jesuit school in Prague. Subsequently he was recalled to Rome to join the first Jesuit mission to England.

Travelling separately and in disguise Fr Campion and Fr Persons entered England during June 1580. Fr Persons wore a mercenary's uniform lent to him by George Chamberlain, exiled brother of Dame Cecily Stonor. The two priests met in London early in July. There they held a secret briefing for the capital's leading Catholics. At this so-called 'Synod of Southwark' they outlined their mission, discussed matters of church discipline and reinforced the official view that attendance at Anglican services was not permissible.

Fr Campion spent the late summer and early autumn of 1580 on a missionary tour of Berkshire and Oxfordshire. One of his guides was John Stonor, Dame Cecily's younger son. Fr Campion received a great welcome from those of the Thames Valley gentry who had remained loyal to the old faith. He wrote 'I ride about some piece of the country every day. The harvest is wonderful great.'

One of the charges later made against him was that 'in a certain room within the manor house of Great Coxwell being vested in alb and other vestments according to papistical rites and ceremonies [he] did say and celebrate one private and detestable mass in the Latin tongue, derogatory to the blood of Christ and contrary to his due allegiance.' Great Coxwell is a village a mile and a half south-west of Faringdon in the Vale of White Horse, noted for its fine medieval tithe barn. The manor house was the home of the Morris family who also owned Little Coxwell Manor. Thomas Morris, who sheltered Fr Campion, was sent to the Fleet prison in London the following year. He died there three years later, leaving an eight year old son.

Another Mass which may have been celebrated by Fr Campion was said that August less than five miles to the south at the chapel of Ashbury Manor. This is a fifteenth century moated farmhouse. Like Great Coxwell, it was a former monastic grange; Great Coxwell having belonged to Beaulieu Abbey, Ashbury to Glastonbury. The widow Alice Wicks was among those indicted for attending the service. During the previous year, a mile and a half to the east, the wife of the exiled Sir Francis Englefield had died at Compton House.

In the autumn of 1580 Fr Persons and Fr Campion met again in Uxbridge where they spent a few weeks resting. Fr Campion then went to Lancashire to write a theological book for distribution at Oxford University. In the meantime Fr Persons began establishing a secret printing press. This was first set up at Greenstreet, between East Ham and Barking. Later it moved to the London house of Sir Francis Browne. He was the brother of Lord Montague, the staunchest Catholic in Elizabeth's first parliament. Sir Francis had a country house, Henley Park, which according to government spies 'was never without three or four priests'. This was probably the Henley Park three miles south of Stonor, although there is another between Aldershot and Woking.

The arrival in England of the two Jesuits resulted in tougher anti-Catholic legislation. The 'Act to retain the Queen's Majesty's subjects in their due obedience' made it treasonable to convert anyone if the intention was to absolve them from allegiance to the Crown. Similarly, anyone so converted was guilty of high treason. Harbouring priests was also made illegal. Fines for celebrating Mass were increased to 200 marks (= £14,400 today) and a year in jail. For merely attending Mass the fine went up to 100 marks (= £7,200 today) and a year in jail. And for refusing to attend Anglican services the fine rose to £20 a month (= £2,200 today). Anyone over sixteen years of age absent from the parish church for a year now had to produce two sureties for at least £200 (= £21,600) until he or she conformed to Anglicanism.

The 'Act against seditious words and rumours uttered against the Queen's most excellent Majesty' raised the penalty for starting slander against the Queen to loss of both ears followed by indefinite imprisonment. For merely repeating the slander the penalty was increased to the loss of an ear followed by three years in jail.

Meanwhile Fr Persons was having great difficulty establishing the secret printing press. He therefore accepted an invitation to site it at Stonor House. This offer came from Dame Cecily Stonor, who was then living nearby at Stonor Lodge. By early 1581 the press was operational.

Stonor House was an ideal site. It was very private, being then surrounded by beechwoods. It was only a few miles from the Thames, giving an easy route to and from London. And it was only twenty-two miles by road from Oxford, the primary target for Fr Campion's new book.

STONOR HOUSE

The Press At Stonor

(1581)

The secret printing press was established at Stonor by a team of Catholic printers disguised as gentry. They were later joined by Fr Edmund Campion, but his superior, Fr Robert Persons, remained in London.

Clandestine liaison with sympathisers at Oxford University was established by Fr William Hartley and Fr Arthur Pitts, a son of the deceased Iffley church papist of the same name. While visiting Oxford Fr Hartley discovered that Roland Jenks, the Catholic stationer and bookbinder of 'Black Assizes' fame, was in trouble with the authorities again.

As Jenks had recently worked for Fr Persons, the Stonor team sent a messenger to London to give warning. It transpired that Fr Person's lodgings had already been raided by a hundred armed soldiers, and that a young Douai priest had been arrested nearby. The priest, Fr Alexander Bryant, was starved and severely tortured, but revealed nothing about the secret press. The former Oxford student's bravery allowed the printing to continue and enabled Fr Persons to escape to Stonor.

The press was probably installed in the large bedroom at Stonor House called Mount Pleasant. This has concealed access through another small room to the vast attics. As the house is built on a slope it was possible to escape from the attics to the then thickly wooded rising land behind the house.

By late June 1581 enough copies of Fr Campion's new book 'Decem Rationes' had been printed for circulation at Oxford. The full title in English was 'Ten Reasons Proposed to his Adversaries for Disputation in the Name of the Faith and Presented to the Illustrious Members of our Universities'. Fr Hartley smuggled more than 400 copies into Oxford, leaving several hundred on the benches of the university church of St Mary. The books caused consternation among the University and Anglican Church authorities.

The work of the Stonor press was now complete, at least for the time being. A fortnight later, on Tuesday 11 July, Fr Campion and Fr Persons left Stonor. Fr Campion intended returning to Lancashire to collect his reference books but had been given permission by Fr Persons to go first to Lyford Grange. Francis Yate, the owner of the house, was in prison for refusing to conform to Anglicanism. His mother remained at Lyford and Yate had managed to get a letter to Fr Campion asking him to visit her. Fr Persons agreed to the Lyford visit on the strict condition that it was for one night only. Ralph Emerson, a

LYFORD GRANGE

Jesuit lay brother, was instructed to go with Fr Campion and make sure that he kept to schedule.

Lyford Grange is a moated manor house near the River Ock, in a part of the Vale of White Horse as flat as Flanders. The house is now smaller than in Fr Campion's time but is strongly evocative of that period.

It has already been noted that one of the Lyford Yates had recently become a Jesuit missionary in Brazil. The family, and their equally Catholic cousins four miles away at Buckland, were descended from John Yate, a Merchant of the Staple in Henry VIII's time. The Yates of Lyford were traditionally buried at St James's church, West Hanney, two miles north of Wantage. One of the monuments to them states that they died 'in the full Catholic Faith'.

At the time of Fr Campion's visit to Lyford Grange the house had two chaplains, Fr Thomas Ford and Fr John Colleton. Fr Colleton had spent three years at the home of James Braybrooke, the expelled Inner Temple lawyer of Sutton Courtenay, jailed for his refusal to conform to Anglicanism.

But there was something more remarkable about Lyford Grange. It was home to what may have been the last remnant of English monasticism still on native soil; a community of Brigittine nuns, still following the religious life. Their convent of Syon in Middlesex (where Syon House now stands) had been suppressed forty-two years earlier. At one time an aunt of Dame Cecily Stonor had been abbess of the community. Queen Mary restored the convent but it was suppressed again by Queen Elizabeth. Since then the nuns had been put in the custody of various unsympathetic people until they ended up at Lyford. Francis Yate's widowed mother had become one of the sisters.

Fr Campion's overnight stay at Lyford passed off peacefully. After lunch he and Bro. Emerson headed towards Oxford, guided by Fr Colleton. Later that day a party of Catholics called at Lyford. They were disappointed to have missed the famous Jesuit, so Fr Ford was sent to bring Fr Campion back to preach to the visitors. Fr Campion and his companions were found at an inn near Oxford where they had met a large group of Catholics from the University, also eager to hear the author of the 'Ten Reasons'.

Bro. Emerson was eventually persuaded to go on to Lancashire alone and to let Fr Campion return to Lyford to preach. So next day the two Lyford chaplains took Fr Campion back to the grange where he preached and celebrated Mass for the people gathered there.

On the Sunday a government spy named Eliot joined the worshippers at Lyford. Eliot had worked in various Catholic households and was known to Mrs Yate's chef, who believed him to be a trustworthy Catholic. However, since they had last met Eliot had been in serious trouble with the law. He had been released from jail only after offering his services as a priest-hunter. This was a lucrative occupation because the priest-hunter could claim a third of the priest's considerable fine.

Eliot was one of thirty or forty people who attended Fr Campion's 10 o'clock Mass that Sunday morning. He then slipped away to call the nearest justice of the peace. As it happened the magistrate was less than enthusiastic. Quite apart from having his Sunday disturbed, he was a member of the then numerous Fettiplace family, some of whom remained Catholic and many of whom seem to have had Catholic sympathies. Indeed the wife of the exiled Catholic activist Sir Francis Englefield was a Fettiplace who had died only two years earlier, eight miles away at Compton Beauchamp. So too were John Yate of Buckland's wife and mother.

The magistrate brought a posse of about a hundred men, who were probably no more enthusiastic than him. The ensuing search was less than thorough, and failed to find the three priests who were in a secret hiding place over a stairwell.

The magistrate and his men were keen to leave but Eliot accused them of being secret Catholics. Justice Fettiplace defended himself by saying that he did not want to damage the house. As the evening wore on a second, more thorough search was made, but with no greater success.

Next morning the search was resumed with more enthusiasm and the priests were captured. Other known Catholics in the house were arrested, including William Hildesley of Beenham. He was probably the youngest son of Margaret Hildesley (nee Stonor) and may have been the Hildesley who, two years earlier, was studying for the priesthood at Douai, but who seems not to have been ordained.

Although Justice Fettiplace's men found the three priests, they seem to have missed some of the incriminating evidence. In 1959 electricians working in the roof void found a wooden box about eight inches in diameter and of similar depth nailed to a joist. It had been there for 372 years. Inside the box was ancient vellum, still soft and pliable, on which was written a list of indulgences. Wrapped inside the vellum was an Agnus Dei (Latin for Lamb of God), a wax medallion issued by the Pope, so-called because it bore a picture of the Lamb of God. In Elizabeth's reign it was a criminal offence to import or possess such a medallion.

The owner of Lyford Grange at the time of this remarkable find was a Miss Whiting who, with her companion Miss Morrell, had the Agnus Dei framed in gold. They presented it, together with its box and vellum wrapping, to the Jesuits of Campion Hall in Brewer Street, Oxford. There it is kept with a copy of a commentary on Aristotle's 'Physics' containing several specimens of Fr Campion's signature.

THE LYFORD AGNUS DEI

COMPTON BEAUCHAMP CHURCH
next to the manor house where Sir Francis Englefield's wife spent her last years

After the arrests Justice Fettiplace summoned the Sheriff of Berkshire, Humphrey Forster of Aldermaston, to take charge of the prisoners. Like Fettiplace, Sheriff Forster must have found the situation embarrassing. He is said to have been an admirer of Campion and 'almost a Catholic', with plenty of Catholic neighbours.

His branch of the Forsters owned Harpsden Court which is only five miles south of Stonor. (His great great great grandmother was Alice Stonor.) And his principal residence, Aldermaston Court, was virtually surrounded by lands controlled by Catholics: the Shalford estates of William Wollascott, Edmund Plowden's Wokefield and Burghfield estates, the Hildesleys' holdings at Beenham, Lady Marvyn's Ufton properties and the sequestrated estates of Sir Francis Englefield.

At first Sheriff Forster stalled and had a message sent back to Lyford saying that he could not be found. Justice Fettiplace had also summoned a fellow magistrate, and it was he, Justice Wiseman, who arrived first, reaching Lyford before dusk with a dozen of his own servants. That night sixty men guarded the house, while the rest slept.

When Sheriff Forster arrived he sent a message to the Privy Council asking what they wanted done with his illustrious prisoner and the other captives. For the next three days, while waiting for the reply, the Sheriff treated the prisoners civilly. The Council's orders put an end to this politeness. The dozen male prisoners were to be taken to London. Fr Campion was to be sat on a tall horse, his arms tied behind his back and his legs tied together under the horse. An inscription was to be fixed round his head to read 'Edmund Campion, the seditious Jesuit'.

The convoy's route took it first through Abingdon where, over dinner, Fr Campion forgave Eliot his treachery. Later it passed through Henley-on-Thames. Fr Persons was hiding nearby, possibly at Henley Lodge in Henley Park. He sent a servant to watch the prisoners pass through the town. The message came back that Fr Campion's morale was high.

But also in the crowd of townspeople was Fr William Filby, a young, recently ordained priest who had helped with the press at Stonor. He was the son of George Filby, a leather worker, who kept open house to Catholic priests at his home in the parish of St Mary Magdalen, Oxford.

Fr Filby broke his cover to speak to Fr Campion, swapped hats with him and was arrested. According to local tradition this took place at the top of the Fair Mile, the road that leads north-west out of Henley towards Stonor. Although the whereabouts of Fr Campion's hat are now uncertain, until earlier this century it was in the possession of the Jesuits of Prague, the city in which he was ordained.

Two days after passing through Henley-on-Thames the prisoners were put in the Tower of London. Fr Campion was confined to Little Ease, a notorious cell where he could neither stand nor lie straight. A week later the rack-master began torturing him. The combination of excruciating torture and false promises that no harm would come to anyone named led Fr Campion to reveal many details of the evolving Catholic underground.

This information was acted upon immediately. In the first week of August 1581 Stonor House was searched and Fr William Hartley, the printers' foreman Stephen Brinkley, and his four assistants were arrested. Stonor Lodge was then raided. Dame Cecily Stonor's younger son John was arrested and charged with having given refuge to a priest. The seven men arrested at Stonor joined the Lyford prisoners in the Tower. A Mr Browne, perhaps a relative of Sir Francis Browne, who was living at Henley Lodge in Henley Park was also arrested.

Fr Robert Persons had left Stonor by the time it was raided. About a fortnight later he escaped to the Continent. For nearly thirty years he was to work in exile for the cause of Catholicism in England. He became a trusted adviser to popes and Catholic rulers such as Philip II of Spain. Shortly after leaving England for the last time he published 'The Christian Directory' which was widely read by Catholics and Protestants. So great was the interest that Protestant publishers edited out the specifically Catholic references and printed pirated copies.

The trial of the priests captured at Lyford and Stonor began in late November 1581 at Westminster Hall. Fr Edmund Campion was charged under the old Treason Act of 1352. He stated 'I will willingly pay to her Majesty what is hers, yet I must pay to God what is his.' At the end of the rigged trial, having been found guilty, he said 'In condemning us you condemn all your own ancestors, all the ancient priests, bishops and kings, all that was once the glory of England, the island of saints, and the most devoted child of the See of Peter.'

On 1 December 1581 Fr Edmund Campion suffered a traitor's death at Tyburn (now Marble Arch) along with Fr Alexander Bryant and Fr Ralph Sherwin, two priests who had helped Fr Persons. Sir Francis Knollys of Greys Court was at the scaffold to ask Campion if he now rejected his Catholic faith. He wasted his breath. A piece of the rope used to hang Fr Campion was retrieved and is now kept at Campion Hall, Oxford.

But the dead Campion was in many ways a greater problem to the government than when he was alive. Even the anti-Catholic Lord Burghley, Elizabeth's close adviser, described him as 'one of the greatest jewels of England'. Numerous pamphlets on his trial and execution were produced, both in England and on the Continent.

Soon after Fr Campion's execution an Oxford Anglican professor of divinity complained that 'in place of one single Campion, champions upon champions have swarmed to keep us engaged.' At Balliol Catholicism was now so strong that the Privy Council ordered an enquiry. And this at the college once controlled by John Wycliffe, founder of the Lollards!

Four centuries later Edmund Campion is far from forgotten. In 1970 he was canonised as one of the forty English martyrs. He is remembered through churches and schools named after him, such as the Oxford area Catholic comprehensive. And every summer, thanks to the ecumenical goodwill of the present Anglican owner of Lyford Grange, a commemorative Mass is celebrated at the scene of his arrest.

Dame Cecily Stonor escaped imprisonment in the Tower. Her younger son John accepted most of the blame for sheltering the priests at Stonor. The authorities considered her old age and her good reputation, and decided to put Dame Cecily and her three daughters in the custody of her elder son Francis. She remained under house arrest or close supervision for the rest of her life. Her death and burial are not recorded.

Francis Stonor, a friend of Lord Burghley, lived at Blount's Court, Rotherfield Peppard. Hitherto he had not been conspicuously Catholic. He was one of six gentry in charge of the muster for the Chiltern Hundreds, the Elizabethan equivalent of the Territorial Army. Two of the other commanders were members of Catholic families, his cousin Robert Chamberlain and Robert Belson.

Francis Stonor was also given custody of John, his younger brother. John Stonor, was about twenty-five years old and had spent eight months in the Tower. There he had fallen in love with Cecily Hopton, the daughter of the Lieutenant of the Tower. She became a Catholic and for four years acted as a messenger between the Catholics in the Tower and their fellows in the more liberal Marshalsea jail at Southwark. Cecily Hopton later married Thomas, Lord Wentworth, whose mother was the daughter of Sir Adrian Fortescue and Anne Stonor.

John Stonor was bailed on the condition that, if he failed to conform to Anglicanism within three months, he would be sent back to jail. He seems to have jumped bail and late the following winter arrived at Douai. There he met his cousin and namesake from North Stoke, who had escaped to Flanders after the Lyford arrests.

A month later they parted company for ever. John Stonor of North Stoke returned to North Stoke Manor, which was probably on the site of the present rectory. His cousin spent the rest of his eventful life on the Continent. There he was kidnapped by the French and later served as a volunteer in an English & Welsh regiment of the Stadtholder of the Netherlands. Later he resigned his commission, settled in Louvain and married a Flemish woman.

He opposed the Jesuits' involvement in political matters but fully supported their spiritual aims. When he died, more than forty years after leaving Blount's Court, he left them 10,000 florins.

What of the others captured following the printing operation at Stonor? Fr William Morris, an old priest who had been the original literary editor, was imprisoned then banished. One of the printers seems to have turned informer. The rest were sent to the Marshalsea prison. So too was Fr William Hartley, who was later banished. He slipped back into England, was recaptured in December 1587 and was subsequently executed at Shoreditch.

Stephen Brinkley, the press foreman, was released from jail after less than eighteen months. He continued printing Catholic books in Normandy, from where they were smuggled into England. William Hildesley was also banished but seems to have returned. He was probably the William Hildesley later arrested for smuggling Catholic books. He had collected them from Amiens in Picardy and intended delivering them to a Mr Reynolds of Corpus Christi College, Oxford on behalf of Mr Reynold's brother living on the Continent. (The Puritan President of Corpus Christi was John Reynolds, one of whose four brothers, William, was a Jesuit.)

Sr Julian Harman and Sr Catherine Kingsmill were sent to Reading Gaol where they are thought to have died. Sr Joan or Philippa Lowe died in the White Lion prison, London nearly eight years after the Lyford incident.

Fr William Filby, the young priest arrested when he tried to speak to Fr Campion at Henley-on-Thames, was executed. So too was Fr Thomas Ford, the Lyford chaplain. His colleague Fr John Colleton, able to disprove the allegation of conspiracy made aginst him, was imprisoned in the Marshalsea for two years then exiled. He returned to England to work as a missionary, and was jailed a number of times. He died more than half a century after the Lyford arrests.

As for Roland Jenks the Oxford bookbinder, he later worked at the English College in Rome and printed Catholic books in Flanders. He is said to have ended his days as a baker at Douai, nearly thirty years after the fateful raids on Lyford Grange and Stonor House.

The Mission Becomes Established

(1582 - 1588)

In 1582, the year following Fr Edmund Campion's execution, Dr William Allen's seminary at Rheims published the first official Catholic English translation of the whole New Testament. Much of the initial print run of 5,000 copies was smuggled into England where it was received enthusiastically.

In the same year Walter Hildesley of East Ilsley and Crowmarsh Gifford, eldest son of Margaret Hildesley and head of the Hildesley dynasty, was among those recorded as being recusants. So too were his wife, manservant and maid. At Reading a Mrs Buckley was jailed for recusancy and the following spring Thomas Edwards, a Reading chandler, was in the Gatehouse prison, Westminster for the same reason.

George Browne, son of the staunchly Catholic first Lord Montague, married Eleanor, daughter of Anthony Bridges of Great Shefford (8 miles NW of Newbury) in 1583. On her marriage her father conveyed to her Great Shefford Manor Farm. It was there that Anthony Bridges sheltered Fr George Snape from about 1584 until 1591. Fr Snape was captured at the farm and abandoned Catholicism, thereby obtaining a pardon. The farm still stands. The Brownes owned Maidencourt Farm, which is less than a mile up the Lambourn Valley from Great Shefford.

There was still much reverence for Catholic vestments, books, furnishings and devotional items, even among ostensibly model Anglicans. There were heavy penalties for being in possession of such things which, according to the law, should have been surrendered or destroyed a quarter of a century earlier.

An Oxfordshire Archdeacon's Court in 1584 tried a number of men for keeping such 'popish trash'. Two had been found in possession of vestments. Another told of numerous items such as crucifixes, bells, vestments and altar cloths kept hidden by local people. Yet another had been given relics by a dying parson, an indication of the mixed feelings of some of the former Catholic priests who conformed to Anglicanism. Four years later the Mayor of Reading found Catholic books and vestments in a house in the town. Oliver Coxhead and a Mr Combes were ordered to be arrested.

In 1585 came further anti-Catholic legislation, prompted by the Throckmorton and Parry plots. Any priest ordained during the Queen Elizabeth's reign was to leave the country within forty days. Any who disobeyed, or who re-entered England, would automatically be guilty of high treason. Any lay person who 'willingly and wittingly' sheltered a priest was liable to the death penalty. Anyone who sent money to English colleges and seminaries abroad could lose their goods and suffer imprisonment. Parents sending their children abroad without a licence could incur heavy fines. Failure to give information on the whereabouts of priests could result in fines and unlimited imprisonment. But, if a missionary priest took the Oath of Supremacy within three days of landing in England, his 'treason' would be pardoned.

Meanwhile some Catholics found 'legitimate' excuses for not taking Communion according to the Anglican rite. For example, Richard East of Swyncombe House (3 miles W. of Stonor) claimed he could not receive Communion because his conscience was troubled by the evil speech of a certain Catherine Ginacre.

Fr Gregory Gunnes was arrested at Henley-on-Thames that summer. He had been ordained towards the end of Queen Mary's reign but for nearly twenty years had been an Anglican parson. In the late 1570s he had abandoned his ministry at Yelford near Witney and had since become a vagrant. At some stage he had been reconciled to the Catholic church.

At the Bell Inn, Henley Fr Gunnes fell into conversation with a member of Sir Francis Knolly's household and betrayed himself by praising Fr Edmund Campion. He was arrested and found to be carrying two consecrated Communion wafers. He was sent to the Marshalsea jail at Southwark.

That autumn the already outlawed Sir Francis Englefield was attainted and convicted of high treason by Parliament. The Privy Council had learned that he had advised Philip II of Spain to invade England. All Englefield's possessions and estates were forfeited to the Crown, which had already sequestrated them. However, having foreseen such problems, the Catholic lawyer Edmund Plowden had arranged the conveyance of the titles in all Sir Francis Englefield's estates and manors to the latter's brother, John. John Englefield had since died, leaving the titles to his young son Francis, who until recently had been Edmund Plowden's ward.

The estates and manors in question included Englefield, Tidmarsh, Tilehurst, Sindlesham, Brimpton, Speenhamland, Hartridge, Ilsley and South Moreton in Berkshire, and Lashbrook, Dunsden, Exlade and Shiplake in Oxfordshire. The conveyance of Sir Francis Englefield's estates drafted by Edmund Plowden included a provision whereby Sir Francis could reclaim the estates if he delivered a gold ring to their holder. This was now the Crown and it was quite unacceptable to the Queen that the seized lands of an attainted traitor could be reclaimed. But Edmund Plowden had done his work well and it was to take eight years of legal wrangling to resolve the situation.

Edmund Plowden died eight months before Sir Francis Englefield's attainder. He was buried in the Temple Church,

EDMUND PLOWDEN & SHIPLAKE COURT – from the bust in the Middle Temple Hall and an old engraving

London, where there is a memorial to him. There is also a bust of him in the Middle Temple Hall.

It was probably Plowden's guardianship of the younger Francis Englefield that enabled the lawyer to lease Shiplake Court from the Crown following its sequestration. After his death there seems to have been no difficulty in renewing the royal lease. Shiplake Court was subsequently occupied by Plowden's Catholic nephew Andrew Blunden, who held a joint interest in the property with Plowden's two sons. There is a bust of Blunden in Shiplake parish church.

Andrew Blunden regarded Sir Francis Englefield's seditious exploits as 'folly' and soon became involved in an acrimonious dispute with Sir Francis's nephew. The young Francis Englefield, backed by members of his family, claimed that Edmund Plowden had acted discreditably in handling Sir Francis's affairs. In contesting this view Andrew Blunden was supported by Plowden's aged brother-in-law Richard Sandford, and Sandford's son Humphrey, the lawyer who had acted as a courier between Edmund Plowden and Sir Francis Englefield. Two other Thames Valley Catholics, Thomas Vachell and Walter Hildesley, were brought into the argument.

During the feud the young Francis Englefield broke a promise he had made to Edmund Plowden. In exchange for Plowden relinquishing Englefield's wardship, Englefield had undertaken to look after Richard Sandford and his family, who lived in a house on the Englefield estate near Shrewsbury. But Englefield had Sandford evicted. The old man was greatly upset and sought refuge with Plowden's son at Plowden Hall, Shropshire where he died a fortnight later.

In July 1586 a remarkable event took place in Buckinghamshire at Harleyford Manor, two miles up the Thames from Marlow. This was the home of Richard Bold, a Catholic former Sheriff of Lancashire and harbourer of Fr Robert Dibdale. Harleyford is opposite Hurley Priory, the name being a corruption of Hurley Ford. It is only four and a half miles over the hills from Stonor and adjoins Danesfield, home of the nineteenth century Catholic convert Charles Scott-Murray.

Despite the fears of Queen Elizabeth's Privy Council there had rarely, if ever, been more than one Jesuit operating in England during the five years following the raid on Lyford Grange. But now three Jesuits came to Harleyford Manor: Fr William Weston, superior of the order in England; Fr Henry Garnet, mathematician, musician and former printer; and Fr Robert Southwell, gifted poet and former head of studies at the English College in Rome.

Others who now gathered at Harleyford included Catholic members of the nobility, and William Byrd, the Court musician. Byrd was the greatest English composer of the time and a staunch Catholic. He shared duties as organist of the Chapel Royal with Thomas Tallis. Because of his outstanding talent he was protected from persecution for his religious beliefs. He therefore wrote musical settings both for the Catholic liturgy and the new Anglican rite. The Harleyford conference gave Byrd a rare opportunity to supervise the performance of his settings for the Latin liturgy.

During the eight days of the conference the mornings were devoted to worship and spiritual improvement, the afternoons to planning the missionary campaign. The conference was safely concluded but three months later Fr Robert Dibdale, Richard Bold's chaplain, was hanged, drawn and quartered at Tyburn.

By this time more than half the 300 seminary priests smuggled into England had been arrested and banished, executed or imprisoned. The Privy Council's intelligence network was becoming increasingly effective. It now intercepted secret letters smuggled to and from Mary Stuart, Queen of Scots, who had been a prisoner of her cousin Elizabeth for eighteen years. Mary Stuart's secret correspondents included Sir Francis Englefield, Fr Robert Persons and a young Catholic courtier, Anthony Babington. He was a distant cousin of Lady Babington of Twyford near Buckingham.

While the Harleyford conference was taking place, in the third week of July 1586, Mary Stuart wrote to Babington making it clear that she fully supported a plot to depose Elizabeth. Early that autumn Babington and thirteen other plotters were executed, and within six months Mary Stuart was beheaded.

George Brome, a Catholic of Boarstall (9 miles NE of Oxford) had little regard for the competence of Babington and his associates. He boasted that he would handle things better if he ever got involved in a plot. His words were reported to the authorities by George Davies, the local parson, whom George Brome, his friend Robert Atkins and Brome's servant Henry Ferris had often tried to convert to Catholicism.

Brome probably thought he was safe talking to Davies. They had been fellow students at Oxford, and Davies wanted the living of Holton parish (3 mile S. of Boarstall) which Brome's family controlled. Nine years earlier George Brome had been imprisoned with his mother in the Gatehouse prison, Westminster for his religious beliefs. Now he was in trouble again.

Parson Davies's report was relayed by a magistrate to the Privy Council. This led to an early morning raid on the Brome's house by the magistrate's men. The family were held captive until the evening while a thorough search was made. The searchers found an Agnus Dei and religious statues which they destroyed. They confiscated 'corrupt and superstitious' books, including works by Thomas More, Edmund Campion and Robert Persons. Similar evidence of Catholicism was found at Robert Atkins's house.

The following month the Reverend Davies complained to the magistrate that Brome and Atkins had threatened him with violence. The case was dropped only after George Brome's

BRIMPTON MANOR & FORMER CHAPEL OF ST. LEONARD

father, a former justice of the peace, put pressure on the Secretary of State.

The execution of the Babington plotters in the autumn of 1586 was celebrated with public bonfires. Scornful remarks by a Berkshire Catholic about the festivities at Reading were reported to the authorities. The man in question was Francis Perkins of Ufton Court, which stands halfway between Padworth and Ufton Nervet (7 miles SW of Reading).

The Perkins family were relative newcomers to the Kennet Valley, having lived in the area for little more than a century. Francis Perkins's father, William Perkins of Brimpton, was gentleman usher to the executed Lady Margaret Pole and later to her son, Cardinal Pole. After the Chantries Act caused the suppression of St Leonard's Chapel at Brimpton, William Perkins occupied Brimpton manor as tenant-at-will of Sir Francis Englefield. This close connection with Queen Mary's regime must have reinforced the family's loyalty to Catholicism. The link was maintained by Francis Perkins who married Anna, the eldest daughter of Edmund Plowden.

Ufton Court was completed in 1576 and included large portions of the original medieval manor house of Ufton Pole. It is a large, timber-framed house with many gables. Woods to the north and west screen the house which stands in a gully and is therefore well hidden. In the year Fr Edmund Campion was executed Francis Perkins's aunt, Lady Marvyn, died. Perkins, who already owned the nearby manor of Ufton Robert, thereby inherited Ufton Court and the family estates in Wiltshire.

Thus Ufton Court became one of a chain of safe houses for missionary priests moving inland from south coast harbours, such as Chichester. One of the volunteers who guided priests between these safe houses was Francis Perkins's uncle, a Wiltshire schoolmaster called Swithun Wells. Shortly after Francis Perkins inherited Ufton Court, Swithun Wells was arrested and the Perkins family put up a surety for him. The underground courier spent the winter of 1586-7 at Ufton Court. Not long afterwards he moved to London where, in 1591, he was hanged for harbouring priests. His wife died in prison more than ten years later. Swithun Wells was canonised in 1970.

The man who accused Francis Perkins of making scornful remarks about Reading's celebration of the Babington Plot executions was Roger Plumpton. He was a tailor from Sulhamstead Abbots (1½ miles E. of Ufton Court). One evening late in the summer of 1586 Plumpton reported Francis Perkins to three local magistrates, one of whom was Humphrey Forster of Aldermaston Court, the former Sheriff of Berkshire who had taken custody of Fr Edmund Campion after his arrest at Lyford Grange. The magistrates somewhat reluctantly sent a report to the Secretary of State, the strongly anti-Catholic Sir Francis Walsingham, who had recently taken possession of Englefield House (3 miles N. of Ufton Court).

Plumpton accused Perkins of harbouring a seminary priest 'in a cock loft or some other secret corner of the house'. The magistrates' report stated that Plumpton 'On various Wednesdays, Fridays and other festival days ... hath seen most of the family, one after another, slipping up in a secret manner to a high chamber in the top of the house, and there continue the space of an hour or more.' and that Plumpton 'hearkening as near as he might to the place, hath often heard a little bell rung, which he imagineth to be a sacring bell, whereby he conjectureth that they resort to hear Mass.'

The informer stated that neither Francis Perkins nor his wife attended Anglican services. Neither did they have a high regard for members of their staff who conformed. Plumpton alleged that various people suspected of being Catholics regularly visited the house, sometimes by day, sometimes by night.

Later he claimed that a priest called George Lingham was likely to be hiding at Ufton Court. Plumpton said that Lingham travelled from one Catholic house to another, 'under cover of teaching in the virginals' (an early keyboard instrument). Apparently he sometimes stayed with William Wollascott II at Tidmarsh and also somewhere at Englefield. Lingham was probably Fr George Lingen, a relative of the Englefields, who had been a priest during the reign of Queen Mary.

Secretary Walsingham instructed the three magistrates to visit Ufton Court and interrogate Francis Perkins. When they arrived he was visiting relatives ten miles away at Ilsley on the Berkshire Downs. A messenger was sent to bring him back. In the meantime the house was searched but nothing incriminating was found.

That evening Francis Perkins arrived home and was questioned by the magistrates. They also interrogated all his servants, a tenant and the parsons of the nearby villages of Padworth and Sulhamstead. The clergymen suspected Perkins of harbouring Catholic priests, but could not prove it.

The immediate result of the investigation was that three of Francis Perkins's servants were jailed and a bond of £500 (= £100,000 today) was taken from Perkins to ensure that he appeared before Walsingham the following Saturday. But Francis Perkins was discharged and it seems that his servants were soon released.

On another occasion the informer Plumpton listed nearly two dozen suspected Catholics who frequented Ufton Court. They included Francis Perkins's mother Mrs Tattersall, his sister-in-law Mary Plowden, his cousins Francis and Richard Perkins of Padworth, Thomas Meysey who had married a daughter of Henry Perkins of Ilsley, Thomas Purcell who many years later bought nearby Wokefield from Edmund Plowden's son Francis, and 'one Taylor, an alehouse-keeper in Englefield, that of long time hath been a courier of letters between Sir Francis Englefield and other papists in Berkshire.' Also named was John Vachell of

Burghfield. He and his Catholic older brother Thomas were sons of Cromwell's commissioner for the suppression of Reading Abbey.

Someone else who had to appear before Secretary Walsingham was Richard Higges, a Berkshire labourer. He was accused of having a child christened 'by a priest at his own house in the Latin service.' Higges said he had met the priest on the Berkshire Downs near Wantage. The priest had been wearing a white sleeveless jacket and white stockings, and had been carrying a pen, ink-horn and a book. Higges refused to name the priest and was imprisoned in the Marshalsea jail.

By the mid 1580s even the richer Catholics were finding it increasingly difficult to pay the fines for non-attendance at Anglican services. The leading Berkshire Catholics pleaded that 'following the private zeal of our consciences we are deprivable of our liberties, and subject to the continual payments of greater sums of money than either our goods or the yearly profits of our lands and livings can discharge or satisfy ...' The practice grew up therefore of making offers of lump sums to clear the backlog of unpaid fines.

In 1586 Berkshire and Oxfordshire were among only ten counties in England where the offers exceeded £100. Berkshire's totalled £138 6s. 8d. (= £14,000 today) while Oxfordshire's came to £202 5s. 0d. (= £20,000 today). That year Berkshire reported 53 recusants and Oxfordshire 79. The Berkshire list included 1 esquire and 3 gentlemen. Oxfordshire listed 3 esquires and 17 gentlemen. An esquire was someone eligible for knighthood because the income from his land was in the order of £200 to £300 a year (= £20,000 to £30,000 today). Gentlemen were lower in status and not necessarily particularly rich.

Among the recusants listed in Oxfordshire were Edmund and Francis Plowden, sons of the famous lawyer. They offered joint composition of £20 (= £2,000 today). Dame Cecily Stonor offered £15 (= £1,500 today). The previous year she, like her brother-in-law Richard Owen of Godstow, had been compelled to pay £25 (= £2,500 today) to provide a light cavalryman for the Queen. Now her income at £100 a year (= £10,000 today) was much reduced, a fifth of what it had been before the Lyford incident. She had probably been carefully assigning her estates to others to reduce her liability.

Harcourt Taverner was the youngest son of Richard Taverner, a former Sheriff of Oxfordshire and of his wife Mary (nee Harcourt) whose family was partly Catholic. The Taverners lived at Woodeaton, a hamlet on the edge of Ot Moor (3½ miles NNE of Oxford). Rather than follow in his father's respectable footsteps, Harcourt Taverner became a highwayman.

In the autumn of 1587, while in Oxford Castle awaiting execution, he was converted to Catholicism by fellow prisoners. They succeeded in getting a message to Fr George Nichols who got into the prison by mingling with the crowd that had come to see the execution. Taverner managed to make his confession to Fr Nichols and was hanged in the Castle Yard shortly afterwards.

The same year the system of fines for non-attendance at Anglican services was tightened up. The new procedures were designed to hit the persistent offender particularly hard. Once a person had been convicted there was no longer any need to bring charges for subsequent offences. Fines were simply to be paid twice a year direct to the Exchequer. Failure to do so could result in the loss of all goods and confiscation of two thirds of the income from estates. Failure to attend the court proceedings meant automatic conviction.

Thomas Vachell was just the sort of person the new procedures were aimed at. In March 1588 he was convicted of not having attended Church of England services for a year. The following month he was ordered to pay £50 (= £5,000 today) to provide two light cavalry. About that time he and his brother John hid a large horde of treasure at Ufton Court.

The Vachells and Perkins were related. In his will, written in the last year of Mary Tudor's reign, Richard Perkins (Francis's uncle) named his 'cousin Thomas Vachell' and Sir Francis Englefield as executors. He left his crossbow to Thomas Vachell as a reward for performing this duty. (Sir Francis Englefield was also named as executor by the secretly Catholic William Wollascott I of Tidmarsh.)

Thomas Vachell had inherited Coley Park, the family seat a mile from the centre of Reading. But, presumably to avoid its loss through his recusancy, the estate was regranted to his Protestant nephew, another Thomas Vachell, who later became Sheriff of Berkshire.

About the time of the Papal Bull of 1570 against Elizabeth I, Thomas Vachell went to live permanently at Ipsden House, Oxfordshire (3 miles SSE of Wallingford). About a quarter of a century earlier he had married Catherine Reade, daughter of Thomas Reade of Barton Manor, Abingdon. (This is in Barton Lane off Radley Road and stands next to a ruined barn that belonged to Abingdon Abbey.) Thomas Reade is said to have built Ipsden House which was to remain in the family for centuries, being altered and extended from time to time. The Victorian novelist and journalist Charles Reade was born there and described it as 'the coldest house in Europe'.

Thomas Vachell was a noted builder of dovecotes, which in those days were useful food sources. That at Coley Park may have been built by him. It survives as part of a housing development based around the old farm buildings. Built into the brickwork is a small stone tablet on which is carved a cross. Perhaps this was saved from Reading Abbey, which Thomas Vachell's father despoiled. There is also a dovecote at Ipsden House. This is ascribed to Vachell and is more elaborate than that at

IPSDEN MANOR & DOVECOTE IN THE SNOW

Coley. Built of brick and flint, it has a conical roof topped by a glazed 'lantern'.

Through his marriage to Catherine Reade, Thomas Vachell acquired the manors of Ipsden, Huntercombe (3 miles ENE of Ipsden) and Ipsden Basset (near Stoke Row). But much of what he gained he lost for refusing to conform to Anglicanism.

In the summer of 1588 Michael Blount of Mapledurham was ordered to arrest Vachell, who also held land at Mapledurham. By the following year Thomas Vachell was having to pay the government £24 15s. 3d. from his Berkshire lands and £13 18s. 4d. from his Oxfordshire estates (together = £3,850 today). His goods had also been seized. The Receiver for the sequestration of his property was none other than his brother-in-law Thomas Reade. This led to a separation from his wife after more than forty years of marriage.

The year of Thomas Vachell's conviction was also the year of the Spanish Armada. Sir Francis Englefield, Fr Robert Persons and William Allen, now a Cardinal, were convinced that English Catholics would support an invasion if it was likely to re-establish Catholicism. In reality most preferred the Queen to a foreign monarch, however much they would have liked a ruler of their own religious outlook. Indeed, some leading Catholics petitioned Queen Elizabeth to be allowed to fight for her against Spain.

The Privy Council was not prepared to take the risk. Prominent Catholics were stripped of their weapons and interned or held under house arrest. They were made to contribute to the Subscription Against the Armada, a sort of enforced loan to the Crown. Most paid £25 to £50. Francis Perkins of Ufton Court, being then relatively wealthy, paid the higher sum (= £5,000 today).

One of the Catholics taken into custody was Dame Cecily Stonor's brother-in-law, Richard Owen of Godstow, who had married her sister, Mary Chamberlain of Shirburn. He occupied the former property of the dissolved Godstow Abbey near Oxford and, like many other Catholic gentry, had benefited financially from the suppression of the religious houses. But he was staunchly Catholic and paid one of the highest fines in the country, £159 2s. 2d. (= £16,000 today). Richard Owen was first imprisoned at Ely and later held under house arrest in London. He was subsequently bound over by the Archbishop of Canterbury. Three years after the Armada he was noted as one of the 'great adversaries of the Spanish practices'.

The reaction of the English Catholics to the Armada finally drove the message home to Sir Francis Englefield. He abandoned any hope of reconverting England by force because 'the Catholics are resolved to resist Spain'. In the last few years of his life he was to advise Philip II against repeating the attempt.

The building of secret hiding places for Catholic priests started in earnest in the year of the Armada. At the Harleyford conference two years earlier Fr William Weston, the Jesuit superior, had presented a list of houses all over England that would shelter priests. He was arrested shortly after the conference and spent the next seventeen years in jail. His strategy of basing missionary priests in the country houses of the Catholic gentry was put into practice by Fr Henry Garnet, who succeeded him as Jesuit superior.

Like Robert Persons before him, Fr Garnet wanted to set up a secret printing press. He still had contacts from his time in the printing trade. Perhaps he met the printer Henry Owen, one of four Catholic sons of Oxford carpenter Walter Owen. If so, it may have been by this means that Henry's brother Nicholas Owen was introduced to Fr Garnet. Nicholas was an extremely skilful mason and carpenter who was to spend the next twenty years working with Fr Garnet as his specialist builder of priest-holes.

All four Owen brothers demonstrated their attachment to Catholicism in practical ways. Henry operated a secret printing press. Walter spent much of his life in seminaries overseas. John served as a missionary priest in England. Nicholas was one of Fr Edmund Campion's young guides, and had been arrested for stating that the Jesuit was executed for his religion.

Now Nicholas Owen was to serve another remarkable Jesuit, becoming known to the authorities simply as 'Garnet's man'. The Catholics he served preferred the more affectionate nickname 'Little John'. The network of safe houses that Fr Garnet and 'Little John' established was to make a major contribution to the survival and character of English Catholicism.

Thomas Belson

(1583 - 1589)

'The Papists ... did proudly advance themselves, as though they ought to be taken for good subjects.' So complained Sir Francis Knollys in the reactionary atmosphere after the Armada. Another crackdown on seminary priests was soon under way.

As part of this drive, just before midnight 18 May 1589, four men were arrested at the Catherine Wheel Inn, Oxford. One of them was a young man called Thomas Belson.

Thomas's family were gentlemen farmers who held land in a number of parishes in the Thame area. Their principal seat was at Aston Rowant (4 miles NE of Watlington) where Thomas's Catholic father had been a churchwarden until the religious changes of Elizabeth's reign.

The family then moved nine miles to the remote Ixhill Lodge (1 mile SE of Oakley) which stood beside a tributary of the River Thame in Bernwood Forest. Although its name has been changed, the house is still there, well hidden by the trees alongside the stream.

Ixhill Lodge was in Buckinghamshire where the magistrates were more tolerant of Catholicism than were their Oxfordshire counterparts. By moving to this remote house across the county border and assigning his lands to sympathetic friends and relatives, Thomas Belson's father considerably reduced his exposure to fines for non-attendance at Anglican services.

The Belsons' new home became a safe house for Catholic priests. One who often stayed there was Fr John Filby, elder brother of the priest captured at Henley-on-Thames when Fr Edmund Campion was paraded through the town. Fr Filby was to exercise his secret ministry in the area for more than thirty years, supported by local Catholics such as the Belsons.

Other Catholics in the area included the Bromes of Boarstall (3 miles NW of Ixhill) the Bethams of Adwell (7 miles SSE) the Easts of Bledlow (9 miles SE) and the Lenthalls and Horsemans of Great Haseley (6 miles S.). The Easts were cousins of the Belsons and Dorothy East's widower, Thomas Fitzherbert, became Rector of the English College in Rome. Margaret Lenthall married Robert Tempest of Holmeside, County Durham who was exiled for taking part in the Northern Rising. Their daughter Anne married Thomas Belson's brother Robert, a commander of the Chiltern musters.

Thomas Belson may have attended the illegal boarding school for Catholics, run by Dr George Etheridge in a medieval hall in

---

Oxford. Etheridge was a skilled physician, musician and professor of Greek. Despite frequent fines and imprisonment he ran his school for a quarter of a century. His pupils included William Giffard, later Archbishop of Rheims, whose sister married Edward Yate of Buckland. Dr Etheridge owned a safe house for Catholics at Stanton St John (5 miles E. of Ixhill Lodge). The Belsons' frequent house guest Fr John Filby often stayed there with the lawyer Ambrose Edmonds, so the Belsons would have been aware of Etheridge's school.

It is known that Thomas Belson studied at St Mary's Hall, Oxford, which was part of Oriel College. This was an unusually independent college, which made it relatively easy for Catholics to gain admission without compromising themselves. Thomas studied under the Spanish Protestant Antonio del Corro, a rare advocate of religious freedom. In 1583 he applied for his Bachelor of Arts degree but did not undergo the final process, which would have necessitated taking the Oath of Supremacy. Instead he gave his lands and property in Brill and Oakley to his brother William and went to Rheims, where he studied at the seminary with his brother-in-law Robert Tempest. In spring 1584 he returned to England. The following summer he was arrested in London and imprisoned in the Tower.

In 1585, while Thomas Belson was still in prison, the Sheriff of Buckinghamshire, Robert Dormer of Wing, was ordered to compile a list of recusants. Each was to pay a fine of £260 (= £28,000 today) and finance a cavalryman for the Queen. Robert Dormer was himself a Catholic, which helps explain the leniency of the Buckinghamshire judiciary towards his co-religionists. The authorities knew that he harboured priests and even that Fr Edmund Campion had celebrated Mass at his house. Dormer also had many Catholic relatives. His brothers-in-law included Francis Browne of Henley Park, George Browne of Shefford, the younger Francis Englefield and the Count of Feria, formerly Philip II's representative in England. The martyred Carthusian monk Sebastian Newdigate, an uncle of Dame Cecily Stonor, was the Sheriff's great uncle.

But despite his religious allegiance, Robert Dormer did not altogether avoid the duties of his office. He named twenty-two Catholics and the threat of the new penalties proved too much for at least one. The widow Avice Lee, a neighbour of the Belsons, had refused to conform for the last two decades. Now, worn down by the struggle, she saved her lands by taking Communion in her parish church. However, two years later she was again listed as a recusant. Her younger son Roger became a guide and helper to the Jesuit Fr John Gerard, and subsequently became a Jesuit priest himself.

In the autumn of 1586 Thomas Belson, still in the Tower, was ordered 'To be banished the realm ... for conveying intelligence between Bridges the priest and others beyond the seas and some in this realm by unknown means.' Bridges was the alias of Edward Grately, a priest who had turned informer, as had Ralph Betham, a young neighbour of the Belsons.

Thomas Belson's father had to put up a bond which would be forfeited if his son illegally re-entered England. The old man promptly transferred what remained of his property to his wife and his eldest son, Robert. This meant that, if Thomas were caught in England, there would be nothing for the authorities to seize. And it seems that Thomas was soon assisting seminary priests again, and acting as a courier between them and the colleges in Rheims and Rome.

In May 1589 the authorities finally caught up with him. He was arrested with Fr George Nichols (confessor of the condemned highwayman Harcourt Taverner), Fr Richard Yaxley and a servant called Humphrey Prichard at the Catherine Wheel Inn, opposite the east end of St Mary Magdalen's Church in Oxford. At the prompting of a spy the arrested men's belongings were searched and among them were found some altar cloths. The two laymen were jailed in Oxford Castle; the priests in the Bocardo, the worst prison in Oxford.

After questioning by notables of the University the four captives were sent to London in the custody of the Sheriff's archers to be interrogated by the Privy Council. The priests had their hands tied behind their backs and their legs tied under their horses. The laymen had their hands tied. Humphrey Prichard, who was probably unused to riding, fell from his horse and suffered head injuries.

A graduate of Magdalen College called Ellis, inspired by their courage, walked alongside the prisoners all the way to London. Afraid that Ellis would tell bystanders how badly the prisoners had been treated, the Sheriff's archers had him consigned to Bedlam, the notorious Bishopsgate lunatic asylum.

The four prisoners were interrogated by Secretary Walsingham and by the Privy Council. Afterwards the two priests were sent to the Bridewell prison, one of the worst in London. They were hung by the hands for fifteen hours. During this time two informer priests confirmed that both Nichols and Yaxley were Catholic clergy.

Other tortures followed. Fr Nichols was transferred to the Tower and put in the Pit, a 20 foot deep unlit underground dungeon, full of vermin. Fr Yaxley was racked every day. Humphrey Prichard was moved to the Bridewell while Thomas Belson was kept in the Gatehouse prison, Westminster. It is probable that both were tortured. But it seems that none of the prisoners revealed any information that would prejudice their fellow Catholics.

By midsummer 1589 the Privy Council had decided to send the prisoners back to Oxford to make an example of them. All four were in such poor condition that they had to be carried in a wagon rather than on horseback.

The Privy Council wanted a show trial and Sir Francis Knollys travelled ahead to stage-manage the operation. On arriving at Oxford he raided the Catherine Wheel where Humphrey Prichard had worked and which, for many years, had been something of a safe house for Catholics. He had the landlady imprisoned for life and confiscated her belongings.

Because there was no evidence whatsoever of treason as normally understood, Thomas Belson and his fellow prisoners were tried under the recent statute imposing the death sentence on any Englishman ordained abroad who entered England, and on anyone helping such a person. The verdicts were a foregone conclusion. The two priests were convicted of high treason and sentenced to be hanged, drawn and quartered. The two laymen, as accomplices, were to be hanged.

The executions took place at Oxford in July 1589. The two priests were each dragged through the streets on a horse-drawn hurdle. The first to die was Fr George Nichols. Having been refused permission to address the crowd, he made his profession of faith. He made it clear that he was being executed merely because he was a priest. Climbing the ladder to the gallows, he made the sign of the cross on each rung and kissed it. Then he was thrown off to his death.

Fr Richard Yaxley was the next to die. He embraced the body of his dead colleague, then climbed the ladder and started to make his own profession of faith. But, before he could finish, he too was pushed off.

It was now Thomas Belson's turn to die. He hugged the bodies of the two priests and prayed that he would share their courage. He climbed the ladder, started his profession of faith and, like Fr Yaxley, was executed before he could finish. He was twenty-six years old.

Finally it was the turn of Humphrey Prichard, the servant from the Catherine Wheel. At the top of the ladder he told the crowd that he died for 'being a Catholic and faithful Christian of Holy Church'. A Puritan minister mocked him for being ignorant. Prichard replied that 'what I cannot explain by mouth, I am ready and prepared to explain and testify to you at the cost of my blood.' Whereupon he was thrown from the ladder.

The priests were decapitated and quartered, their heads and quarters being parboiled in a cauldron. Their remains were then fixed to the wall of Oxford Castle where they were mutilated by Puritan extremists. A couple of days later the remains were fixed to the town gates. The right arm of Fr Nichols is reported to have swivelled round of its own accord. Some said it pointed accusingly at the city.

Within a year of their deaths, the story of the Oxford Martyrs had been published in Italy, Spain and France. Four eye-witnesses of the executions had related the story to Richard Verstegan, an English writer, poet and publisher based in

Antwerp. Verstegan relayed the reports to Cardinal William Allen in Rome and sent additional information to Spain. The story was published in Rome early in 1590. Within three months a French translation was available. Later in the year Fr Robert Persons issued the Spanish version. The incident had generated international interest and much bad publicity for Queen Elizabeth's regime.

In 1987 Thomas Belson, Humphrey Prichard, Fr Nichols and Fr Yaxley were among eighty-five English and Welsh martyrs beatified by the Pope.

Elizabeth's Later Years

(1589 - 1603)

After the Oxford executions of 1589 searches took place all over the Thames Valley area. At Aston Rowant a priest-catcher who had been involved in Thomas Belson's arrest accused a Mr Randall of being a Catholic priest.

Randall was a lawyer of the Middle Temple. He and his mother and sister were Catholics, held under house arrest in the home of his brother-in-law, John English. Mrs English was a Catholic and English himself was probably a church papist. He worked for the Lord Chancellor, Sir Christopher Hatton, a Protestant who allowed the Catholic Mass to be celebrated in his London house.

It seems that Randall mischievously encouraged the priest-catcher's suspicions. Later, when interrogated by Sir Francis Knollys, Randall completely denied any suggestion that he was a priest. He admitted being a Catholic but said he was 'as ready man to fight the Spaniards as my Lord Montague was.' (The Catholic second Lord Montague, nephew of George Browne of Shefford and Francis Browne of Henley Park, had volunteered to fight for the Queen against the Spanish.)

John English's house was searched and a large collection of suspected 'popish' literature was found. English told Knollys that it belonged to the exiled George Chamberlain, whose nephew owned Shirburn Castle, a few miles down the road towards Watlington. Eventually the threat of legal action was dropped for lack of evidence.

The Oxford Catholic martyrdoms seem to have inspired Francis Stonor to become more open in the practice of his Catholicism. No doubt the execution of the brother of a fellow militia commander made a great impact. Two years earlier Francis Stonor had been Member of Parliament for New Woodstock. Yet eight months after the Oxford executions he was examined by the Privy Council and the following year was paying recusancy fines of £30 a year for himself (= £2,750 today), and twice that sum towards £340 (= £31,000 today) owed by his mother, Dame Cecily Stonor. By the end of the year his fine was even higher and he was also expected to provide on demand two light cavalry and two lancers for the Queen.

However, Francis Stonor's recusancy did not prevent him from serving as Sheriff of Oxfordshire in 1593 nor from being knighted by the Queen when she visited Basing House, near Basingstoke, in 1601. Francis Stonor's wife Martha was a staunch Catholic. Her father, judge John Southcote, had resigned in open court rather than sentence a priest.

It has already been noted that Catholicism survived strongly among the gentry of the Kennet Valley. At Henwick, between Thatcham and Newbury, lived another Catholic, John Winchcombe. The Winchcombes were descended from John Smallwood of Winchcombe, Gloucestershire, better known as Jack O'Newbury. He was 'the richest clothier England ever beheld', and it seems that the Catholic John Winchcombe was his great grandson.

In 1591 Winchcombe was reported by the spy Robert Weston for being a harbourer of priests. Weston described a hiding place used by fugitive clergy, a great hollow oak in the hedgerow near Winchcombe's house (probably Henwick Manor). According to the spy 'church stuff' was hidden upstairs in the house, in a cupboard by the pickling trough for pigs' offal.

By 1592 the income from fines for recusancy was so great that a special department was established by the Exchequer to handle it. The following year the Five Mile Act was introduced. This compelled recusants to remain within five miles of their homes or else forfeit their goods and the income from their estates. They had to report regularly to the parson and parish constable, and their names had to be recorded in the parish register and notified to the justices of the peace. Failure to pay the fines could result in banishment. Any Catholic even suspected of being a priest, but refusing to admit it, could be imprisoned without trial.

Not long after this new legislation Francis Stonor's sister-in-law, Lady Ann Curson of Waterperry House, was fined £260 for recusancy (= £24,000 today). Her husband Sir Francis was not a recusant but may have been a church papist. As the parish church of St Mary stands next door to Waterperry House the pressure on him to attend Anglican services must have been considerable. (The present Waterperry House is a Georgian replacement for the house in which Sir Francis and Lady Ann lived.)

Lady Ann Curson is thought to have entertained the Jesuit Fr John Gerard. He had studied briefly at Oxford before being imprisoned for his faith and subsequently becoming a priest. For seventeen years he travelled England setting up Catholic communities with resident chaplains based in country houses. Waterperry House formed the core of one of Fr Gerard's communities. With his help Lady Ann Curson established a chapel in the house, and another Jesuit, Fr Edward Walpole, became the chaplain. At this time there were still only some eighteen Jesuits working in England.

John Vachell of Burghfield had until this time been a Catholic and was one of those suspected of attending Mass at Ufton Court. However, in 1593, during imprisonment in the Marshalsea, he conformed to Anglicanism. Perhaps he was influenced by what he saw in his own family. His recusant elder brother Thomas was head of the family but had felt compelled to regrant the family seat at Coley Park, Reading to his conformist nephew. While

WATERPERRY HOUSE

Thomas suffered sequestration, fines and consequent marital discord, his nephew married a daughter of Sir Francis Knollys, was knighted and became Sheriff of Berkshire.

In the spring of 1593 an Act Confirming the Queen's Title to the Lands of Sir Francis Englefield was passed. This was the culmination of eight years of attempts by the Crown to circumvent the cunning conveyances devised by the late Edmund Plowden on behalf of Sir Francis. Now virtually all the manor of Englefield was forfeited to the Queen. According to the Englefields it had been theirs for almost 800 years.

Sir Francis Walsingham, the Secretary of State who had moved into Englefield House, had subsequently died. The estate passed to his son-in-law, the Earl of Essex. Although Walsingham is said to have built a gallery especially for a visit by the Queen, much of what approximates to the present mansion seems to have been built during the Earl of Essex's tenancy. The reported discovery in 1838 of a roof timber dated 1558 suggests that at least part of Sir Francis Englefield's manor house was incorporated. However, there was a major fire in 1886, and much of what we see today is a Victorian reconstruction.

The Englefields retained a small foothold in the village from which they took their name. Margaret Englefield, mother of the younger Francis, owned Englefield Farm near Cranemoor Lake, a little to the south-east of the manor house. The family also continued to be buried in their former chantry in the parish church.

In 1593 a Recusant Roll was produced. This listed known Catholic non-conformists and the fines imposed on them. Further rolls were produced annually for the following three years. In most cases the authorities had sequestrated some or all of the recusants' estates. Usually two thirds of the estate income was taken by the Exchequer.

The Recusant Roll for 1592-3 reveals that in Oxfordshire Thomas Vachell of Ipsden lost all the income from a farm, and two thirds from the manors of Ipsden, Huntercombe and Basset, and from a parcel of land in Mapledurham called 'Payges'. (Basset Manor stands between Stoke Row and Checkendon and there is still a wood called Page's Shaw at Chazey Heath, Mapledurham.) Vachell's Berkshire estates were also sequestrated. In the area immediately to the south-west of Reading he lost the income from Beansheaves near Calcot and from other properties in Burghfield, Grazeley, Shinfield and North Street, Englefield.

Francis Perkins of Ufton Court was apparently living at Langford, Wiltshire at this time. He owed fines of £80 (= £7,000 today) and lost the income from estates at Buscot and Snowswick near Faringdon. He also lost two thirds of the income from his estates at Bathampton in Wiltshire and Ufton Court. His cousin Richard Perkins and Richard's mother Margaret, widow of Henry Perkins of Ilsley, each owed a massive £260 in fines (= £23,000 today). Richard Perkins, usually referred to as being of Beenham, was described in the Recusant Roll as being of Fieldhouse Farm, Ufton; probably a mistake for what is now Field Barn Farm, Beenham, just over the parish boundary from Ufton.

Walter Hildesley lost two thirds of the income from Ilsley Farm. With his mother he lost two thirds of the income from estates at Howbery and Newnham Murren, both near Crowmarsh Gifford.

Francis Plowden, son of the famous lawyer, lost the income from a farm at Wokefield and two thirds of the income from 'Migheals' at nearby Burghfield. This was perhaps what is now called Meales Farm, actually in nearby Sulhamstead. Roger Astell, a yeoman of Basildon, lost two thirds of the income from a farm at Peasemore (6 miles N. of Newbury).

Thomas Hulse lost two thirds of the income from a holding called Le Poole at Sutton Courtenay. (A few years later his widow Mary married Edmund Wollascott, a son of William Wollascott II. The Hulse estates at Sutton Courtenay thereby became Wollascott property.)

Martha Braybrooke was presumably the widow of the expelled Catholic lawyer James Braybrooke of Sutton Courtenay. She was then living at Brightwalton, a village on the Berkshire Downs (5 miles S. of Wantage). Her losses were enormous: two thirds of the income from the manors of Marlston (Bucklebury), Fulscot (between Didcot and South Moreton) and Adresham (South Moreton), eight tenements in Abingdon, another in Sutton Courtenay and land at Sparsholt (3 miles W. of Wantage).

Others listed on the Recusant Roll included men and women from Oxford, Watlington, Waterperry, Aston Rowant, Crowmarsh, Chinnor, Great Haseley, Checkendon, Wolvercote and Garsington. Church papists such as the Wollascotts avoided sequestration. Hence William Wollascott II's son William was able to buy the manor of Brimpton, which adjoined his Shalford estates.

In 1594 Nicholas Owen, the Oxford craftsman and builder of priest-holes, was arrested with Fr John Gerard. Owen was taken to the Counter prison in Poultry in the City of London. Despite being hung by the hands for three hours he revealed nothing to his captors. Fortunately they did not realise who he was and released him on payment of a large bribe.

Late in the summer of 1596 Sir Francis Englefield died. He is buried at Valladolid, Spain where he had retired to the English College. He had been blind for the last twenty-four years of his life.

Ironically the other Sir Francis, his Puritan opponent Knollys, died in the same year. Their lives contained a number of parallels. Both had gone into exile for their religious beliefs and both had suffered great frustration. Neither had enjoyed the support they felt their causes deserved.

But whereas Sir Francis Englefield died far away from his native Berkshire, Sir Francis Knollys died on home ground. His funeral took place across the valley from his home, Greys Court, at Rotherfield Greys parish church. His son William, the first Earl of Banbury, built the north chapel on to the church. Inside he erected a huge, freestanding monument to his father and mother. (Sir Francis is also commemorated by the road in Reading called Great Knollys Street.)

One of those who attended the funeral of Sir Francis Knollys was Sir Richard Blount of Mapledurham. The Blounts were ostensibly conformists in religious matters and were relatively wealthy. Six years before the Armada Sir Richard had bought the adjoining Chazey manor from Anthony Bridges, presumably the man who sheltered Fr George Snape at Great Shefford Manor Farm.

At the time of Sir Francis Knollys' funeral it seems that Sir Richard's father had recently converted to Catholicism. Sir Michael Blount was a former Sheriff of Oxfordshire and Member of Parliament who had become Lieutenant of the Tower of London six years earlier. He was deeply impressed by two of his Catholic prisoners, both of whom were sentenced to death. One was Fr Robert Southwell, the Jesuit priest and poet, who had played a major role in the Harleyford conference. The other was Philip Howard, Earl of Arundel. Fr Southwell was executed early in 1595 and Philip Howard died later that year while awaiting execution. Both were canonised in 1970.

Evidence of Sir Michael's conversion to Catholicism is found in the mansion he was then building at Mapledurham. In the year of the Armada he had raised a loan of £1,500 (= £140,000 today) to build it. The original, relatively humble manor house was then anything up to four hundred years old and did not befit a man of Sir Michael's status. (A corner of the old manor house quadrangle still exists.)

The new house was not completed until 1612, two years after Sir Michael's death. Yet not long after he ceased to be Lieutenant of the Tower, he had two secret hiding places constructed off a first floor bedroom. Their distinctive features show that they were built by the same craftsman who had earlier constructed hides at Ufton Court, someone involved in the local Catholic underground.

As secret Catholics the Blounts had a useful facility within the parish church at Mapledurham which stands immediately behind the manor house. They owned the Bardolf Aisle and it was therefore possible for them to pray privately in the family aisle during Anglican services. As far as the Church of England authorities were concerned, this would constitute attendance at an Anglican service. But as far as the family were concerned they could merely be making proper use of their aisle for private prayer. Thus the Blounts had an unusual opportunity to avoid the labels 'recusant' <u>and</u> 'church papist', if they so

MAPLEDURHAM HOUSE

wished. The Bardolf Aisle remains, to this day, a private aisle owned by Catholics within an Anglican church.

Many people in the Reading area know the attractive road from Caversham to Mapledurham called The Warren. At the Caversham end it is a pleasant residential road, whereas towards Mapledurham it becomes a farm track and bridleway. It came into existence about the year 1600 as a result of a land deal by which Sir Richard Blount acquired a parcel of land below Chazey Wood. This allowed him to complete a relatively level route from his home to Caversham. The parcel in question had formed part of the estate of Caversham rectory.

At this time the rectory was leased to a Catholic family called the Alexanders. The house was later renamed Caversham Court and survived until 1933. Its site is now a public garden. Evidence of the Alexanders' tenure is provided by a surviving photograph of the Old Rectory's ornate staircase. It shows a ceiling plaque with the initials WIA, said to stand for William Alexander.

The Alexanders were succeeded by another Catholic family, the Brownes. It appears that the Browne in question was George of Shefford, who was knighted three years after the Armada.

In 1597 Nicholas Williamson, an Oxfordshire Catholic, wrote to Lord Burghley from Liege. He urged that the Queen grant religious freedom so that people with differing religious viewpoints could more readily unite to defend England.

Williamson cited France, Germany and Poland as places where relative freedom of conscience had been granted. He argued that:

'If a man does a lawful act, yet against his conscience (as thousands in England do to avoid the penalty of the law) he damneth his own soul. Therefore men that have a care for their souls will rather suffer their country to be a spoil to the enemy and themselves brought into bondage, than their souls to be led daily to damnation ...'

The plea was ignored. The following year a Levy of Horses was introduced to fund cavalry to combat the threat of a Spanish invasion of Ireland. In 1601 fourteen Berkshire Catholics were compelled to contribute to this fund.

In 1599 Ufton Court was raided again. This time the informer was a man called Gayler, whose brother had worked for the Perkins family. Gayler persuaded the Lord Chamberlain to draw up three warrants. Two were for the apprehension of the Jesuit Fr John Gerard and his superior Fr Henry Garnet. A third authorised seizure of 'a great store of treasure and money deposed at Ufton Court by persons of ill repute for the relief of ill-disposed persons'.

On a summer night the officers brought the warrants from London to the Member of Parliament for Reading, Sir Francis Knollys.

He was a son of the recently deceased Puritan leader and lived in the small royal palace that had been created out of what remained of Reading Abbey. The officers refused to tell him the name of the house to be raided and did not mention the treasure. Nonetheless, they insisted that a raid be carried out without delay. Although it was already dark Knollys agreed and set off from Reading with the two officers and about forty men.

On arrival at Ufton Court early next morning it took nearly an hour to get a reply from the occupants. Francis Perkins was not living there at the time, but his cousin Thomas Perkins was acting as housekeeper and eventually opened the door to the search party.

Knollys' men broke into a secret chapel in the attic of the south-west wing. There they found 'divers relics and popish trash, as namely, holy water with a sprinkler therein and a cross at the end of the sprinkler, besides which, there was a little box with divers small white wafer cakes like Agnus Dei fit for the saying or singing of Mass, and candles half burnt out such as usually Mass is said withall, and divers pictures and such other things whereby it seemed unto them that some Mass had been said or sung not long before.'

Thomas Perkins denied all knowledge of the chapel. Then one of the officers from London produced the third warrant, declaring that he had found the hidden treasure. He revealed two locked chests in a hide under the passage floor in the attic. They were found to contain gold and silver plate worth some £1,850 (= £145,000 today). The treasure was confiscated and the male servants put in Reading Gaol.

The Perkins family subsequently used a man called Peter Beaconsawe in an effort to recover the treasure. He claimed, falsely, that it represented his proceeds from cattle dealings, and had been hidden at Ufton Court for safekeeping. The Perkins's also implied that Sir Francis Knollys, or one or more of his men, had stolen a further £751 15s. 7d. (= £58,000 today) in silver that had gone missing from the secret hiding place. Beaconsawe brought a successful legal action against Knollys but was later jailed for contempt of court.

The legal wrangling lasted for ten years and ended with Sir Francis Knollys being exonerated. The disappearance of the silver was never properly explained but it is thought that two of the Ufton servants may have taken it, perhaps in collusion with Richard Perkins who had been given custody of the treasure by its real owner.

That owner was Thomas Vachell of Ipsden. His formerly Catholic brother John was called as a witness for the defence of Sir Francis Knollys. John Vachell revealed that he and Thomas had put the treasure in the hide at Ufton Court when Thomas was facing sequestration of his estates and seizure of his goods. The seized treasure was eventually put in the custody of Thomas Vachell's nephew and heir, Sir Thomas Vachell of Coley, who was

PART OF UFTON COURT – the chapel was in the south-east wing on the left of the picture

also Knollys' brother-in-law. This was done 'out of pity for the distressed state' of the elder Thomas, who was by then senile.

Francis Perkins was fortunate in living away from Ufton Court at the time of the raid. Two years after, he was listed as a justice of the peace, despite being a known Catholic.

The year following the Ufton raid an old priest called Fr Moore died at Water Eaton, a hamlet on the River Cherwell near Kidlington. He is mentioned in the parish register and may have been sheltered by the Anglican owner of the local manor, which had been built only fourteen years previously, and which still stands.

By the late 1590s the deaths of many of the Queen's long-serving advisers left a power vacuum. This aided the rapid rise of Robert Devereux, Earl of Essex who held Englefield House by virtue of his marriage to Lord Walsingham's daughter Frances. In 1597 he disposed of Englefield to Lord Norris. Two years later he attempted what was virtually a coup d'etat. He failed but survived to make a second attempt early in 1601.

Two of his fellow plotters were Catholics. One was Sir Christopher Blount, Essex's stepfather and a distant relative of the Blounts of Mapledurham. The other was Sir John Davis.

Davis was an eminent mathematician who had studied at Gloucester Hall, Oxford, where Catholic influence remained strong. He had been knighted by Essex at Cadiz, southern Spain, after taking part in the English raid on the city in 1596. Two years later he was appointed Surveyor of Ordnance, hence his importance in the Essex plot. Davis saved himself from the death sentence by abandoning his friends and his faith. He became a witness against his co-conspirators, blaming Sir Christopher Blount for his conversion to Catholicism. Twelve years later Davis bought Bere Court, adding to the unhappy associations that house has for Catholics. There is a monument to him in Pangbourne parish church.

Another Thames Valley Catholic who took part in the Cadiz raid was the great poet John Donne, then about twenty-four years old. He had studied at Hart Hall, Oxford and his uncle Fr Jasper Heywood was a Jesuit working on the English mission. Donne later conformed to Anglicanism and eventually became Dean of St Paul's, London. His Catholic past greatly influenced his poetry and his Anglicanism.

During the late Elizabethan era it was still possible for discreet Catholics to benefit from an Oxford University education, especially if sympathetic tutors could be found. But conscientious Catholics could not receive their degrees because to do so would require taking the Oath of Supremacy.

In 1602 the oldest and youngest sons of the late John Eyston of East Hendred were admitted to Magdalen College, Oxford. William was eighteen, his brother Thomas fifteen. Both were described as being of Catmore, one of the manors long held by their family. The parish of Catmore, high on the Berkshire Downs, is one of the least populated in England. It includes the hamlet of Lilley where most of the fifty or so inhabitants live. Catmore itself is nearly 600 feet above sea level. Today it consists of little more than a farmstead and an ancient Norman church, illuminated by candlelight. Catmore was not always so small; in Saxon times it was a market town.

Catmore's remote location (5 miles S. of East Hendred) made it a good refuge for the Catholic Eystons. In the 1970s evidence of a hiding place and pre-Reformation chapel was found in the farmhouse, which still belongs to the family. An early fifteenth century statue was discovered hidden under the floor, the head missing but the body carefully wrapped in silk. According to family tradition there was a second hiding place at Catmore and an escape tunnel.

William Eyston, the older of the two Magdalen students, married in 1610 and continued to live at Catmore. Centuries later a small silver ring was dug up in Catmore churchyard. It was inscribed 'William Eyston, Esquire, of Catmore near Wantage, in Berkshire'.

By the end of Elizabeth's reign some 800 seminary priests had been smuggled into England of whom about 300 were still at large and exercising their ministry. Yet there had been no proper leadership of the Catholic church in England for forty years. By the late 1590s it was becoming increasingly necessary to establish some sort of formal organisation. Fr George Blackwell, a former scholar of Trinity College, Oxford, was therefore appointed to the new post of Archpriest of England. He was to report to the papal nuncio in Brussels and to consult the Jesuit superior on all matters of importance. There were many objections from English Catholics to this appointment and an appeal was made to Rome to appoint a bishop instead, who would be free of Jesuit influence.

This first appeal failed but a second attempt was aided by the government which saw an opportunity to divide Catholic opinion and curb Jesuit influence. The Pope subsequently agreed that the Archpriest need not consult the Jesuit superior.

Those who presented the appeal also tried to negotiate a measure of religious freedom, but this was rejected by both Queen and Pope. The Queen said that it would 'disturb the peace of the Church' and 'bring this our State into confusion', whereas the Pope felt that 'persecution was profitable to the church'.

One of the leading supporters of the appeal was Fr Thomas Bluet. He had been ordained at Dr Allen's seminary in 1578 and later that year was arrested in Berkshire. Fr Bluet spent most of the rest of his life in internment, campaigning against the Jesuits. He complained that the mission of Fr Campion and

Fr Persons had been 'like a tempest, with sundry great brags and challenges', the main effect of which was harsher anti-Catholic legislation. Fr Bluet was regarded as something of a crank. He left the priesthood in 1602 and died two years later.

Queen Elizabeth died in 1603, nearly seventy years after her father's break with Rome. At the beginning of her reign England was a nominally Catholic country with a minority of committed Protestants; at her death, forty-five years later, the country was nominally Anglican with Puritan and Catholic minorities.

Elizabeth had executed 123 priest and more than sixty lay Catholics. She had made it socially disadvantageous and potentially financially ruinous to be a Catholic. And she had tried hard to avoid accusations of religious persecution by equating Catholicism with treason.

Estimates of how many English people remained Catholic at the end of Elizabeth's reign vary from 1½ per cent to 25 per cent. There may well be an element of truth in both figures. It is probable that only 1½ per cent were Catholics who would make no concessions whatsoever to state-enforced religious conformity. It is equally likely that 25 per cent would have been prepared to describe themselves as Catholic, given the freedom to do so.

In the Thames Valley area Catholicism survived strongly among the gentry, particularly in southern Oxfordshire and western Berkshire. The Catholic occupants of manor houses along the river valleys and ancient downland pathways were rarely more than a few miles from a recusant or church papist neighbour of similar social standing. And they had many good Anglican relatives and neighbours who would rather turn a blind eye than report them to the authorities.

The Gunpowder Plot

(1604 - 1606)

'Now we have a king who is of our religion and will restore us to our rights.' So said an Oxfordshire Catholic lady on the accession of the son of Mary Queen of Scots to the English throne. She was wrong on both counts.

It is true that James Stuart had been baptised a Catholic. He had, however, been raised a Protestant. And although he had given the impression that he would relax anti-Catholic legislation, his performance was a grave disappointment to most Catholics.

The first signs were promising. On his accession in March 1603 he knighted Henry Stonor, eldest son of Sir Francis. But two months later he instructed that the recusancy fines be collected.

Among those fined as a result was Lady Margaret Clarke, daughter of Mary Tudor's Secretary of State, Sir John Bourne. She and her husband, Sir William Clarke, lived at North Weston, a mile and a half west of Thame.

The following year she was reported to be sheltering a priest. It is said that, for the last twenty years of her life, Mass was regularly celebrated at her home, North Weston Manor Farm, or in a 15th century chapel which stood just to the west of it. A small portion of the east wing of Lady Clarke's house survives as part of the present farmhouse. The chapel was demolished in the last century but a few moulded stones from it remain.

Early in 1604, following the Bye Plot, the King commanded all Catholic clergy to leave England and never return. About this time Francis Plowden, son of the famous lawyer went into exile for six years. He left his son Francis and the rest of his family in the care of Andrew Blunden at Shiplake Court.

The disappointment at the King's treatment of Catholics led a small group of them to organise the Gunpowder Plot. None of the principal plotters came from Berkshire or southern Oxfordshire, but there is evidence that there may have been some knowledge of the plot among Catholics in the area.

The Earl of Salisbury, Robert Cecil, was head of the secret service at this time. He seems to have infiltrated the plot at an early stage and to have manipulated it for propaganda purposes.

One of his informants was a mysterious Davies. Could this have been Sir John Davis who later bought Bere Court? His name is

---

sometimes spelt with an 'e'. Until recently he had been a Catholic and perhaps some Catholics believed him still to be one at heart. He and the Gunpowder plotter Robert Catesby had been co-conspirators with the Earl of Essex. Did Catesby mistakenly confide in him? Davis had already shown his preparedness to inform on his colleagues.

In January 1605 a number of the Gunpowder plotters, including Catesby, met at the Catherine Wheel Inn, Oxford. An ominous location perhaps, as this was the same tavern in which Thomas Belson and his companions had been arrested sixteen years earlier.

At the time of the Gunpowder Plot the Member of Parliament for Reading was Francis Moore. He was forty-seven years old, a barrister of the Middle Temple and one of the ablest lawyers of his day. He was also one of the lawyers to whom the younger Francis Englefield had been bound when Edmund Plowden had him admitted to the Middle Temple.

The Moores came from East Ilsley and had built Ilsley Hall. (The present building is later, at least externally.) The Catholic Englefields, Hildesleys and Perkins all held land in the village. Francis Moore had formerly acted as a lawyer for the Catholic Earl of Northumberland and Moore's daughter Elizabeth later became the second wife of Sir Richard Blount of Mapledurham. Moore therefore had plenty of Catholic connections and his family seems to have been Catholic.

Nine years after the Gunpowder Plot he built the remotely sited South Fawley manor, on the Berkshire Downs between Hungerford and Wantage. It had a Catholic chapel at the top of the tower. The manor formed an outpost of discreet Catholicism which was to endure into the following century. A number of Francis Moore's descendants became monks or nuns.

Francis Moore left intriguing evidence of the government's infiltration of the Gunpowder Plot. At the time of the conspiracy he often had to work into the small hours with a client in London. Several times during 1605, on his way home at about two o'clock in the morning, he saw Thomas Percy leaving the home of the Earl of Salisbury, the head of the secret service. Francis Moore knew Percy, who was the Earl of Northumberland's steward. It later transpired that Percy was one of the Gunpowder plotters.

Francis Moore told all this to Dr Godfrey Goodman who moved to West Ilsley fifteen years after the Gunpowder Plot. Goodman later became Bishop of Gloucester and is said to have become a secret Catholic.

Francis Moore was knighted in 1616. He was a Member of Parliament five times and a steward of Oxford University. He amassed considerable property in Berkshire. Among his many acquisitions were the rectory of the vanished medieval village of Whatcombe (1 mile S. of South Fawley) and Maidencourt Farm

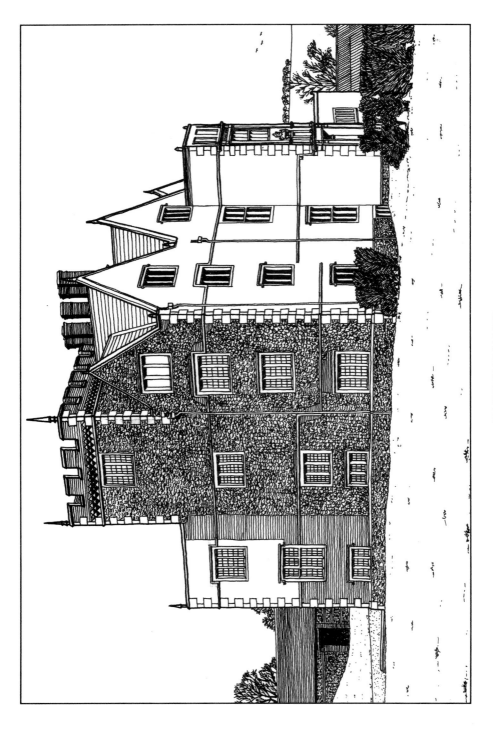

FAWLEY MANOR

on the River Lambourn (1½ miles SSW of Whatcombe). Both of these were sold to him by the Catholic Sir George Browne of Great Shefford.

In the summer before the Gunpowder Plot a Thomas Hildesley became a Jesuit on his deathbed in Rome. The following winter the head of the East Ilsley line, Walter Hildesley, and his wife were to find themselves dangerously close to the Privy Council's investigations.

Walter and his wife Honour were staying with her father, Henry Carey, at Hamworthy near Poole in Dorset. On 2 January 1606, eight weeks after Guy Fawkes was arrested, the house was visited by two servants of Lord Howard of Bindon, a member of the Privy Council. They had come to arrest Honour's brother Henry.

At first she refused to open the door, answering the men from an upstairs window. But eventually, having been joined by her husband Walter, she let them in. It seems that at the time she was wearing a jewelled crucifix given to her by the Spanish ambassador who had visited the Hildesleys at East Ilsley.

The reason for the Privy Council's suspicion was that the younger Henry Carey knew Thomas Percy and Robert Catesby, and had been in London with his armour the day after the King and Parliament were to have been blown up.

Henry Carey's apparently successful defence was that, while in London, he had offered to join Sir Christopher Blount, the Earl of Devonshire, who was heading for Warwickshire, heartland of the plotters. Although a Catholic and former co-conspirator of the executed Earl of Essex, Blount was now Master of the Ordnance and a member of the Special Commission for High Treason that investigated and condemned the Gunpowder Plotters.

Walter Hildesley himself had also been in contact with a plotter. Five weeks before the planned explosion he had sold a horse to Ambrose Rookwood. It must have been a good one because £30 changed hands (= £2,000 today). However, as Rookwood's main interest in life was horse breeding, this was hardly evidence of conspiracy.

When the Gunpowder plotter Robert Winter was convicted, the Crown seized the main manor of Didcot, which a group of people including Winter held from the Stonors. But Winter may never have actually been there and the property was recovered by the Stonors in 1616.

The Catholic Alexander family of Caversham Rectory (later Caversham Court) were also drawn into the aftermath of the Gunpowder Plot. Robert Newport, a Catholic servant of the Earl of Northumberland, had been living with them for two years. He was alleged to know much about the conspiracy and would certainly have known Thomas Percy, Northumberland's steward.

During his stay with the Alexanders (who were also known as the Milwards), Newport had never attended an Anglican service at the adjoining parish church. But the rector had been afraid to report him because William Alexander controlled the tenancy of the parsonage. Situations like this led shortly afterwards to legislation preventing Catholics controlling the patronage of Anglican benefices.

The family that were to succeed the Alexanders at Caversham Rectory, the Brownes, were also implicated in the Gunpowder Plot. The plotter Robert Catesby's sister Anne was the sister-in-law of Sir George Browne of Shefford. But it was Sir George's nephew, the second Lord Montague, who was arrested and put in the tower. It transpired that, thirteen years earlier, Guy Fawkes had been one of his servants. And apparently, a few weeks before the planned explosion, Robert Catesby had advised Lord Montague to avoid visiting Parliament for the time being.

Lady Agnes Wenman of Thame Park, site of the former Cistercian abbey, was also in trouble as a result of the Gunpowder Plot. Her husband Sir Richard Wenman was a Protestant, but she was a member of the Catholic Fermor family and related to Elizabeth Vaux, a great supporter of the Jesuit superior, Fr Henry Garnet. (Interestingly, Fawkes is a variant of the name Vaux.)

A letter Elizabeth Vaux had written to Agnes Wenman implied inside knowledge of Jesuit operations. Unfortunately it was found by her mother-in-law, who passed it to the authorities.

Subsequently Elizabeth Vaux and Agnes Wenman met to discuss their position. The venue was the home of Elizabeth Vaux's son-in-law, Sir George Simeon, at Brightwell Baldwin (3 miles W. of Watlington). This was presumably the former residence of Sir Adrian Fortescue.

John Fortescue, a grandson of Sir Adrian, had a marginal involvement in the Gunpowder Plot. But the man who arrested Guy Fawkes, Sir Thomas Knyvett, married the daughter of Sir Adrian's widow. The lantern that Fawkes was using at the time of his arrest can be seen in the Ashmolean Museum, Oxford.

Early on 20 January 1606 more than a hundred armed men surrounded Hindlip Hall, a Catholic safe house near Worcester. Inside, in a secret hiding place, were Fr Henry Garnet and another Jesuit, Fr Edward Oldcorne. In another hide were Nicholas Owen, the Oxfordshire master builder of priest-holes, and a fellow Jesuit lay brother, Ralph Ashley.

After a week the two lay brothers surrendered and tried to pass themselves off as the priests. This ploy was foiled by the informer Anthony Sherlock, who had been Dame Cecily Stonor's chaplain and who knew Fr Garnet. The search therefore continued until the priests were eventually captured.

Nicholas Owen had ruptured himself while single-handedly building priest-holes. An iron plate was therefore fitted around his body so that he could be racked without ripping his body open. It did not work. In early March 1606 his bowels burst and he died, taking his secrets with him.

Two months later Fr Garnet was executed as an accessory to the Gunpowder Plot. He had known of its existence but had warned Robert Catesby against 'rushing headlong into mischief'.

Since the Harleyford conference Fr Garnet and Nicholas Owen had worked solidly for twenty years to establish mission bases in country houses. The government may have rid itself of this troublesome pair, but it could not undo their work.

The Jacobean Period

(1606 - 1625)

In the aftermath of the Gunpowder Plot came new anti-Catholic legislation. Catholics were forbidden to appear at Court, despite the fact that the Queen, Anne of Denmark, had recently converted to Catholicism. They were also banned from coming within ten miles of the City of London, and had to remain within five miles of their homes, unless granted a special licence. They were excluded from many professions, including medicine and the law. All holders of public office were now required to take Communion annually according to the Anglican rite. And the penalties for secret Catholic baptisms were increased by an additional £100 fine (= £6,800 today).

It was also made illegal for Catholics to hold the patronage of Anglican benefices. Many Catholic landowners retained these ancient rights from pre-Reformation times. Henceforth these rights were to be divided between the universities of Oxford and Cambridge.

The 1606 version of the Oath of Allegiance contained a declaration that the Pope had no political authority in England. This seemed reasonable and some Catholic priests, including the Archpriest of England, took the oath. However, the new wording could also be construed as rejecting the Pope's spiritual authority. The Pope therefore condemned it and the Archpriest was replaced.

With the stiffening of anti-Catholic legislation John Perkins of Beenham, brother of the recently deceased recusant Richard Perkins and cousin of the recusant Francis Perkins of Ufton Court, claimed exemption from recusancy fines on the grounds that he had become an Anglican.

In 1606 Francis Englefield and William Wollascott together bought the manor of Earley Whiteknights near Reading for £7,500 (= £½m today). Six years later Francis Englefield achieved knighthood by becoming a baronet. After a further seven years he bought out Wollascott's interest in Whiteknights for £5,600, (= £336,000 today). This Wollascott seems to have been William Wollascott III. Whiteknights was to become an important Catholic centre for the Reading area. Today it is the main campus of Reading University.

Walter Hildesley's mother, Margaret nee Stonor, died early in 1607. Her youngest daughter Catherine had a brass plate erected to her memory in the parish church at East Ilsley. Margaret Hildesley is not named but is referred to as the widow of William who had died some thirty years earlier. In the text on the plate Catherine refers to herself as 'shining with a virgin's diadem', thus seeming to imply that she was a nun. If so, she was not the only Hildesley nun about that time. In 1601 a Mary Hildesley had joined the Franciscan nuns of Brussels. Also in Brussels, but at a Benedictine convent, was one of Lady Ann Curson's daughters, who professed in spring 1605. Another of Lady Ann's daughters professed at the same convent seven years later.

In 1609 Mary Ward from Yorkshire founded a female equivalent of the Jesuits, which became known as the Companions of Mary Ward. They worked among the poor and established schools for girls at Hammersmith and York. An early Companion was Jane or Joanna Browne, daughter of Sir George Browne of Shefford and Caversham. One of her aunts was the wife of the younger Francis Englefield, another the wife of Sir Robert Dormer, the Catholic former Sheriff of Buckinghamshire.

Catherine Hildesley's brother Walter married twice. As previously noted, one of his wives was Honour Carey. The other was Dorothy, daughter of Humphrey Burdett of Sonning. The Burdetts were Catholics, friends of the Vachells and close relatives of the Englefields. In 1608 Dorothy Burdett's brother William gave thirty-one manuscripts to the recently refurbished Bodleian Library. Most came from Reading Abbey.

It may well be that Thomas Vachell rescued the manuscripts when his father oversaw the suppression of Reading Abbey. Perhaps half a century later, when threatened with seizure of his goods, he had secreted the documents with the Burdetts at Sonning, just as he had hidden his treasure with the Perkins at Ufton Court. The Burdetts passed other Reading Abbey manuscripts to another Catholic, John Stonor of North Stoke, who gave them to St John's College, Oxford.

About 1609 the Catholic Francis Hyde completed construction of Hyde Hall, Purley. The Hydes were a family with branches in many parts of Berkshire, some of which remained Catholic long after the Reformation. In Elizabethan times their principal seat was Denchworth (2 miles SSW of Lyford Grange) where they held three manors. The road from Denchworth towards Lyford is still called Hyde Road and almost half way between the two villages is Hyde Farm.

In Denchworth parish church is a monument to William Hyde whose fourth son Hugh lived at Letcombe Regis (3 miles SW of Wantage). Through marriage Hugh Hyde acquired the manor of La Hyde at Purley (1 mile E. of Pangbourne) which had been held by his medieval ancestors (hence presumably the family name).

Hugh Hyde's son Francis became lord of La Hyde manor in 1605. About four years later he finished building Hyde Hall, now known as Purley Hall. Although the house was altered in later centuries, the symmetrical facade, with its bay windows, appears to be as Francis Hyde built it.

PURLEY (FORMERLY HYDE) HALL

The parish boundaries in the area are somewhat convoluted and it is said that until about a century ago four parish boundaries converged in the dining room: Pangbourne, Purley, an enclave of Whitchurch that no longer exists, and a neck of Sulham.

An old account in the Reading Mercury describes a smoke-blackened room adjacent to the kitchen chimneys, 'accessible only through a trap door in the ceiling of a cupboard'. The article suggests that this may once have been a priest-hole but it might merely have been for smoking bacon.

Francis Hyde's first wife was Anne Tempest, said to have been the daughter of Robert Tempest of Holmeside, Durham. This Anne was too young to have been the widow of Robert Belson and therefore can not have been the daughter of the Robert Tempest of Holmeside attainted for involvement in the Northern Rebellion of 1569. It is more likely that she was the daughter of his eldest son Michael, who was also attainted and who died in exile working for the Spanish in Flanders. She must have died relatively young, probably in childbirth, and certainly before Francis Hyde inherited La Hyde, Purley.

In 1610, about a year after the completion of Hyde Hall, Sir Robert Chamberlain of Shirburn obtained a licence to travel abroad for three years, with three servants, two nags and £50 (= £3,000 today). The permit was later extended by two years which enabled him to visit his exiled relative Jane Dormer on her deathbed in Spain. Jane Dormer, half-sister of the Catholic former Sheriff of Buckinghamshire, had been the loyal companion of Mary Tudor. She had become a Spanish duchess by her marriage to the Duke of Feria, Philip II's former representative in England. She urged Chamberlain to 'stand strong and firm in the Catholic faith'. However, he never saw England again because, a year or two later, he was drowned or murdered in the Mediterranean.

Another Oxfordshire Catholic who travelled abroad at this time was Robert Harcourt of Stanton Harcourt (6 miles W. of Oxford). In 1609 he sailed to Guyana in South America where, with his brother Michael, he established a settlement. After a few years it failed and, despite publishing a book on his voyage, he was unable to raise enough capital to revive the venture. However, in 1626 he and Captain Roger North founded the Guyana Company. Robert Harcourt left for Guyana two years later and is thought to have died there not long afterwards.

The remains of Stanton Harcourt Manor, the Harcourt family seat at this time, include a fifteenth century tower (of which more later) and the Great Kitchen, described as 'one of the most complete medieval domestic kitchens in England'.

Finchampstead (3 miles S. of Wokingham) lies on the Devil's Highway, the old Roman Road from Silchester to London. In the late thirteenth century the original manor was divided into two, known as East Court and West Court. The Perkins of Ufton acquired West Court in the late fifteenth century. By the time James I came to the throne West Court had passed to George Tattersall through his marriage to Francis Perkins's daughter Catherine. Two of George and Catherine Tattersall's great granddaughters married Howards and thereby became ancestors of the Dukes of Norfolk. West Court today presents a late seventeenth century appearance.

The Tattersalls were not the only Catholics in Finchampstead at this time. Thomas Eyston, youngest brother of William Eyston of Catmore (he of the ring), also lived there. He was a lawyer who had married Mary Yate of Lyford. Thomas Eyston was such a patient sufferer for his faith that he was given the nickname 'Old Job'. He was born in the year of the Armada and lived to the age of eighty-one.

Old Thomas Vachell lived to much the same age. He too had suffered greatly for his religious beliefs. His only child, a daughter, had died young. He passed away at Ipsden in the spring of 1610.

The appointment of his brother-in-law, Thomas Reade, as receiver for his sequestrated estates and seized goods, had resulted in a separation from his wife, Catherine. In 1595 she was boarding with her husband's tenant at Basset Manor near Stoke Row. But before her death in 1604 Catherine and Thomas were reconciled.

During his last few years Thomas was senile and was cared for by his widowed sister, Anne Montague. This led to charges of undue influence against her by Thomas's Protestant heir, Sir Thomas Vachell of Coley. He claimed she had retained a will and appropriated some of his valuables.

Old Thomas of Ipsden was buried on 10 May 1610, in accordance with family tradition, at St Mary's in the Butts, Reading. This was the church where, sixty-four years earlier, he had married, and to which he had recently made a donation for a new bell. But until the end of his life he was fined for being a Catholic.

Perhaps the most traumatic event of 1610 for Catholics in the Thames Valley was the execution of Fr George Napper at Oxford.

The Nappers were said to be descended from the Earls of Lennox. They lived at Holywell Manor, which they leased from Merton College. The house stands on what was then the eastern outskirts of Oxford, near the River Cherwell. Originally an early sixteenth century building, it is now much altered and part of Balliol College. The Nappers also leased Rectory Farm at Temple Cowley from Christ Church College.

George Napper's father was a fellow and benefactor of All Souls; his mother the niece of a Franciscan Cardinal. Towards the end of Elizabeth's reign, George's elder brother William had sublet a plot of land at Temple Cowley to a Catholic mason called Badger, who built a safe house for Catholics on it.

George Napper was born during the reign of Edward VI. At the age of thirty he was arrested on his return from a year at Rheims. He was in prison about the time of the Armada in 1588. The following year he took his own version of the Oath of Allegiance which seems to have satisfied the authorities without compromising his own conscience. He later studied at Douai and was ordained in his mid forties. He spent the rest of Elizabeth's reign at Douai and Antwerp.

On the accession of James I in 1603, Fr George Napper joined the English mission. He worked in England for seven years, travelling on foot, poorly dressed. One summer's day in 1610 he was in the village of Kirtlington (8 miles N. of Oxford). The holders of the manor house, the Arden family, were Catholic about this time, but that night Fr Napper stayed at the house of Henry Tredwell. Two young men saw him enter and told the vicar.

The following morning Fr Napper was arrested, taken to the local constable and then to the nearest justice of the peace, Sir Francis Evers. Sir Francis treated him well and contrived not to find the small bag of relics and the pyx containing two consecrated hosts which were concealed in the old priest's clothing.

Fr Napper was tried at Oxford Assizes. The judge, Sir John Croke, was a son-in-law of Sir Michael Blount of Mapledurham. He told the jury that, if Fr Napper were to say he was not a priest, he would believe him. But the priest was not prepared to deny his calling and so was sentenced to death.

He might have been granted a reprieve but for the fact that, soon after his conviction, a criminal revealed on the scaffold that Fr Napper had reconciled him to Catholicism. This enraged the militant Puritans who pressed for an early execution.

However, this was prevented by the Sheriff, Sir Michael Dormer, whose elaborate tomb can be seen in Great Milton parish church (8 miles ESE of Oxford). Fr Napper was interrogated by Sheriff Dormer (a Protestant relative of the Catholic Dormers of Buckinghamshire) and by the Vice Chancellor of the University. He was urged to take the Oath of Allegiance and thereby save his life. The priest was prepared to take his own version of the oath, but this time the ploy was rejected. His family petitioned the King for a reprieve but to no avail.

Early one November morning in 1610 Fr Napper was told he would be hanged between one and two o'clock that afternoon. He responded by celebrating Mass in his cell. Later the Proproctor of the University made a final unsuccessful attempt to persuade him to take the Oath of Allegiance.

Fr Napper was then dragged through the streets on a hurdle and taken to the scaffold. A Protestant clergyman told him to confess his treason. He replied 'I thank God I never knew what treason meant.' An argument followed in which Fr Napper maintained that only Catholics could achieve salvation. Then the old priest prayed that the King might be made a saint.

The crowd were sympathetic to Fr Napper. When he was thrown off the scaffold they pulled on his legs so that he would not have to live through his own disembowelling.

Each of the four quarters of his body was fixed to a gate of the city. According to tradition at least one of his quarters ended up in the Thames. A miller at Sandford (3 miles S. of Oxford) saw it and told Edmund Powell, whose sister was Fr George Napper's sister-in-law.

The Powells were a Catholic family of Welsh origin who had bought Sandford Manor during the reign of Henry VIII. The house had been a regional base, first for the Knights Templars and later for the Knights Hospitallers. It is said that Edmund Powell had Fr Napper's remains retrieved from the river and buried in the Knights' old chapel on the south side of the manor house. At some stage the chapel was converted into a barn but it still exists.

Two of Edmund Powell's daughters later became Franciscan nuns. Through the Powells' influence Sandford-on-Thames was to remain an important Catholic mission throughout the seventeenth century. The manor house became known as Temple Farm. It is now part of Templars' Court Country Club, a Thameside caravan park and leisure complex. Fr Napper was beatified by the Pope in 1929.

By the time Fr Napper was executed Sir Michael Dormer's term of office as Sheriff of Oxfordshire had expired. His successor was Benedict Winchcombe, a Catholic. Sheriff Winchcombe was related to the Berkshire Winchcombes and lived at Noke, on the edge of Ot Moor (4 miles NE of Oxford). He also held land at Chalgrove (3 miles WNW of Watlington). Towards the end of Elizabeth's reign his family had built their own chapel on to the north side of Noke parish church. This chapel no longer exists, having been demolished in the mid eighteenth century.

Two years after Fr Napper's execution the Privy Council made an order that all holders of public office with recusant wives, children or servants should be dismissed. Benedict Winchcombe's wife was a known but unconvicted recusant and he promised to receive Communion according to the Anglican rite in the near future.

Benedict Winchcombe was probably a church papist but it seems unlikely that he ever fully conformed. He died in 1623, leaving his estates to Benedict Hall, his Catholic nephew. The overseers of the will included the notable Catholics Francis Plowden and Sir Richard Fermor.

Catholicism meanwhile persisted in the Henwick branch of the Winchcombes. This is evidenced by William Winchcombe of

SANDFORD MANOR (NOW TEMPLARS COURT)

Henwick, who became a Benedictine two years after Benedict Winchcombe promised to conform.

The heads of the Bucklebury branch of the family conformed to Anglicanism, at least outwardly. Yet throughout the seventeenth century the Bucklebury Winchcombes frequently intermarried with neighbouring Catholics. Jane married Edward Perkins, son of Francis Perkins I of Ufton Court. Her brother Henry married Mary Wollascott of Woolhampton. Henry's daughter Frances married another Francis Perkins, grandson of Francis Perkins I. Frances's sister Mary married Francis Hildesley of East Ilsley and Littlestoke. Her son Francis became a Jesuit. And Sir Henry Winchcombe of Bucklebury married Frances Howard, the Catholic daughter of the third Earl of Berkshire, who lived at Ewelme Manor. The Winchcombes' Bucklebury home was built on the site of a retreat of the martyred abbot Hugh Faringdon. It burned down in 1830 but the monastic fishponds still exist.

In 1611, the year after Fr Napper's execution, the authorities sequestrated an estate known as Bullocks at Cookham. This was the property of Sir Edward Manfield who had been convicted of recusancy. It is now called White Place and is on the Thames two miles upstream of Maidenhead, and almost opposite Cliveden.

In the summer of 1611 Sir Francis Stonor's wife, daughter, sister and daughter-in-law were imprisoned in Banbury Castle for refusing to take the Oath of Allegiance. The daughter-in-law was his youngest son William's wife, Elizabeth. Her father was the Secretary of State, Sir Thomas Lake. Her brother Arthur married Anne Plowden, granddaughter of Edmund Plowden.

In 1615 the trial took place of another kinsman of the Stonors, John Owen of Godstow. The Owens of Godstow were gentry and do not appear to have been closely related to the family of the martyred Oxford craftsman Nicholas Owen.

Although not a priest, John Owen was said to have spent time at seminaries in Seville, Rome and in Flanders. He was alleged to have stated that the King, being excommunicated, could lawfully be deposed and killed. John Owen was sentenced to death, but after three years in jail, he was exiled following the intervention of the Spanish ambassador.

In 1616 Marcus Antonio De Dominis, Archbishop of Spalato (now Split, Yugoslavia) fled to England, renouncing the Catholic Church. James I made him Dean of Windsor and Rector of West Ilsley.

Initially De Dominis wrote against Catholicism, but after six years without promotion, he turned against Anglicanism. One wonders what contact he had with his Catholic neighbours such as the Moores and Hildesleys.

De Dominis was expelled from England in 1622 and made his way to Rome. Despite writing against Anglicanism he was imprisoned by the Church authorities. He died in the Castle of St Angelo two or three years later. De Dominis was noted for his advanced explanation of rainbows. But soon after his death his body was disinterred and burned with all his writings.

His successor at West Ilsley was Dr Godfrey Goodman, who later became Bishop of Gloucester. Although Goodman never formally left the Church of England, he is said to have become a secret Catholic, the only Anglican bishop to do so.

In 1617 Thomas Plowden of Shiplake became a Jesuit. He was the third son of Francis Plowden and hence a grandson of the Elizabethan lawyer Edmund Plowden.

Another Edmund Plowden now comes into the story, Thomas's elder brother. In 1620, about the time that the Puritan 'Pilgrim Fathers' set up their American colony, Edmund Plowden II established the Plantation of New Albion. This consisted of a huge area around Chesapeake Bay, including what is now Delaware, part of Pennsylvania, New York, and Cape Cod. Long Island was first known to English-speaking people as Isle Plowden, after Edmund Plowden II of Shiplake.

Edmund and his wife Mary stayed in America for ten years. During this time his sister Margaret became a nun at the Augustinian convent, Louvain. She had been taken there at the age of twelve by her mother. Edmund Plowden II later became Earl Plowden, Governor of New Albion, and took the radical step of offering religious freedom to his settlers.

Francis Perkins II, son of the first of that name, succeeded his father at Ufton Court. In 1620 he did a deal with his Catholic neighbour, Thomas Purcell of Wokefield, whereby Purcell applied to the Crown for the lease of Perkins's sequestrated lands.

Since 1606 it had been standard practice for the authorities to offer the sequestrated lands of Catholics, to their Protestant neighbours for a nominal rent. This was to encourage Protestants to inform on Catholics.

The authorities thought Purcell was a Protestant and so granted him Perkins's estates for a token rent. The plan was that Purcell would then pay Perkins the difference between the true rental value and the nominal rent. Unfortunately an informer told the authorities and the plan was foiled.

William Eyston of Catmore, owner of the ring found in Catmore churchyard, was Francis Perkins II's brother-in-law. William Eyston's fourteen children added to the financial burden of being a recusant. He was forced to sell the manors of Burford in Gloucestershire and Seymours, West Hanney (3 miles N. of Wantage). However, in 1623 he was able to buy the Abbey Manor, East Hendred from the Dutch merchant Sir Peter Vanlore, whose alabaster monument is in Tilehurst parish church.

To what extent he used these lands is hard to ascertain. Many years later it was reported that former monastic lands at East Hendred were uncultivated because it was felt wrong to do so.

Five years after his purchase of the Abbey Manor, it seems that William Eyston was able to achieve for his brother-in-law what the informer had prevented Thomas Purcell from doing. The Crown issued letters patent to William granting him use of Perkins's estate. Richard Hyde of Purley also managed to negotiate an advantageous arrangement. The Hydes' sequestrated land was leased to Richard's father-in-law, William Smith of Whitchurch.

In 1623 the role of Archpriest was superseded by that of Vicar Apostolic. The first to hold the new post was the aptly named William Bishop, who was given the title Bishop of Chalcedon, all the traditional English Catholic sees being occupied by Anglican bishops. In the same year the English Province of the Jesuits was established and Fr Thomas Plowden of Shiplake was sent on the mission to England. Oxfordshire formed part of the Jesuits' 'Residence of St Mary', often referred to as 'Mrs Oxon', whereas Berkshire formed part of their 'College of St Ignatius'.

Towards the end of his reign James I tried to arrange a Spanish Catholic marriage for his son Charles. In 1623, during these negotiations, Catholics in England first became known officially as Roman Catholics. This was at the insistence of the Spaniards who appreciated that the Church of England claimed to be the Catholic Church in England.

James I died in 1625. At the end of his reign there were still some eighty Catholic justices of the peace, and two high sheriffs. Within the last four years, old Sir Francis Stonor had served another term as Sheriff of Oxfordshire, and Edward Yate II of Buckland had become a baronet.

Although the hopes of the Oxfordshire woman expressed at James's accession had not been met, during his reign the number of Catholics in England had increased by about a quarter. Even more remarkably, the number of Catholic priests had doubled.

Charles I

(1625 - 1642)

James I died in 1625 and was succeeded by his son Charles I. The new king had married a French princess, Henrietta Maria, and the wedding treaty included secret clauses providing toleration for English Catholics.

Queen Henrietta Maria expressed her Catholicism more exuberantly and openly than her predecessor. The Court became a centre of cosmopolitan Counter-Reformation Catholicism, somewhat at odds with the discreet English Catholicism that survived in the country houses of Berkshire, Oxfordshire and elsewhere.

In the year of Charles's accession, Peter Curtis of Andover, Hampshire became a Jesuit after four years studying at the English College at Rome. His father was a member of the Curtis family of Enborne (2 miles WSW of Newbury). The elder Curtis was 'a Catholic of respectability ... who, on account of his poor circumstances, for many years was occupied in the trade of a fuller.' Downward mobility was something many Catholic families were having to come to terms with.

Sequestration of estates was quite common. For example, Sir George Browne's Great Shefford Manor was sequestrated about 1627. But some Catholics could still afford to purchase property. One such was Francis Fettiplace who, in 1627, bought Swyncombe Manor from the Crown. Previously his family had leased it from the Fortescues. The house stood in a fold of the Chilterns on the Ridgeway, three and a half miles west of Stonor. (The present Swyncombe Manor is a twentieth century replacement.)

In 1630 a churchwarden of Mapledurham was in trouble for not reporting Sir Charles Blount for being a Catholic. The churchwarden's defence was that he did not know how to write. Sir Charles had succeeded his father Sir Richard on the latter's death two years previously.

An incident in 1630 gives an insight into the problems faced by Catholics when it came to burying their dead. Clandestine baptisms and weddings were relatively easy to arrange, but with funerals there was always the problem of what to do with the body. Any Catholic who died without being admitted or reconciled to the Church of England could be refused burial.

In practice gentry were rarely refused interment alongside their ancestors in the parish church. Often the rules were also bent for lowlier folk and blind eyes were turned, but occasionally the Anglican authorities felt it necessary to

SWYNCOMBE HOUSE – the Elizabethan house, based on an old unfinished drawing

record the fact that an unauthorised funeral had taken place. For instance, it was noted in 1624 that Agnes Tull, a Catholic from Burcot (1 mile NW of Dorchester) had been buried illegally in the churchyard at Dorchester.

The most celebrated clandestine funeral in the Thames Valley was that of Elizabeth Horseman, a convicted recusant who lived at Wheatley (4½ miles E. of Oxford). She died at the end of December 1629. Her friends had promised to bury her in church but were not prepared to lie to the Anglican archdeacon that she had repudiated Catholicism. Consequently the archdeacon would not give permission for a church burial. The vicar of the nearest parish church, at Holton half a mile north of Wheatley, was sympathetic to the dead woman's friends, but could not be seen to disobey the archdeacon.

One morning a week later it was discovered that the door of Holton parish church had been forced; Mrs Horseman had been buried under the Communion table.

There had been a wake the previous night and the servants said they had left the coffin in the garden for hygiene reasons. Persons 'unknown' had removed it. The authorities could find no witnesses but the whole village seemed to approve what had happened. 'God's blessing on the hands that buried the dead', said one woman.

Elizabeth Horseman was related to the Belsons and the Powells. Almost a century earlier a John Horseman was one of the servants imprisoned with Sir Adrian Fortescue. She therefore had links with at least two, and probably three Thames Valley martyrs, all now beatified; Thomas Belson, Fr George Napper and Sir Adrian Fortsecue.

The clandestine burial was organised by a Mr Powell, believed to be Richard Powell of Forest Hill (1 mile NW of Holton). And it is probable that the Jesuit chaplain from Waterperry House made the short journey to Holton to officiate at the secret funeral.

Lady Ann Curson of Waterperry died in 1631 after twenty years of widowhood. Most of this had been spent at the Stonors' manor house at North Stoke. There is a monument to Lady Ann and her husband in Waterperry parish church, next to Waterperry House. Their effigies kneel facing each other at a prayer-desk, on which is an hourglass to symbolise the brevity of life.

Also in 1631 Sir Francis Knollys's second son, William Lord Knollys, sold Greys Court. Shakespeare is said to have based Twelfth Night's Malvolio on William Knollys, who was also Viscount Wallingford and Earl of Banbury.

Despite his father's ardent anti-Catholicism, William Knollys's second wife Elizabeth was a Catholic. Her father, Sir Thomas Howard, was Viscount Andover and Earl of Berkshire. He and his brother Charles were keepers of the royal manor of Ewelme.

Had he been alive Sir Francis Knollys would have been even more shocked to discover that another son, Sir Thomas, had apparently become a Catholic and was having his daughter educated at a convent in Flanders.

Mary Yate, wife of Sir John Yate of Buckland, inherited Harvington Hall, Worcestershire in 1631. She was the daughter of the Catholic Humphrey Packington of Chaddesley Corbett. She harboured priests at the moated hall which now belongs to the Catholic Archdiocese of Birmingham and is open to the public.

Sir Francis Englefield the younger died in 1631. He was buried at Englefield parish church in accordance with family tradition. In his will he left not only Whiteknights and Englefield Farm, but other property at Englefield, Beenham and Bucklebury. He was succeeded at Whiteknights by his fifth son, Anthony.

Whiteknights was served by the Franciscans, who in 1630, had established two English districts. One was based in London, the other in the Reading area. The latter covered Berkshire, Hampshire and Sussex. The choice of Reading probably reflected the presence in the locality of three houses served by Franciscans; Whiteknights, Ufton Court and Mapledurham. However, the order soon relocated their base to Oxford. A young Franciscan chaplain, known as Stephen of the Holy Cross, is believed to have died at Whiteknights in 1640.

Bishop Richard Smith, the Vicar Apostolic, fled from England in 1631. A group of Catholic gentry had petitioned the Privy Council for his arrest because they saw him as a threat to their authority over their chaplains.

Bishop Smith made his way to Paris. He wrote to the Pope suggesting that England should have three Catholic dioceses, the senior one to be based at Dorchester-on-Thames. The plan was rejected but the country was later divided into four districts, each with its own bishop who was known as a Vicar Apostolic.

During the mid 1630s relations between the Crown and the Vatican improved. In 1633 the Queen's representative took up residence in Rome, ninety-nine years after Henry VIII's break with Rome.

In the following year papal representation was re-established in London. This was because Charles I wanted the diplomatic assistance of the Vatican in his European affairs, but there were also beneficial side effects for English Catholics.

The mid 1630s saw the deaths of some notable Catholic churchmen with Thames Valley connections. Bishop George Chamberlain of Ypres in Flanders died in 1634. He had been dean of the chapter of St Bavo's Cathedral, Ghent and was buried in St Martin's Cathedral at Ypres. Before his death he had returned to England to confirm his sister's title to the Shirburn estate. She married John Neville, Lord Abergavenny.

Dom John Curre, a Berkshire-born Benedictine died in Gloucestershire in 1634. He had been banished but had secretly returned to work on the mission.

Fr Arthur Pitts was a son of the church papist Arthur Pitts of Iffley. As noted earlier, Fr Pitts worked with the martyred Fr Edmund Campion. He later became chancellor to the Cardinal of Lorraine in eastern France before becoming Archdeacon of London. Fr Pitts spent the end of his life as a house guest of William Stonor at Blount's Court, Rotherfield Peppard. He is said to have been buried secretly at Rotherfield Peppard parish church about 1634.

William Stonor had succeeded to the Stonor estates on the death of his father, Sir Francis in 1625. William's recusant wife, Lady Elizabeth, had been released from jail after the accession of Charles I and the authorities now treated her more leniently. She suffered from a serious illness and in 1630 was excused from appearing before the Oxford magistrates. Eight years later the King granted her exemption from further prosecution. It may have helped that the Queen's private physician, Doctor William Gibbes, was a Catholic convert and William Stonor's brother-in-law.

In 1635 the parson of Pyrton wrote in the parish register that, at the request of William Stonor's curate, he had entered therein the christenings of William's children. However, he added that he did not know where, when or by whom they had been baptised. Pyrton was the parish then serving Stonor and William Stonor's 'curate' was his Catholic chaplain.

In the absence of civil registration of births it was important to register children at the parish church to avoid legal complications concerning their legitimacy. Where the Anglican clergy refused to compromise in the way the parson of Pyrton did, the Catholic clergy would often allow a second baptism according to the Anglican rite to ensure registration.

The 1630s saw further seizures of Catholic estates. John Dancastle, who had married Anne Fettiplace, was a recusant who owned the manor of Wellhouse. This is a small farming settlement on the Berkshire Downs (4 miles NE of Newbury). The site of Wellhouse Farm was occupied by the Romans and evidence of a Roman building more than 100 feet long has been found there. Wellhouse manor was sequestrated in 1635. It had been leased to John Dancastle's uncle, Griffin Dancastle, who also held The Grange at Shaw (1 mile NE of Newbury). Griffin's daughter Elizabeth married John Eyston, who became a Royalist major and was a son of William Eyston of Catmore.

John Dancastle's grandfather, also John, had married Mary Browne, a cousin of Sir George Browne of Great Shefford. This elder John Dancastle had purchased Binfield manor in east

BLOUNTS COURT, ROTHERFIELD PEPPARD

Berkshire. Binfield was in Windsor Forest, an area full of squatters and dissidents who were unlikely to be concerned about a neighbour's religion. The Dancastles held Binfield until the family died out in the second half of the eighteenth century. They forfeited a property there called Cliftons to the Crown during the reign of Charles I.

In 1635 George Tattersall's West Court estate at Finchampstead was seized by the Crown. He subsequently leased the property back and continued paying £20 a month in recusancy fines (= £1,100 today). Later he paid a lump sum to clear his backlog of fines and regained full possession of the estate.

William Wollascott III died in 1637. He had built a separate aisle with a chapel on to the parish church at Brimpton. This was therefore another Anglican church with a Catholic-owned private aisle, as at Mapledurham, Noke and Pishill (the latter serving the Catholics of Stonor village). Wollascott was buried in a vault attached to his chapel. He was succeeded by his son, William Wollascott VI, whose wife Susan Fryer was also a Catholic. (The Wollascotts' aisle no longer exists.)

The Wollascotts held the right to appoint the parson of Brimpton. However, legislation now prevented Catholics from exercising such rights. William Wollascott III had successfully done so, probably because he was a church papist who, in the Wollascott tradition, managed to conceal his Catholicism. In 1638, however, three men who were not members of the family made the presentation. They may have been William Wollascott III's executors. One of them was Sir Thomas Vachell, the Protestant heir of the old recusant, Thomas Vachell of Ipsden.

In 1637 the Archbishop of Canterbury, William Laud, thought he had converted the heir of the Wollascott family to Anglicanism. This was presumably William Wollascott V who died young. Archbishop Laud was a Reading man and had placed the young Wollascott at Wadham College, Oxford.

The Archbishop had been appointed to the See of Canterbury in 1633 and tried to reintroduce to the Church of England a semblance of pre-Reformation liturgy. This was in keeping with the King's high church ideas, but was bitterly opposed by the Puritans. Ludovic Bowyer, also a Reading man, spread rumours that Laud was in league with the Pope. Laud was indeed invited by the Pope to join the Catholic Church and become a cardinal, but he did not accept the offer. The unfortunate Bowyer had the letters L for liar and R for rogue branded on his forehead. He was pilloried in Reading and London, being nailed by the ears. He was then sentenced to hard labour for life. During the Civil War Archbishop Laud was beheaded by the Parliamentarians, on Tower Hill, London in 1645.

The survival of Catholicism along the three mile stretch of the Thames from Clifton Hampden through Burcot to Dorchester was unusual for the Thames Valley area. It was centred not on one or two gentry homes, but on a group of yeomen families. Yeomen were middle class holders of small estates, typically farmers.

At Dorchester it seems that there was only one gentleman recusant in the early seventeenth century. George Beauforest was listed in 1612, exactly a century after the death of an Abbot of Dorchester of the same surname. When Dorchester Abbey was suppressed Sir Richard and Lady Beauforest had bought the monastic church as a gift for the parish, thus saving it from destruction. George may have been Sir Richard's son.

The Catholic yeomen of the Dorchester district were predominantly members of the Davey, Day and Prince families. The first record of the Days as Catholics is when a member of the family died in 1639. Day's Lock at Little Wittenham was named after this family.

The Princes, some of whom lived at Clifton Hampden, were listed as recusants as early as 1604. In the 1620s George Prince of Clifton Hampden was a churchwarden but, nonetheless, seems to have been a Catholic. His appointment probably reflected the high standing of his family in the village. Some forty years later one of the Days of Dorchester also served as a churchwarden.

The Daveys of Dorchester and nearby Overy eventually became the most prominent and enduring recusants of the area. Ann, wife of Richard Davey, was listed for recusancy in 1641.

About 1640 the ratio of priests to Catholic laity in England was perhaps at its all time peak. It is estimated that there was one priest for every eighty lay people. Vocations were numerous. In 1641, for instance, Francis Bruning became a Jesuit. Although he was not a Thames Valley man, his mother was a Simeon from Brightwell near Watlington, and he used her surname as an alias. In the previous year Isett Moleyns became a Benedictine lay sister at Cambrai in northern France. The principal seat of her family was at Mongewell (now the site of Carmel College) a mile up the Thames from the Stonor manor of North Stoke.

A mile downstream from North Stoke was another Catholic house where vocations were nurtured. Littlestoke Manor was then the principal residence of the main East Ilsley line of the Hildesleys. It was only two and a half miles downstream from their previous seat at Newnham Murren.

Littlestoke Manor today is a much altered farmhouse with a Georgian facade, but one or two traces of Tudor construction can still be found. A branch of the Hildesleys had lived there as early as the reign of Edward VI when Archbishop Cranmer granted Francis Hildesley a dispensation to eat meat during Lent.

Littlestoke is on a narrow finger of Checkendon parish that gave the latter Chiltern village direct access to the Thames. The house stands where the Ridgeway, having crossed the Thames

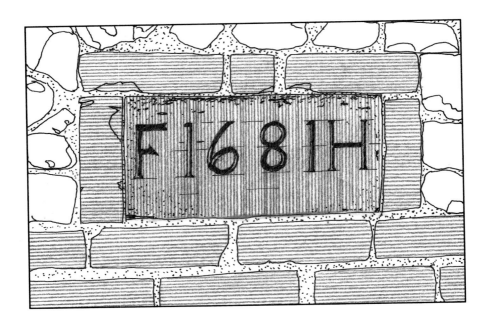

LITTLESTOKE BARN
with foundation stone above showing Francis Hildesley's initials

at Goring, passes through the meadows alongside the river on its way to North Stoke, Mongewell and Swyncombe; all places where Catholic families lived in the seventeenth century. From Swyncombe it was only three and a half miles to Stonor.

Formerly there was a ferry across the Thames at Littlestoke. The road from the ferry on the opposite bank at Cholsey today passes through the grounds of Fair Mile Hospital, becoming a public road to the west of its junction with the Reading to Wallingford road. Significantly it is called Papist Way and points towards the Hildesleys ancestral home at East Ilsley, about eight miles away. It also leads towards East Hendred, home of the Eyston family, some ten miles distant.

Using the Thames as a highway the Hildesleys could reach fellow Catholics eight miles upstream in the Dorchester area and nine miles downstream at Mapledurham. Littlestoke was therefore at a meeting of the ways for Catholics in the area.

Walter Hildesley, head of the East Ilsley and Crowmarsh line, was apparently succeeded by his younger brother William, probably the Hildesley who was at Lyford Grange when Fr Edmund Campion was arrested. He in turn was succeeded by his son, another William.

This William Hildesley married Anne Hawkins who, between 1618 and 1631, gave birth to two sons and four daughters. The family lived at Littlestoke. The girls - Mary, Anne, Catherine and Susannah - all became nuns at Liege. (Littlestoke in Oxfordshire should not be confused with Little Stoke near Chipping Sodbury in Gloucestershire, which was a Benedictine mission.)

In 1641 the last known Catholic Vachell died. This was John Vachell who must have been the youngest brother of Sir Thomas and therefore a nephew of old Thomas Vachell of Ipsden. John Vachell was buried with his wife Mary at Warfield parish church (1½ miles N. of Bracknell). Their epitaph reads:

'While they lived together they were living apart, and death itself has neither joined them nor separated them. They were both of them Catholics, she of the Anglican, he of the Roman faith. Both, nevertheless, lived temperately, piously, virtuously; and, which is a riddle, were friends with one another.'

Anglican and Catholic co-operation was also necessary between the King and Queen's chaplains. Charles I's chaplain, Bishop Jeremy Taylor, developed a close working relationship with the Queen's chaplain, Fr Christopher Davenport, who later served Charles II's queen, Catherine of Braganza. Fr Davenport was a Franciscan theologian, often known by his religious name, Franciscus a Sancta Clara. As the Queen's chaplain he enjoyed much greater liberty than other Catholic priests, and was said to 'pervade' Oxford. He was also an ecumenist and tried to show that the Church of England's Thirty-Nine Articles could be interpreted in accordance with Catholic tradition, two centuries before John Henry Newman tried to make the same case.

At Oxford in 1640 Charles Green, innkeeper of the Mitre, was dismissed from the city council for being a Catholic. Two years later his house and that of another prominent Catholic family, the Nappers, were raided. Bonfires were made of their Catholic books and pictures. This reflected the growing influence of Puritanism.

That spring the Puritan poet John Milton travelled to Stanton St John (4½ miles NE of Oxford) to get married. His late grandfather, Richard Milton, was a Catholic who lived in the village and worked as an under-ranger of Shotover Forest. Vestiges of the forest remain on and around Shotover Hill two miles south of Stanton St John.

Although raised a Catholic, John Milton's father had become a Protestant whilst studying at Christ Church College, and had therefore been disinherited. He had subsequently moved to London where he made a comfortable living as a scrivener.

John Milton's bride was seventeen year old Mary Powell. She was one of eleven children of Richard Powell, the man implicated in the clandestine Catholic burial of Elizabeth Horseman twelve years earlier.

As previously noted, Richard Powell lived at Forest Hill (1 mile SE of Stanton St John). He had bought Forest Hill Manor, which stands north of the parish church, from John Brome, a member of another family who were, or recently had been, Catholic. Powell was plagued by financial problems. He failed to pay Mary's dowry of £1,000 (= £50,000 today) and Milton's father had previously lent him £300 (= £15,000 today).

John Milton is generally regarded as having been anti-Catholic. Yet, as we will see later, he had many friendly contacts with Catholics, even including a cardinal in Rome. It is not known, though, to what extent the Powells of Forest Hill were Catholic when Milton married into the family. Richard Powell was certainly not in a position to pay recusancy fines, although he may have been a church papist.

The marriage got off to a bad start. Milton's bride deserted him after a few weeks and went home. Three months later the Civil War broke out. John Milton was a Parliamentarian, and the Powells were Royalists. Consequently there was to be no reunion between John and Mary Milton until after the war.

Meanwhile at Purley, Richard Hyde, who had inherited Hyde Hall from his father Francis, must have seen the way the Puritan wind was blowing. A month before the King raised his standard, Richard Hyde had his new son John baptised at Purley parish church. During the 111 years that the Hydes lived at Purley, baby John Hyde was the only member of the family recorded as having been christened according to the Anglican rite.

The Civil War

(1642 - 1646)

In the Civil War most Thames Valley Catholics preferred the Royalists to the Parliamentarians; but relatively few actively supported Charles I. One of those who did was Major John Eyston, a son of William Eyston of Catmore. Another was Sir Charles Blount of Mapledurham, who was Scout Master General in the King's army. At various times Catholics were Royal Governors of Oxford and Reading, but these men came from outside the area.

The Protestant descendants of families which, a generation or two earlier, had been Catholic recusants tended to support the Parliamentarians. One such was the poet John Milton. Another was the Speaker of Parliament, William Lenthall, the son of a west Oxfordshire Catholic and nephew of the Jesuit martyr Fr Robert Southwell. (Speaker Lenthall's house stands in Hart Street, Henley-on-Thames.)

The war broke out in August 1642 and the following month Richard Deane brought two men suspected of being Catholic priests before the Mayor of Reading. They were ordered to take the Oaths of Supremacy and Allegiance.

Late in October Oxford became the temporary royal capital and hence the largest Royalist garrison. In early November Reading, hitherto held by Parliament, fell to the Royalists. It became their second largest garrison, with more than 3,000 soldiers stationed in and around the town.

The Governor of Reading was Sir Arthur Aston, a Catholic professional soldier. Parliamentary spies reported that he regularly dined with the local Catholics Sir Charles Blount of Mapledurham and Anthony Englefield of Whiteknights. The spies also reported 'One W. Dolmer or Dormer, a Papist' of Caversham who harboured Royalist soldiers.

The third Earl of Essex besieged Reading in April 1643. One of the Royalists in the town was John Milton's younger brother Christopher. He later became a Catholic and claimed that his brother had died one.

On the second day of the siege Essex sent some of his forces to attack Mapledurham House, which had been fortified by the Royalists. The Parliamentary forces breached the defences and pillaged the house. However, it is unlikely that they found much worth taking. Sir Charles Blount was an extravagant man who, eight years previously, had been forced to sell his household goods to pay his debts. Mapledurham was sequestrated by Parliament and Sir Charles Blount later died during the siege of Oxford. According to the diarist Anthony à Wood, he 'was killed by the sentinel, for not standing at his command'. There is a fine portrait of Sir Charles in the entrance hall of Mapledurham House.

It seems that Mapledurham was not the only local Catholic house to suffer from Parliamentary incursions. According to tradition, at some time during the Civil War Parliamentary troops burned down part of Blount's Court, the Stonor residence. It is also said that the Parliamentary Fane family, who lived some four miles north of Stonor, raided Stonor House, stabled their horses in its chapel of the Holy Trinity, and trained a cannon on the house from the top of the hill opposite.

Four days into the siege of Reading, Governor Aston was struck on the head by a piece of building debris dislodged by a cannon shot. Nine days later the garrison surrendered. Sir Arthur Aston subsequently recovered and became Governor of Oxford.

Francis Plowden (brother of Edmund Plowden II), his family and their servants had taken refuge in Reading. When the town fell they tried to escape back to Shiplake. Their coach, carrying valuables and £500 in cash (= £25,000 today) was ambushed by Parliamentary forces who stole everything except their clothes. The Plowdens spent the rest of the war in comparative safety at Oxford.

About five months after the fall of Reading, in September 1643, the first Battle of Newbury took place. There fell Robert Dormer, first Earl of Caernarfon, and grandson of the Catholic former Sheriff of Buckinghamshire. Robert Dormer had been raised as a Protestant, but had converted to Catholicism, possibly through the influence of Fr Thomas Fitzherbert, Rector of the English College in Rome. (Fr Fitzherbert was the widower of Dorothy East of Bledlow, Buckinghamshire.)

Robert Dormer expired on the battlefield proclaiming his happiness to die a Catholic serving the King. However, his dying wish, that his son be raised a Catholic, was ignored by his widow.

In November 1643 Sir William Waller's Parliamentary troops besieged Basing House. This mansion stood by the River Loddon, a tributary of the Thames, at Old Basing (12 miles S. of Reading). It was the largest private residence in England, the site covering fifteen acres within a mile and half of enclosing walls and earthworks. The 'Old House' was a medieval fortress on a defensive mound. Next to it stood the palatial 'New House' which had 380 rooms and was five storeys high.

Basing House had been converted into a palace by Sir William Paulet, first Marquis of Winchester and Treasurer to Henry VIII, Edward VI and Elizabeth I. His successor John Paulet, the fifth marquis, now owned the house. He was one of the richest landowners in England, despite being a Catholic.

The Marquis's first wife was Jane, the daughter of Sir Thomas Savage. Her sister Dorothy later married the second Earl of Berkshire, Charles Howard, and maintained a Catholic presence in Ewelme for more than thirty years. Another sister, Catherine, became a Benedictine nun at Ghent and founded the English convent at Dunkirk. But Jane herself died young. Her epitaph was composed by John Milton.

At the time of the siege of Basing House the Marquis was married to Lady Honora de Burgh, the Catholic daughter of Lord Clanricarde and Frances Walsingham.

The Marquis of Winchester had been irritated by minor Parliamentary attacks on Basing House. He had therefore obtained permission from the King to garrison the house. Many of the occupants were Catholics and the Parliamentarians regarded it as 'the only rendezvous for the Cavaliers and Papists hereabouts'.

Sir William Waller's siege lasted only nine days. It was abandoned because of bad autumn weather and a rumour that 5,000 Royalist troops were coming to relieve the garrison.

In June the following year, 1644, Basing House was besieged again. Colonel Richard Norton had greater success than Waller and was supported by a heavy mortar bombardment. By early September the Marquis's garrison had been reduced from 400 to 250 men. He therefore sent a message to Oxford saying that he could hold out for no more than ten days.

Colonel Henry Gage, the Catholic commander of the Oxford garrison, raised a relief force consisting of Colonel Hawkins's regiment, a hundred volunteers and various servants. They disguised themselves as Parliamentarians and Colonel Gage, who as a young man had fought in the Spanish army, led them the forty miles to Basing.

The relief force succeeded in breaking through to Basing House, replenishing the garrison's ammunition and food. Colonel Gage and his party escaped by night and headed back to Oxford, swimming their horses across the Kennet and the Thames. The Colonel received a knighthood for this exploit.

During the siege Lord Edward Paulet, younger brother of the Marquis, tried to betray the house. He was foiled and made to execute his accomplices before being expelled from the fortress.

Less than a fortnight after Colonel Gage relieved Basing House, Colonel Norton resumed the siege. More than seven weeks were to pass until Colonel Gage again relieved the garrison. By that time Norton had retreated to Farnham. It was November 1644 and two thirds of Norton's 2,000 strong force were dead, injured, ill or absent without leave. Basing House had withstood a six month siege with only the brief respite following Colonel Gage's first relief mission.

MAIN GATEWAY, BASING HOUSE RUINS

On Christmas Day 1644 the King made Colonel Henry Gage Governor of Oxford, in place of Sir Arthur Aston. The following month Gage was killed in a skirmish at Culham Bridge near Abingdon. He was given an impressive military funeral at Christ Church Cathedral, Oxford where he is buried. He was a devout man who attended Mass daily. Three of his brothers were Catholic priests. A fourth, Thomas, had been a Dominican missionary to the West Indies and Central America, but had subsequently become a Puritan adviser to Oliver Cromwell.

Colonel Gage's chaplain, the Jesuit Fr Peter Wright, was later executed by the Parliamentarians at Tyburn (now Marble Arch).

The Civil War was all but lost for the King when Basing House was besieged for the third and last time. In August 1645 the Dutch siege engineer Colonel John Dalbier arrived at Basing with about 800 Parliamentary troops. He was soon joined by a company of soldiers from Reading, and later by a hundred musketeers from Southwark.

Dalbier spent a month scientifically planning his attack. He then went into action with devastating effect, causing much more severe damage than the previous random bombardment. He even tried an early form of poison gas, burning wet straw mixed with sulphur and arsenic upwind of the house.

About a fortnight after Dalbier commenced his onslaught he was joined by Oliver Cromwell, who brought state of the art heavy artillery. His largest gun is thought to have fired shot weighing between forty-eight and sixty-three pounds.

A final surrender demand was rejected outright. Paulet's motto was 'Aimez Loyauté' (Love Loyalty) and he is said to have scratched it on every pane of glass in the huge mansion. This supremely loyal Catholic Royalist had no intention of surrendering 'Loyalty House' to what he called the 'pretended authority of Parliament'.

On Friday 10 October 1645 Cromwell and Dalbier commenced a concerted artillery bombardment. By Monday evening the walls of Basing House were well and truly breached. At dawn the following morning the Parliamentarians made their final attack, spurred on by rumours of treasure stored in the House and tales of numerous Catholic priests harboured there.

The storming of the house was ferocious. Between forty and a hundred of the inmates were killed, including six Catholic priests and many noblemen. Among those captured were the historian Thomas Fuller, the engravers William Fairthorne and Wenceslaus Hollar, and the great architect Inigo Jones. According to the Parliamentarians, Jones had gone to Basing House to advise on preparing it for the siege. He was seventy-two when the house fell and was brought out naked, wrapped in a blanket. It was said that the Marquis himself was found saying his rosary in a bread-oven.

The Parliamentary soldiers were given free rein to pillage Basing House. The loot was estimated to be worth about £200,000 (= £10m today). The troops raided the cellars and it may have been here that the fire started that burned for twenty hours and completed the destruction of the palatial fortress.

The Marquis was still defiantly protesting his loyalty to the King as the house burned. The Great Loyalist, as Paulet was known, was sent to the Tower of London on a charge of high treason and his estates were sequestrated. His two sons were taken away to be brought up as Protestants. The treason charge was later dropped, but he spent years in prison and suffered huge financial loss.

Cromwell ordered demolition of what remained of Basing House. The villagers of Basing were encouraged to loot the building for materials to repair their houses, damaged during the sieges. Some of the rebuilt cottages still exist

The remains of Basing House are now in the care of Hampshire County Council and are open to the public from April to September. Outside the main complex is the superb tithe barn, where Colonel Dalbier's Parliamentary regiment was stationed. Access to the ruins is through the gateway used by Colonel Gage when he relieved the garrison. The earthworks are clearly visible, including the medieval mound on which the Old House stood. It is possible to walk among the foundations and cellars of the New House, and through the old walled garden with its dovecotes.

The defenders of 'Loyalty House' responded to the Civil War very differently to the majority of Thames Valley Catholics, but it cost them dearly.

The Commonwealth

(1646 -1660)

Charles I surrendered in the spring of 1646. He was executed in 1649, the monarchy being replaced with a republican Commonwealth.

During the following year Parliament repealed the act requiring compulsory attendance at Anglican services. This was intended to undermine the Church of England, rather than help the Catholics. The Oaths of Allegiance and Supremacy were abandoned in favour of an Oath of Abjuration, even more offensive to Catholics.

After the fall of Oxford the Plowdens returned to Shiplake, much impoverished. Their property, like other Royalist estates, had been sequestrated by Parliament and rented out to neighbours. Fortunately the Plowdens' neighbours returned the property voluntarily. Francis Plowden responded by helping them with their legal problems, while his wife Mary provided medical aid.

In 1649 Richard Godric Blount became a Benedictine monk of St Gregory's, Douai. He had been born at Fawley, Berkshire and was presumably a son of Sir Richard Blount by his second wife, Elizabeth, nee Moore.

Sir Richard's grandson Michael Blount, nineteen year old heir to Mapledurham, was murdered by a footman at Charing Cross, also in 1649. He was succeeded by his brother Walter who, two years after Michael's murder, had the Mapledurham estates released from sequestration. Walter later married Philippa Benlowes, an Essex Catholic. Her uncle, the poet Edward Benlowes, had abandoned Catholicism a quarter of a century earlier and was now bitterly opposed to it. Despite this he mortgaged his estates to raise her a huge dowry of £6,000 (= £280,000 today). Not surprisingly he was destitute within a few years. The Blounts therefore provided accommodation for him at Mapledurham until the poet could arrange lodgings with more convenient access to the Bodleian Library at Oxford.

Another poet, William D'Avenant, was born at 3 Cornmarket, Oxford, once the Crown Inn. Sixteenth century murals have been found there, including a large IHS, the monogram of Jesus. Officially D'Avenant was the son of the innkeeper, but William Shakespeare admitted to being his godfather and may have been his natural father. D'Avenant was a Catholic, Royalist and sometime Poet Laureate.

As a Royalist William D'Avenant had been imprisoned at Cowes on the Isle of Wight. In 1650 he sailed for Virginia on behalf of the Queen, who had returned to her native France during the Civil War. He was captured by the Parliamentarians and it is said that his fellow poet John Milton intervened and saved him from execution. At the Restoration D'Avenant was to return the favour for Milton.

By 1650 all Stonor estates outside Oxfordshire, except Didcot in Berkshire and Penton Mewsey, Hampshire, had been sold. The remainder were worth about £1,600 a year (= £75,000 today), of which £300 went to pay recusancy fines (= £14,000 today). Most of this residue consisted of woodland. Fortunately for the Stonors, the county commissioners were unable to find a tenant whom they could trust not to strip the timber for a quick profit. The family were therefore allowed to retain these estates.

Nonetheless, William Stonor had to borrow considerable sums from, among others, his cousin Sir John Curson of Waterperry. Sir John had been involved in the defence of Oxford and had been captured when Ascott House, near Stadhampton, fell to John Hampden's Parliamentary troops. Despite his mother Lady Ann's strong Catholicism, Sir John was not ostensibly a Catholic. He had, however, married a daughter of the Catholic Sir Robert Dormer, sometime Sheriff of Buckinghamshire.

William Stonor died in 1652. That Christmas Eve (the year in which Christmas was 'abolished') Sir John Curson was one of three men who petitioned Parliament on behalf of themselves and other creditors of William's surviving sons, Francis and Thomas. (Another son, William, had been killed defending Basing House.)

Sir John and his colleagues asked for the release for eight years of the rents of the sequestrated manors of Stonor, Bix, Pishill, Shiplake, Dunsden and Blount's Court. Parliament had leased these estates to three men, one of whom was Sir George Simeon, then in his seventies. Sir George was a member of the Catholic Brightwell branch of the Simeons. His grandmother was a Stonor, and he had married three times, on each occasion to a bride from a Catholic family.

Sir John Curson and Sir George Simeon seem to have been able skilfully to interpose themselves, with the assistance of Protestant colleagues, to protect the interests of the Stonors.

Francis Stonor died in 1653, only a year after his father. Thomas Stonor, then twenty-eight years old, succeeded his brother as head of the family. In the same year he was appointed proof-master of all saltpetre in the country. Apart from being a food preservative, saltpetre was an important constituent of gunpowder. The appointment of a Catholic Royalist was therefore somewhat surprising. It reflected the high regard in which the Stonors were held, even by their religious and political opponents.

In 1653, the year of this appointment, Thomas married Lady Elizabeth Neville, daughter of the ninth Lord Abergavenny. She had been living at Shirburn Castle, the former home of the Catholic Chamberlain family, which had been sequestrated. The Chamberlain male line had failed and the castle had recently been inherited by two daughters of John Chamberlain, Elizabeth who married the tenth Lord Abergavenny, and Mary who married Sir Thomas Gage of Firle, Sussex.

Despite his new appointment Thomas Stonor had to lease the manors of Didcot, North Stoke, Stoke Mules and one of the Ipsden manors. Three-quarters of the income from these had already been seized by the authorities. He also sold Penton Mewsey in Hampshire and leased out Watlington Park and Newnham Murren. Even these measures were not enough to resolve his financial situation and a few years later he sold the Stonor lands at Shiplake.

The Hildesleys were also in financial difficulties at this time. In 1650 the mortgagees of Ilsley Farm applied to the county commissioners to compound (pay a lump sum) for the estate. However, the following year William Young, a member of a Catholic family living at Whatcombe, near Fawley, Berkshire petitioned the Commissioners that the mortgage had been assigned to him and that the interest had been paid. This seems to have saved Ilsley Farm for the Hildesleys, who continued to hold it until the following century.

The Ufton estates of Francis Perkins II did not escape sequestration. As Mary Sharp, the historian of Ufton Court, put it 'the unfortunate lords of Ufton, after having so long suffered as traitors at the hands of the King, were severely taxed with the rest of their Royalist neighbours as malignants for their loyalty.'

Consequently the parishioners of Ufton and Padworth almost lost the benefit of the 'Ufton Dole'. This annual charity had been instigated by Lady Marvyn, aunt of Francis Perkins I. It consisted of gifts of bread, calico and flannel. The overseers of the two parishes successfully petitioned the Commissioners to allow the charity to continue so that the poor families for whom it was intended 'may not starve and perish for want thereof.' Consequently the Ufton Dole is still distributed today.

Augustine Belson of Brill and Aston Rowant, great nephew of the martyr Thomas Belson, was among those whose estates were seized. So too was Benedict Hall of Noke, whose estates included West Ginge Manor near Wantage and property at Chalgrove.

Humphrey Hyde had acquired part of Marlston Manor (2 miles N. of Bucklebury) through his marriage to Margaret Braybrooke. She had inherited it from her father Richard, presumably a descendant of the Elizabethan recusant lawyer James Braybrooke.

The estate had been sequestrated and, as was usually the case, two thirds of its income had been seized by Parliament.

In 1652 Humphrey Hyde, probably the head of the Kingston Lisle branch of the family, successfully petitioned for the return of Marlston Manor, presumably by taking the Oath of Abjuration. However, he died shortly afterwards and the property was again sequestrated, because his widow refused to take the oath.

Lowbrook Manor at Bray was sequestrated from William Englefield, a son of the younger Sir Francis. Another son, Henry, had inherited the family's property at Englefield and complained when it, too, was seized. He protested that 'though a papist' he was 'not a papist delinquent', that is, an active supporter of the Royalist cause. In fact, no Berkshire Catholics were convicted of 'delinquency' by the Parliamentary courts, an indication of their lukewarm support for the King.

Amidst this gloomy economic situation the Catholic families of the Thames Valley continued to provide vocations to the religious life. While the Nappers of Oxford suffered the sequestration of their property, Edmund Napper joined the English College at Rome. He had been educated by the English Jesuits at St Omer in the Pas de Calais, and had subsequently taken the Jesuit novitiate at Tournai in Flanders. Edmund Napper was ordained in 1653 but lameness is said to have impeded his ministry. He left Rome for England a few years later and was never seen again.

John Eyston, son of Thomas Eyston of Finchampstead, became a Franciscan friar in 1653. He took the name Fr Bernard Francis and had a distinguished career, mostly on the Continent, as Professor of Philosophy and Theology, and Doctor of Divinity.

Elizabeth Plowden, daughter of Francis Plowden of Shiplake, became a nun at Louvain in 1656. She eventually became Mother Superior. In Victorian times parts of the dress she wore when she became a 'bride of Christ' were kept at the Augustinian Convent at Newton Abbot, Devon (now closed). The dress was made of silver cloth decorated with the Plowden family arms.

In 1658, the year of Oliver Cromwell's death, some London men were bound over for distributing Catholic books in Oxford. At the time there were forty known recusants in the city.

That year Sir John Yate of Buckland died. His estates had been sequestrated and his widow Mary retired to Harvington Hall near Kidderminster. She raised a monument to Sir John in Buckland parish church. It bears a remarkable Latin description which translates as:

'The said Mary, widowed and most tearful, erected this monument as a memorial to her most famous husband who died piously with the sacrament of the Holy Roman Church.'

The Restoration

(1660 - 1685)

By June 1660 the Commonwealth had collapsed. Shortly afterwards the monarchy was restored and Charles II, son of the executed king, acceded to the throne.

For some Catholics there was an immediate improvement in their situation. Within a few weeks of the King's accession a writ was issued stating that there would be no further levy for recusancy on the manor of Whiteknights and lands nearby owned by Anthony Englefield. By the end of the year the Stonors had regained full possession of Stonor and Blount's Court. Thomas Stonor seems to have marked the Restoration by presenting a bell to Watlington parish church.

In the Restoration year Francis Perkins II revised his will, his son and heir Francis having died. He cut out his relative John Perkins of Beenham, who had recently conformed to Anglicanism.

Francis Perkins II died the following year and, in accordance with family tradition, was buried in Ufton Nervet parish church. A marble slab on his tombstone was later placed under the altar. There was already a monument in the church to his parents, Francis Perkins I and Anna, daughter of the Elizabethan lawyer Edmund Plowden. This still exists, although it is in bad condition.

One of Francis Perkins II's daughters married John Hyde of Hyde End on the River Enborne near Brimpton (5 miles WSW of Ufton Court). Even today Hyde End is a quiet backwater. The former Hyde mansion, subsequently restyled in the Georgian manner but now derelict, stands a few hundred yards from the Enborne, which there forms the boundary between Hampshire and Berkshire. A small detached building at the back of the house is said to have been the Catholic chapel.

In the year Francis Perkins II died, 1661, Fr Richard Hyde, a Berkshire Jesuit, abandoned Catholicism. He may have been the brother of Perkins's son-in-law, John Hyde.

Like Francis Perkins, William Wollascott IV's son, heir and namesake predeceased him. He was therefore succeeded by his daughter Catherine. She married Thomas Wollascott of the Sutton Courtenay branch of the family. Thomas and Catherine had a common great grandfather in William Wollascott II. Their son and heir Martin was born shortly after the Restoration.

A month or two after the Restoration the Royalist administration proposed to compensate John Paulet, Marquis of

THE DERELICT HYDE HALL, BRIMPTON

Winchester, for losses resulting from the siege and fall of Basing House. At first the sum suggested was £19,000 (= £890,000 today) but in the end he received nothing.

However, his lands were restored and he retired to Englefield House, which he had acquired through his second wife, Honora de Burgh. Her mother was Frances Walsingham. Hence a Catholic known as the Great Loyalist inherited the former house of a Catholic attainted as a traitor via the granddaughter of the head of Elizabeth I's secret service.

The Marquis greatly enlarged Englefield House where he lived a life of privacy, concentrating on literature and agriculture. But he continued to be dogged by sadness. In his first three years at Englefield he lost his wife, a son and a daughter. He also fell out with his eldest son Charles, later Duke of Bolton, who had been forcibly converted to Protestantism. Their differences were settled only by the passing of a parliamentary bill in 1663.

John Paulet married again, his third wife being Isabella Howard, daughter of the first Viscount Stafford. He fathered no more children and died in 1675, first marquis of England. His sepulchral slab lies in the floor before the altar of Englefield parish church. On the north wall of the nave is a monument erected to him by his widow. It bears an inscription by the poet Dryden, who later became a Catholic. The Great Loyalist was laid to rest a few yards from the private chapel of the Englefields, where the father and nephew of the attainted Sir Francis lie.

The new King, Charles II, wanted to improve the position of all nonconformists, whether Catholic or Protestant. He had declared at Breda in Holland that he proposed 'liberty to tender consciences' for 'differences of opinion in matters of religion which do not disturb the peace of the Kingdom'.

In 1662, two years after the Restoration, the King married a Portuguese Catholic princess, Catherine of Braganza. Fr Richard Russell, born at Buckland in 1629, had a major role in negotiating the marriage treaty. He also escorted Catherine to England and officiated at the wedding. (He later became Bishop of Vizeu, Portugal.) Catholics now expected a real improvement in their position. They were to be disappointed.

The Corporation Act of 1661 had already been passed, compelling holders of town office to take Communion in the Church of England at least once a year. Mayors, aldermen, recorders, bailiffs, town clerks, councillors and magistrates could therefore no longer in good conscience be non-Anglicans.

A new Act of Uniformity, passed in 1662, re-established the Church of England. It also led to the parting of the ways between Anglicanism and the descendants of what had hitherto been known as Puritanism. Some 2,000 ministers, mainly Presbyterians, were expelled by the Church of England. In

Reading, for example, the Puritan vicar of St Mary's, Christopher Fowler, was ejected in 1662. The Independents who met in his house formed the basis of Reading's first Congregational church, the Broad Street chapel.

The Conventicle Act of 1664 prohibited more than four persons assembling for non-Anglican worship. The following year a new Five Mile Act restricted the movement of non-Anglican clergy and imposed strict licensing on schoolteachers.

Despite this, three years after the Restoration a priest was able openly to visit Oxford, stay at the Mitre Inn and administer the laying on of hands to the sick. And even after the passing of the Five Mile Act there were said to be many priests in the city, keeping company with scholars.

Charles II's religious legislation was known as the 'Clarendon Code' after Edward Hyde, Lord Chancellor Clarendon. Although a Wiltshire man, he was descended from a Cheshire family, not closely related to the Catholic Hydes of Berkshire. Yet, by a strange coincidence, in 1632 his first wife Anne had died at Purley, the village in which the Catholic Francis Hyde lived. There is a memorial to her in the parish church.

Anne, Lord Clarendon's daughter by his second wife, was born at Windsor and married Charles II's brother, the Duke of York, later James II. She converted to Catholicism and is said, somewhat improbably, to have visited the Catholic Hydes at Hyde End, Brimpton. A pane of glass there is alleged to have her name and a date scratched on it.

In 1664, four years after the Restoration, John Eyston of Leigh Farm near Lambourn died. He had also held property at Hanney and Streatley. He was a brother of William Eyston of Catmore and had at least five children. He was succeeded at Leigh Farm by his eldest son John, who married Honor, daughter of Francis Hyde of Hyde Hall, Purley. (This would appear to be Francis Hyde II, grandson of the first Francis Hyde.)

The elder John Eyston's youngest daughter, Anne, married Richard Perkins of Beenham, who became a Justice of the Peace under James II. Her sister Margaret married George Phillipson of Streatley. Two of the Phillipsons' sons became Benedictines. John was twice prior of the English Benedictines at Douai, his younger brother William was their second president.

George Napper of Holywell Manor, Oxford was the great nephew of his martyred namesake. He was summonsed with his wife to appear before the Bishop's Court on a charge of recusancy in 1664. On being instructed to conform to Anglicanism, he diplomatically asked for time to consider his position, 'having been trained up in the opinion of the Roman Church'. His implied willingness to consider the matter seems to have satisfied the authorities. Two of George's brothers were Franciscans and a sister may have been a nun. (In the 1680s the Napper family left Oxford and moved to York.)

About 1665 Thomas Stonor established a grammar school for boys at Watlington. The school building doubled as a covered market and later served as a town hall and fire station. It stands to this day, a steeply gabled, brick building on an 'island' site, with traffic flowing around it.

Sir John Browne, son of the second George Browne and of Elizabeth, nee Blount, became a baronet in May 1665. This seems to have been his cue to dispose of Caversham Court. He died fifteen years later, his Great Shefford estate passing to his three sons in turn. He was a great grandson of the first Viscount Montague.

Charles I had made Edmund Plowden II (now Sir Edmund) Governor of New Albion in North America. Charles II, however, ignored his father's charter and gave the colony to his brother James, making him Duke of Albany. Sir Edmund's nephew, Edmund Plowden III of Shiplake died in 1666. Two of Edmund III's sons became priests in the mid 1670s. His daughter Elizabeth married Walter Blount of Mapledurham.

In his will Edmund III left property to Anthony Englefield of Whiteknights, thus maintaining the links established in Shropshire well over a century earlier. Sir Thomas Englefield of Whiteknights also maintained links with another old Catholic family. In 1666 Sir Thomas assigned to Francis Hildesley of Littlestoke and another man £50 a year (= £240 today) from the rents of land at Wootton Bassett in settlement of various debts to third parties.

Meanwhile another descendant of the Elizabethan Edmund Plowden was causing a stir. His daughter Mary, sister-in-law of Francis Perkins I of Ufton Court, married Richard White of Essex. Their son Thomas was a priest educated at St Omer, Valladolid, Douai and Paris. Fr Thomas White wrote numerous books and was commonly known by his literary name, Blacklo. His friends included the scientist Galileo, the philosopher Hobbes and Kenelm Digby, son of an executed Gunpowder Plotter. Digby, though a Catholic, had served Cromwell as a diplomat and Blacklo had himself urged the Catholic clergy to come to terms with the Commonwealth.

Blacklo spent some years after the Restoration in colleges on the Continent but returned to England in 1667. He supported the reintroduction of a proper Catholic hierarchy and dominated the chapter of English Catholic clergy. Because he tried to integrate Catholicism with the current intellectual climate, many Catholics regarded him as an unorthodox sceptic.

Blacklo died in 1676. So too did Fr Benedict Brychan, the first Benedictine chaplain of Fawley Manor. He served the Moores of Fawley for about six years. Fawley is noteworthy as the only Benedictine chaplaincy in Berkshire to survive for any appreciable time between the Reformation and the Catholic Emancipation Act.

Ten years after the Restoration a secret treaty was signed at Dover between Charles II and the French king, Louis XIV. It included a provision for Charles II publicly to adopt Catholicism. Being 'convinced of the truth of the Roman Catholic religion' he was 'to reconcile himself with the Church of Rome as soon as his country's affairs permit.' Timing was left to Charles's discretion and Louis was to pay £150,000 (= £7.7m today) and provide 6,000 troops to suppress any resulting civil disturbance. However, it was not until Charles was on his deathbed that he formally became a Catholic.

In 1672 Charles issued a Declaration of Indulgence. This suspended 'all penal laws in matters ecclesiastical, against whatsoever sort of non-conformists, or, recusants ...' At long last it looked as if England had been granted something resembling religious liberty. However, in the following year Parliament countered the Declaration by passing the Test Act. This prevented the suspension of anti-Catholic laws and actually worsened the position of Catholics. Now all holders of public office had to take Communion according to the Anglican rite, swear the Oaths of Allegiance and Supremacy, and formally deny the Catholic doctrine concerning the nature of Holy Communion.

That year a Catholic master at Magdalen College school, Oxford was forced to flee. He was said to have made sixty converts to Catholicism. In the same city it was noted that Thomas Napper had two grandsons in the French army. Two others were priests, one a Benedictine, the other a Jesuit.

Three years later Lady Mary Yate endowed the Catholic chaplaincy at Buckland, where she had lived until the death of her husband, Sir John Yate. It seems that the endowment started as a £25 a year rent charge (= £1,300 today) on an estate on the Isle of Dogs, in what is now the East End of London.

The Stonors had leased Watlington Park to a tenant but by the mid 1670s the lease had expired. Thomas Stonor built a mansion there and moved into it in 1676. He left Blount's Court to his eldest son John, who married Lady Mary Talbot, only child of the eleventh Earl of Shrewsbury.

The new mansion at Watlington Park was at the top of the steep Chiltern escarpment more than 700 feet above sea-level. It therefore afforded extensive views westwards towards Watlington and Britwell. Although much altered, the present house incorporates parts of Thomas Stonor's mansion.

In the same year that he built the house, Thomas Stonor had Widmere Pond near Blount's Court cleaned out. About two years later an intriguing account of what was found was published in 'The Natural History of Oxfordshire' by Dr R Plot, Professor of Chemistry at Oxford University and Keeper of the Ashmolean Museum, Oxford. He was fascinated by 'many whole Oaks' found in the pond (now known as Widmore Pond and part of Sonning Common, rather than Rotherfield Peppard). It seems that the trees were each fifty to sixty feet high and upside down in the water. All were 'dyed through of a black hue like Ebony, yet much of the Timber sound enough, and fit for many uses ... and all receiving a very good polish'. This, and the discovery of two Roman urns, seems to have sparked off an improbable rumour that the pond covered the entrance to an ancient silver mine.

Despite the persistence of anti-Catholic legislation some pockets of Catholicism in the Thames Valley remained large enough to be regarded as communities rather than merely extended households. The 1676 Recusant Lists show there were almost 200 Catholics within an eight mile radius of Woolhampton. This included 28 at Ufton where Perkins influence was strong, and 21 at Hampstead Norreys which was Dancastle territory. Binfield near Bracknell, also a Dancastle area, had 24 Catholics. Buckland, the chaplaincy of which had recently been endowed by Lady Mary Yate, had 32 Catholics, the most in any single parish in Berkshire. Cookham and Englefield each had 16. Shirburn near Watlington, Oxfordshire had 24.

The percentage of the population that was known to be Catholic varied enormously. In Reading it was 0.1 per cent whereas at Ufton Nervet it was 22 per cent.

The numbers convicted of recusancy reflected the fact that it was not worth the authorities prosecuting those who could not afford the fines, and who might even become a burden on the parish if further impoverished. In the reign of Charles II Cookham near Maidenhead was the Berkshire parish with the most convictions (10), followed by Binfield (8), Englefield and Buckland (7 each), and Wasing and Padworth (5 each). Twenty-four other Berkshire parishes had from one to four convictions.

In 1678 a second Test Act was passed. This removed Catholics from the House of Lords. They had been expelled from the Commons 115 years earlier. Parliament now became increasingly anti-Catholic. So too did public opinion, spurred on by the efforts of the poet Andrew Marvell, who at one time was John Milton's assistant. Marvell's 'Account of the Growth of Popery and Arbitrary Government' blamed Catholics for all kinds of horrors, including the 1666 Great Fire of London.

Matters went from bad to worse with the revelation in 1678 by Titus Oates of an alleged Popish Plot. Oates was a former Anglican minister who had converted to Catholicism and studied for the priesthood at the English College, Valladolid. He brought with him a long tradition of being expelled from places of learning and consolidated this by being ordered to leave the college. His reaction was to return to the Church of England and become an informer against Catholics.

Marvell's book had begun with the statement:'There has now for divers years a design been carried on to change the lawful government of England into an absolute tyranny, and to convert the established Protestant religion into downright Popery.' The allegations of Oates and his co-conspirator Israel Tonge seemed to bear this out and something approaching a national anti-Catholic hysteria erupted.

Titus Oates, who died a Baptist, was later convicted of perjury. However, at the time of the allegations Parliament and the Protestant public were prepared to believe almost anything, and Catholics suffered badly as a result. More than a quarter of the Catholic peers were imprisoned for alleged treason. One was executed and another died in the Tower of London. About a sixth of the Catholic clergy were arrested. Seventeen were executed and twenty-three died in prison.

The Newbury Chamberlain's accounts for this period include payment of £1 (= £50 today) to the Mayor and Justices 'for conveying up a Jesuit to the King and Council'. Francis Hildesley of Littlestoke, a Jesuit lay brother in his mid twenties and later a priest, returned from the Continent to be a defence witness for five Jesuits subsequently executed.

In 1678 Catholic houses were searched for arms. Scholars burned an effigy of the Pope and there were anti-Catholic demonstrations at St Clement's in east Oxford. The Popish Plot hysteria caused the poet William Joyner to flee from his home at Horspath near Cowley. He was captured on suspicion of being a priest but released when it became clear he was not. William Joyner had previously been a fellow of Magdalen College but had renounced his fellowship on becoming a Catholic.

Titus Oates was made a freeman of the City of Oxford in 1679 and at the Oxford Quarter Sessions fifty-one people were indicted for recusancy.

Elizabeth, Lady Abergavenny of Shirburn Castle, widow of the tenth Lord Abergavenny, was accused of recusancy in 1678, along with her servants. She was arrested the following year on information received from Francesco de Feria (was presumably a relative of her kinswoman, the late Lady Jane Dormer, Duchess of Feria). It was alleged that Lady Abergavenny had sent money to a religious establishment overseas and that she had corresponded with a Jesuit called Harcourt. She was acquitted for lack of evidence.

Lady Abergavenny's sister Mary was the wife of Sir Thomas Gage of Firle, Sussex. Lady Mary Gage's relative Frances Gage had married Sir Charles Yate of Buckland, who died in 1680 during the Oates hysteria. Their son and heir John was in Rome at the time of his father's death but wisely postponed his return for four years. When he finally came home he travelled with Fr Thomas Codrington who became chaplain to James II.

The Oates affair forced the sixty year old Franciscan Fr Bernard Francis, alias John Eyston of Finchampstead, to leave England after only a year on the mission. He returned to his former academic career on the Continent and died at Douai more than twenty years later.

Fr Richard Prince was sent to Flanders to escape the persecution following the Oates Plot. He returned after only five months - too soon - and was arrested at Dover. Oxford born, he was in his late twenties and a member of the Catholic yeoman family of the Clifton Hampden district.

After his arrest he was put in Newgate prison, where the Central Criminal Court now stands. His cell was filthy and very narrow. Not surprisingly during five months in prison without medical attention he contracted jail fever. Having been condemned to death, he was allowed a visit on the eve of his execution from Fr Edward Petre. Fr Prince died in Fr Petre's arms and thus escaped the gallows.

The young Oxfordshire priest, Fr Richard Prince, was one of the last Catholic clergy to die for their faith in England. Fr Edward Petre, a member of the famous Essex Catholic family, was later a strong influence on James II and became a member of his Privy Council.

Another Thames Valley Catholic imprisoned during the hysteria generated by the Oates Plot was George Eyston of East Hendred. His lands were sequestrated and the fine for Catmore alone was £80 a year (= £4,000 today). He was listed as owing £233 6s. 8d. in fines (= £12,000 today). His brother John was also imprisoned.

In 1680 the Inns of Court certified that they had no papist members except a Mr Stonor Crouch of Wallingford and Francis Hyde of Hyde End. It was stated that both had absented themselves since a proclamation banishing Catholics. This was Francis Hyde II, then about sixty years old.

Three years later an Oxford Jesuit, Fr Lovell, died. Shortly after the Restoration Fr Lovell had been accused of embezzling £40,000 worth of the King's jewels (= £1.9m today) by a Mrs Curson, then in Newgate jail. However, there is no record of him being tried, nor of exactly who Mrs Curson was.

It has been suggested that, because of the anti-Catholic feeling prevailing at the time of his death, Fr Lovell's body was taken to the Curson home, Waterperry House, for secret burial. By this time the Catholic Sir John Curson had succeeded his openly Protestant father Sir Thomas.

Thirty years later, during the rebuilding of Waterperry House, several coffins were discovered under the house. One at least seems to have been that of a Jesuit chaplain. It was covered in black velvet and contained a silver crucifix and candlesticks.

Although the Jesuits lost one of their number through the death of Fr Lovell, they gained three more through the Plowdens of Shiplake. Edmund Plowden IV, the great great grandson of the Elizabethan lawyer, now held Shiplake Court. Three of his sons were ordained about this time.

The harsher enforcement of anti-Catholic legislation after the Titus Oates affair hit the Stonors hard. Thomas Stonor had to relet all the northern part of his estates, including Watlington Park. By 1684 he was dead and the lease of the manor of Blount's Court (the village of Rotherfield Peppard) was assigned to Martin Hildesley of the Inner Temple, London for £2,766 12s. 0d. (= £144,000 today). Martin Hildesley was the third son of Francis Hildesley of East Ilsley and Littlestoke. Although not listed as a Papist by the Inns of Court, Martin appears to have maintained the family's religious tradition.

The Hildesleys of Littlestoke had been enjoying a resurgence of prosperity at this time, as is evidenced by foundation stones at Littlestoke Manor. A brick and flint barn bears the date 1681 and the initials of Francis Hildesley, whose wife was Mary Winchcombe of Bucklebury. Another stone, dated a year later and built into the garden wall facing the road, has the inititials of their son William and his wife Mary.

In 1685 the dying King was finally received into the Catholic Church by Fr John Huddleston. A branch of his Cumberland-based family held Haseley Court in the remote village of Little Haseley (3½ miles SSE of Waterperry). Haseley Court is a medieval house subsequently altered and extended, with gardens noted for their topiary since Tudor times. The Haseley Brook runs nearby on its way to join the River Thame.

During the Civil War the Huddlestons of Haseley Court mortgaged the estate to help provide a troop of Royalist cavalry. The family never recovered financially from this display of loyalty to the Crown. Their chapel was subsequently used as a stable.

After the Parliamentary victory at Worcester, Fr Huddleston had hidden with the future King at Moseley Old Hall in Staffordshire. Mr Anthony Mockler of Milton Manor, near Abingdon, is a descendant of the Whitgreave family who lived at the Old Hall. A missal of Henry VIII's time, used by Fr Huddleston, can be seen at Milton Manor.

The Huddlestons of Sawston Hall, Cambridgeshire have loaned their authentic portrait of Fr John Huddleston, together with a companion portrait of Charles II, to Stonor House where both are on display to visitors.

The End of a Dream

(1685 - 1700)

Charles II was succeeded by his Catholic brother the Duke of York, who became King James II in 1685. Not long after his coronation the rule of the Vicars Apostolic was reinstated. England had not had a Vicar Apostolic since Bishop Smith fled to France more than half a century earlier.

Any idea of regaining the original pre-Reformation bishoprics was abandoned. Instead England was divided into four districts, each with its own Vicar Apostolic. Each district was to be funded by the King with £1,000 a year (= £52,000 today). Berkshire was in the London District, which included the Home Counties, Isle of Wight, Channel Islands and the American colonies; Oxfordshire was in the Midland District, the Thames forming the border between the two. This division has continued to the present day, the Thames forming the boundary between the diocese of Portsmouth and the archdiocese of Birmingham.

The new King, James II, began a programme of positive discrimination in favour of Catholics. Thirteen were appointed to the Privy Council and four were made judges. Others were given commissions in the army or senior appointments in the universities.

James set up a Catholic royal chapel in London and this led to the opening of many other Catholic chapels across the country. At Oxford Mass was celebrated in the chapel of Magdalen College and in the oratory of Christ Church Cathedral. In 1686 Obadiah Walker, master of University College, Oxford, had a private Mass said at the college, thus provoking a minor riot.

In Easter Week 1687 George Eyston of East Hendred began repairing the ancient thirteenth century chapel of St Amand attached to Hendred House. Before the Reformation the chapel had its own chaplain and parsonage, and had been financed by tithe income and a dozen acres of land. Now the interior was derelict and only the base of the altar remained.

Five days after the refurbishment began the King issued a Declaration of Indulgence suspending anti-Catholic legislation. Thus the Catholic Thomas Kimber was able to join Oxford City Council. That summer the Papal Nuncio, the Pope's ambassador, was formally received by the King at Windsor.

The refitting of the Eyston's chapel was completed a week before Christmas 1687. On Christmas Eve three Franciscans, including the Eystons' chaplain Fr Pacificus, blessed the altar stone and celebrated vespers. On Christmas Day seven priests said Mass. One of the celebrants was the Jesuit Fr Francis

---

Hildesley, whose brothers William, the heir of Littlestoke, and Martin, purchaser of the manor of Blount's Court, were also present. Others attending included Sir Henry Moore of Fawley and John Massey, the Catholic Dean of Christ Church, Oxford.

The following April James II issued a second Declaration of Indulgence giving rights of public worship to Catholics and Protestant Nonconformists. The King stated:'We cannot but heartily wish ... that all the people of our dominions were members of the Catholic Church; yet ... conscience ought not to be constrained nor people forced in matters of mere religion ...'

Seven Anglican bishops, including Tilehurst born William Lloyd, were imprisoned for signing a petition against the Declaration.

It was becoming clear that the King's attempts to improve the lot of his fellow Catholics were moving too fast. The situation was not helped by Catholics such as the landlord of the Mitre at Oxford, whose inflammatory anti-Protestant comments led to the mob breaking the windows of every known Catholic house in the city.

The backlash was not confined to the Oxford rabble. Fifty miles downstream Protestant gentry and nobility were plotting at Ladye Place, a Tudor riverside mansion on part of the site of Hurley Priory. Ladye Place was the home of Lord Lovelace, a friend of Titus Oates.

Earlier in the year Lord Lovelace had been brought before the King and Privy Council for telling constables to ignore the instructions of a Catholic Justice of the Peace. He was released for lack of evidence and promptly joined a plot to depose James II and replace him with his Dutch Protestant son-in-law, William, Prince of Orange. Lord Lovelace allowed the old Benedictine cellars of Ladye Place to be used for midnight meetings of the conspirators. These included Lady Mary Stonor's stepbrother, the Earl of Shrewsbury, who had left the Catholic Church after the Titus Oates affair.

Although the original Ladye Place was long ago demolished, the cellars still exist to the east of Hurley parish church. They are not normally open to the public. (The present Ladye Place stands to the west of the church and is the modernised sixteenth century farmhouse of the Tudor mansion.)

In September 1688 Lord Lovelace visited Holland and in November William of Orange landed at Torbay with 15,000 troops. On Friday 7 December he reached Hungerford and stayed at the Bear Inn, which stands on the old London to Bath road. There he was visited by James's Commissioners, who wanted to negotiate. William wished to be seen as the protector of parliamentary independence rather than the rightful King's usurper. He therefore withdrew three miles up the Kennet Valley to Littlecote House while the negotiations took place at Hungerford.

HENDRED HOUSE IN THE LATE 17th CENTURY – from an old engraving

William of Orange's visit to Hungerford entered the town's folklore. The traditional Hocktide festivities, which take place in the second week after Easter, were modified to include the distribution of oranges and orange flowers. And the Town Clerk's staff bears a silver ferrule engraved with the date 1688.

On Sunday 9 December, two days after William arrived at Hungerford, hundreds of Irish troops loyal to James II moved into Reading to defend the town against the Dutch. But the people of Reading supported William and appealed to him for help. The Prince responded by sending a relief force of some 300 Dutch troops.

Irish cavalry were stationed at the bottom of Castle Street where the road from the west enters the old town centre. Other Irish troops were in Broad Street and St Mary's churchyard, but most were in the Market Place. The townspeople sent details of the Irish strategy to William. The Dutch soldiers therefore approached Reading not down Castle Street as expected, but from the Pangbourne direction, thus catching the Irish off guard.

The fighting that followed resulted in the Irish being forced out of town towards Twyford. About fifty were killed, whereas the Dutch suffered a mere half dozen fatalities. Some of the dead were buried in St Giles's churchyard, a few hundred yards south of where much of the fighting took place.

The event was remembered by the people of Reading who added their own verses to the then popular anti-Irish song Lillibulero. These told of how 'Five hundred Papishes (sic) came there' to destroy the town 'in time of prayer, But God did them defend.'

On Tuesday 11 December 1688, two days after the Reading skirmish, the Dutch army reached Abingdon. William of Orange stayed at the recently built Milton Manor, four miles south of the town. There he heard that James II had fled from London, throwing the Great Seal of office into the Thames to prevent Parliament being called in his name.

This news soon reached a party of Dutch troops quartered at East Hendred, two miles south of Milton. They celebrated by desecrating the Eyston's newly reopened chapel of St Amand. They smashed the fittings, celebrated a travesty of the Mass and stole a set of vestments. These they took to Oxford which Lord Lovelace now held on William's behalf. There they dressed a dummy to represent a Catholic priest and burned it on a bonfire.

This was one of many anti-Catholic incidents that occurred that 'wild Popish night' as it became known. George Eyston's aunt Jane, a daughter of William Eyston of Catmore, died that Christmas 'of a fright she took at the mob when they plundered the Spanish Ambassador's chapel and house' in London. Her husband was Robert Smeaton, an attorney from Henwick near

Thatcham where a Catholic branch of the Winchcombes had lived before the Civil War.

A few days after the 'wild Popish night' William of Orange reached London. James II, having been captured, was allowed to escape on 23 December 1688 and went into exile in France. There he joined his second wife Mary of Modena, the last Catholic Queen of England.

James's Court was re-established at the great fortress of Saint-Germain-en-Laye near Paris. Several hundred Catholic gentry joined the King, including the Comptroller of the Royal Household, Francis Plowden, a great great grandson of the Elizabethan lawyer.

Francis Plowden's young nephew, Lieutenant William Plowden of Shiplake, quit the Thames Valley for Saint-Germain-en-Laye. He left his mother to supervise the disposal of Shiplake Court which was sold to Robert Jennings, a former head of Reading School, for £5,800 (= £313,000 today) and a life income of £60 a year (= £3,250 today) for William's grandmother. She was probably the Mrs Plowden who lived on at Shiplake until 1694 in a house called Grovelands, later known as Ship House.

Two hundred years later, in 1894, a secret cupboard was found in a farmhouse near the site of Shiplake Court. It has been suggested that this may have been used to conceal Mass materials after the Plowdens sold the Court.

Nothing now remains of Shiplake Court except a silted-up fish pond. The site is divided between Shiplake College and the former kitchen garden of Shiplake House. Three hundred years after they left the village the Plowdens are commemorated in the name of an inn on the Reading to Henley road, the Plowden Arms.

In 1689 William of Orange and his wife Mary, daughter of James II and his Catholic convert wife Anne Hyde, were recognised by Parliament as joint monarchs. The penal laws against Catholics were harshly re-enforced and Catholic landowners were again badly hit.

The same year George, second son of George Eyston of East Hendred, joined the Jesuits at Watten in Flanders. He seems to have spent the rest of his life there or at Ghent.

James II tried in 1690 to regain the Crown by invading Ireland and raising an army there. In July his troops were defeated by William's at the Battle of the Boyne. Commanding James's Second Regiment of Foot was twenty-two year old William Plowden, late of Shiplake, who after the battle returned to exile in France.

In 1692 William Plowden's mother obtained a pass for him to visit England. Four years later he married his second wife Mary Stonor, daughter of John Stonor and Lady Mary Stonor of Watlington Park. The following year he was officially pardoned and allowed to return to England where he lived a quiet life.

William Plowden's marriage and pardon were arranged with the assistance of Lady Mary Stonor's stepbrother, the Earl of Shrewsbury. He had been well rewarded by William of Orange for his part in the plot to usurp James II and was the only person ever to be made simultaneously Lord Lieutenant of Ireland, Lord Chancellor and Lord High Treasurer. But despite having abandoned Catholicism, he used his influence to help his Catholic relatives.

In 1690, the year of the Battle of the Boyne, Sir John Yate of Buckland died in Paris. He was succeeded by his sister Mary who soon afterwards married Sir Robert Throckmorton. The Throckmortons were an old Catholic family with estates in Warwickshire and north Buckinghamshire, and Sir Robert spent little time at Buckland.

1692 saw the imposition of double land tax on Catholics. That same year Maryland, established as a North American refuge for English Catholics, was transformed into an Anglican colony with anti-Catholic legislation.

Two years later William, son of the John Eyston imprisoned in the aftermath of the Popish Plot, was jailed for going into exile with James II. He spent four years in prison and was then banished. He returned to spend his last years in England and was buried in the Eyston aisle of East Hendred parish church. A Latin inscription refers to his loyalty to the Catholic Church and to the King. We are left to guess whether the king in question was James II or William III.

William Eyston's three younger brothers all went into exile and served in the Duke of Orleans' regiment. All three had died unmarried by 1705.

For Catholic gentry the choice of marriage partners was now reducing. A significant minority had become nuns or priests, who were therefore ineligible for marriage and produced no children for the next generation. Others had followed James II into exile on the Continent. In 1693 the widowed Francis Perkins III of Ufton Court married his distant cousin Anne Perkins, daughter of Richard Perkins of Beenham. (Francis Perkins III was the grandson of Francis Perkins II.) Anne gave birth to a daughter whose birth was, for legal reasons, recorded in the registers of Beenham parish church, despite not being baptised there. Out of habit the parson started to write 'baptised' but crossed it out and wrote 'born' instead.

About this time the Perkins of Beenham had a Jesuit chaplain, whereas their Ufton cousins' chaplain was a secular priest, that is, one who was not a member of a religious order.

In 1696 Fr Francis Hildesley was forty-one and Superior of the Jesuits' Residence of St Mary, which included Oxfordshire. Two years later his aunt Catherine died. She was the last survivor of four daughters of William Hildesley of Littlestoke who had become nuns at Liege. More than twenty years earlier William

Hildesley, together with a Mr Dolman, had made a donation to the convent at Liege and paid for a stained glass window in its chapel. Another Hildesley nun, Frances, died in 1693 aged thirty-one. She was probably Fr Francis Hildesley's youngest sister.

In the same year that Frances Hildesley died so too did Elizabeth, wife of Joseph Gage of Shirburn Castle near Watlington. She was buried in Shirburn parish church, next to the castle. Joseph Gage was the nephew of Lady Abergavenny and in 1698 was indicted with some of his servants for recusancy, just as his aunt had been in the past. Similar indictments were made the two following years.

In 1700 an investigation was carried out into an alleged boast of Lady Abergavenny and Joseph Gage. It was claimed that they had said that, when the Catholic Stuart monarchy was re-established, Catholics would reclaim £100,000 (= £4.8m today) from Protestant estates. This seems to have referred to the costs of maintaining English seminaries and religious houses abroad.

Allegations and rumours of this sort were rife at this time. The villagers of Great Milton (7 miles ESE of Oxford) claimed that the Simeons' estate at nearby Chilworth and Coombe was held secretly for the Dominicans. John Stonor was said to have made over part of his estate to the Jesuits of Douai. Sir John Curson of Waterperry was accused of mortgaging his estates for £450 a year (= £21,600 today) to provide £6,000 (= £288,000 today) for the same Jesuits. Ten years earlier an informer had reported that a small estate at Garford near Lyford had been granted, presumably by the Yates, as a site for a nunnery 'when Popish times should come'. Even earlier, in the 1670s, an informer had claimed that a farm at East Garston in the Lambourn Valley (presumably Maidencourt) was being held in trust, also as a site for a convent.

And so the century ended. Having set out to establish a religious freedom in which Catholicism enjoyed favoured status, James II had lost the Crown and left a legacy of anti-Catholicism that took centuries to dispel. His Dutch son-in-law had given a solemn assurance that Catholics would be 'put out of fear of being persecuted on account of their religion'. Yet by the end of the seventeenth century their lot was, in many ways, worse than ever.

The days of martyrdom and glory were over and the expectation of the re-establishment of Catholicism as the national religion had gone. From now on all that Catholics could expect was financial ruin, exclusion from public life and deprivation of civil rights; a subtle form of internal exile.

When Alexander Pope
Lived in Berkshire

(1700 - 1715)

In the eighteenth century many of the gentry families that had
been pillars of Catholicism died out. The natural tendency for
the male line of any family ultimately to fail was exacerbated
by the relatively high proportion of celibate religious
vocations and by economic decline affecting marriage prospects.
And Anglicanism became increasingly attractive to those wishing
to retain their social gentry status.

The decline of the Catholic gentry gave them the impression
that English Catholicism as a whole was declining. In reality
it was slowly growing, for as the Catholic squires died out,
there was a simultaneous growth of the Catholic middle class.

As the century started, further anti-Catholic legislation was
introduced. Anyone responsible for the arrest and conviction of
a Catholic priest could now claim £100 (= £4,800 today).
Catholics were forbidden to acquire an interest of any kind in
land or property. Any they would have gained through marriage
or inheritance was to go instead to their Protestant next of
kin. Only by renouncing Catholicism could the interest be
recovered.

One who had to cope with the new property laws was Alexander
Pope, a London linen merchant. He was the son of a Hampshire
rector and a convert to Catholicism. Having been widowed, he
married a Yorkshire woman, Editha Turner, whose family was
partly Catholic.

Shortly after William and Mary became joint monarchs, Catholics
were expelled from the City of London. The Popes moved up river
to Hammersmith, but in 1700 they relocated to Binfield near
Bracknell. There the principal manor house, Binfield Place, was
held by the Catholic Dancastle family. The village was also
only seven miles across the heath from Hall Grove, Bagshot in
Surrey. This was the home of Magdalen Rackett, Mr Pope's
daughter by his first wife.

It was through Magdalen's husband Charles Rackett that Pope had
been able in 1698 to purchase Whitehill House, a small manor
house in fourteen acres of land at Binfield. The house has been
known successively as Binfield Lodge, The Firs and Arthurstone.
Now much altered, and renamed Pope's Manor, it is (1991) the
headquarters of the construction company Bryant Southern.

The Racketts kept a Catholic chaplain, Fr William Mannock. So
too did the Popes, whose priest sometimes acted as tutor to

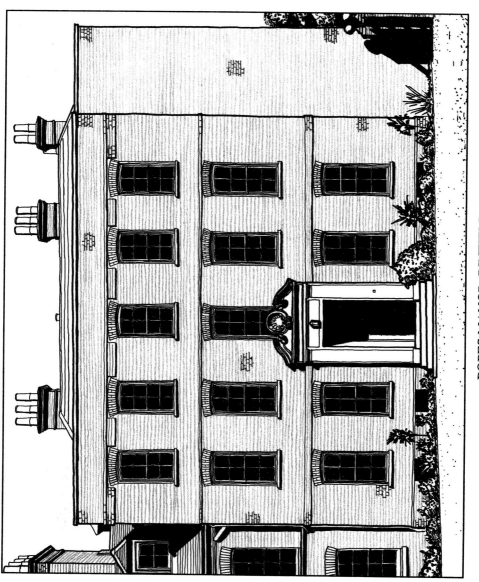

POPES MANOR, BINFIELD

their son Alexander, who was to become one of England's greatest poets. At the time of the Popes' relocation to Binfield in 1700, young Alexander was twelve years old. Fr Mannock described him as having 'a great deal of sweetness in his look'. However, shortly after the move the boy drank some infected milk which gave him Pott's Disease, an infection of the spine which was ultimately to deform his whole body.

In 1701 both William of Orange and the deposed James II died. William's wife Mary, who was James's daughter, had died some years earlier. The new monarch was her Anglican sister Anne, wife of Prince George of Denmark, and an opponent of any nonconformity, whether Catholic or Protestant.

The last record of the Stonors in connection with Blount's Court, Rotherfield Peppard dates from this time. Thereafter the estate was sold to James Jennings, probably a relative of the man who bought Shiplake Court from the Plowdens. The Stonors had long-established links with Shiplake, and as late as 1696 Henry and his brother Thomas were described as justices of Shiplake. Presumably it was only through the influence of their formerly Catholic uncle the Earl of Shrewsbury that they were able to hold these positions. The Stonors retained land at Shiplake Row called Holmwood until the 1830s, including Holmwood House, a Georgian residence that still stands.

Blount's Court was later altered and now presents an early nineteenth century appearance. It is part of the Johnson Matthey Technology Centre and has a Sonning Common postal address. Company security and the twentieth century offices and laboratories adjacent to the old house make viewing difficult but the seventeenth century chimney hides still remain.

In 1704 the sixteen year old Alexander Pope met the poet William Wycherley, then sixty-four. Wycherley had been a successful Restoration dramatist but had since lost royal favour and spent four years in jail for debt. Fr Mannock described the old man as Pope's 'first poet-friend'.

Pope and Wycherley met at Whiteknights, seat of Anthony Englefield II since his father Anthony's death in 1667. Englefield often played host to leading literary figures and lived only ten miles from Alexander Pope's home at Binfield.

The friendship between Pope and Wycherley initially proved good for both of them. Pope corrected Wycherley's work and suggested improvements, while Wycherley provided Pope with numerous literary contacts in London. But after six years the old man tired of Pope's corrections and the friendship cooled. Nonetheless Pope visited Wycherley on his deathbed, where the old dramatist became a Catholic.

In the spring of 1704 Austin Belson of Aston Rowant was heavily in debt. He set out for the Netherlands pending resolution of his financial situation. However, he was arrested at Hull on suspicion of being a subversive. He wrote from prison seeking character references from two Members of Parliament, Tanfield Vachell of Coley Park and Sir Richard Neville of Billingbear near Twyford, Berkshire.

Austin Belson was not the only Catholic suspected of being a subversive. In the following year four properties in the south Chilterns were searched for arms. These were the Stonor residences at Stonor and Watlington Park, a shepherd's house at Greenfield (½ mile SE of Watlington Park) and Shirburn Castle. But nothing more subversive than a 'birding gun' was discovered.

Also in 1705 John Talbot Stonor returned to Paris to resume studying for the priesthood after a break of seven years. He had previously concluded that he did not have a vocation. His change of heart was to have a profound influence on Catholicism, both locally and nationally.

The head of the Stonor family at this time was John Talbot's brother Thomas Stonor, whose deceased first wife, Isabella Bellasis, was a granddaughter of the Great Loyalist, John Paulet. Thomas had subsequently remarried, his new wife being Winifred Roper, a member of the family into which Sir Thomas More's eldest daughter Margaret had married. Winifred Roper was also a granddaughter of the Catholic Viscount Montague of Cowdray, Sussex.

Thomas Stonor's uncle, William Stonor, had gone into exile with James II. Eighteen years had since elapsed. He was now in his mid forties and wanted to return home. Thomas asked the Duke of Marlborough to intercede with Queen Anne and a pardon was obtained. Thus William Stonor was able to retire quietly to Cornwall.

But if Queen Anne was capable of acts of clemency towards individual Catholics, she showed no compromise to Catholics in general. In 1706 she made it a treasonable offence to convert anyone to Catholicism. She ordered the enforcement of the laws against Catholics and had a census made 'of the Number of Papists in every Parish, with their Qualities, Estates and Places of Abode'. The Catholic population of the Thames Valley area remained fairly static at about 1 per cent. In Berkshire, for example, there were 293 known or suspected Catholics. In the city of Oxford there were fourteen. That year Thomas and Winifred Stonor, along with ten servants and three other people, were fined at the Oxford Quarter Sessions for being Catholics.

Catholicism generally continued to be based around the country homes of Catholic gentry. The village of Noke on the edge of Ot Moor provides an example. The estate had probably been in Catholic hands continuously since Elizabethan times, having been held successively by the Fermors, Winchcombes and Halls. In 1706 John Palmer from the nearby village of Islip headed the Catholics of Noke, probably as lessee of the manor. The rest of the Catholic community of the village seems to have consisted of his family and servants, and a pair of yeoman families.

A year or so later Henry Benedict Hall of High Meadow, Gloucestershire, sold the Noke estate. Most of it, including the manorial rights, passed to the first Duke of Marlborough. His wife Lady Sarah Churchill, the confidante of Queen Anne, subsequently demolished Noke manor house. However, as late as 1767 a Catholic priest visited the village to 'mutter dirges over the dead'.

Anthony Englefield's daughter Martha had married Lyster Blount of Mapledurham. They had two daughters: Teresa, who called herself Zephelinda; and her younger sister Martha, who styled herself Parthenia, but was otherwise known as Patty. Martha and Teresa Blount were introduced to Alexander Pope at Whiteknights in 1707. Pope and Teresa were both nineteen, Martha seventeen.

Pope had a puzzling relationship with the girls that lasted all his life. He was a frequent visitor to them at Whiteknights and Mapledurham. More attracted to Teresa at first, he later became closer to Martha.

He frequently wrote romantic and outrageously libertine letters to them. It seems that the correspondence was permitted partly because no one took the content seriously, partly because of his genius for poetry and partly because he was an increasingly hopeless invalid.

Until the early nineteenth century the parish of Ufton had consisted of two separate manors, Ufton Nervet and the Perkins's estate, Ufton Robert. In 1709 Ufton Nervet was purchased from Lord Abingdon on behalf of Francis Perkins IV by two trustees, Lord Stawell of Aldermaston and Leonard Belson. At the same time a 35 acre plot of meadowland belonging to James Bertie was bought on Perkins's behalf by his bailiff, John Berrington. (The use of Protestant or ostensibly Protestant intermediaries to purchase the land was necessary to evade the anti-Catholic property laws.) Thus, apart from a few smallholdings, all the land in the parish now formed one estate controlled by Francis Perkins.

In November 1709 Mary Eyston died aged thirty. She was a daughter and coheiress of William Hildesley of East Ilsley and Littlestoke. He had died two years before leaving no male heir. She was buried in the Eyston family aisle in East Hendred parish church where she lies alongside her husband Robert Eyston. He survived her by seventeen years and was the son of the George Eyston who restored St Amand's Chapel at Hendred House. They had three sons, the oldest being named George Hildesley Eyston, so that he would perpetuate the Hildesley name as a descendant of the main Ilsley branch of the family. What became of him is a mystery.

In spring 1711 John Talbot Stonor was ordained at Paris at the age of thirty-three. He was the first priest in the family for

250 years. After his ordination he stayed at Paris for a further three years studying for a university degree and a doctorate in divinity.

The year after John Talbot Stonor's ordination Alexander Pope's famous poem 'The Rape of the Lock' was published. It caused a storm, especially among some of the senior Catholic families.

In the previous year a feud had broken out between the Fermors of north Oxfordshire and the Petres of Essex. Lord Robert Petre, a ward of Pope's friend John Caryll of Sussex, had stolen a lock of hair from the head of his attractive relative Arabella Fermor. She was then about twenty-two years old and one of the most eligible beauties in London.

Miss Fermor was enraged and her family took great exception to the incident. Caryll therefore suggested that Pope should write a humorous poem to defuse the situation. Pope contacted Lord Petre and Miss Fermor before publication and both appeared happy with the idea. However, when the poem was published she objected strongly. Her second cousin, the pompous Sir George Browne, even threatened to cane Pope!

By the end of 1713 the fuss had died down and shortly afterwards Pope published an expanded version dedicated to Arabella Fermor. Within two years 'Bell' Fermor had married the forty year old Francis Perkins IV of Ufton Court. The house was 'much-refashioned and enlarged' for her. The frontage was updated and the hall and dining room repanelled. She is said to have played literary hostess at Ufton to wits such as Pope, Arbuthnot and Lord Bolingbroke.

About the time that 'The Rape of the Lock' was first published the yeoman Catholic community of the Dorchester district witnessed the completion of Overy Manor House. Overy is a hamlet which faces Dorchester across the River Thame, the two communities being linked by Dorchester Bridge. Overy Manor House was built by William Davey for his second wife Helen. Their initials can still be seen on the building. Before its construction the Daveys, by then the leading Catholic family of the area, had lived in a substantial old house which stood a hundred and fifty yards south-west of the present building.

The old house contained a room which served as a Catholic chapel. It was fully equipped with altar furniture and was used for Mass about seven times a year. A few relics of this chapel still exist; some ancient vestments now on display in Dorchester Abbey, an oil painting later presented to an Oxford convent, and an old mission chalice. The chalice is kept at the Catholic church of St Birinus opposite the abbey. It is small and takes apart for easy concealment. (In 1583 a priest wrote to Cardinal Allen telling him that he had ordered thirty such chalices to be made.)

In the summer of 1713 Alexander Pope wrote to his friend John Caryll. He complained that Henry Englefield, who had inherited

Whiteknights from his father Anthony, had 'not shown the least common civility to my father and mother by sending, or inquiring of them from our nearest neighbours, his visitants, these five months.' Pope wrote that he would take the hint and Englefield would be 'as much a stranger to me as he desires'.

The following spring Alexander Pope returned to his parents' home at Binfield from one of his frequent periods in London. With him came the poet Thomas Parnell, a charming Irish Anglican clergyman who was greatly liked by the Catholic household. Two months later Parnell revisited Binfield and from there he and Pope travelled to Letcombe Bassett (3 miles SW of Wantage). There another Irish Anglican clergyman, Dean Jonathan Swift, was living at the rectory. Pope already knew Swift, both being founder members of a literary club. However, their close friendship only lasted a short time.

In the autumn of 1713 Martin Wollascott died aged fifty-two. He was buried in Brimpton parish church. He had succeeded to the manor of Woolhampton two years after William and Mary came to the throne. Martin Wollascott had married Mary Throckmorton, daughter of Sir Francis Throckmorton of Coughton Court. At least two of their sons were educated at Douai. Two daughters became nuns, one at Louvain, another at Paris: portraits of them in their habits are in the National Gallery of Art, Washington DC.

Martin Wollascott owned a 1684 missal (Mass book) printed in Paris. On the flyleaf he recorded the birth dates, names, christenings, godparents and confirmations of his seven children. One of his manor houses was Shalford House, an old Wollascott property now known as Shalford Farm. It stands less than a mile east of Brimpton and is said to have had secret hiding places, including a chimney with a double flue offering an escape route to the roof. Martin was succeeded by his son William Wollascott V.

Queen Anne died in the summer of 1714 and the Crown passed to George I, a Hanoverian Lutheran descendant of James I. However, for some weeks he was unable to get to London from Germany. In the meantime the authorities grew ever fearful of a coup by the Jacobites, supporters of the Stuart cause. The reward for the capture of Prince James Edward Stuart, son of James II and pretender to the throne, was therefore raised to a staggering £100,000 (= £4.8m today).

George I was crowned in October 1714. Alexander Pope's friends Martha and Teresa Blount of Mapledurham were in London for the coronation. Martha, however, seems to have missed it through catching smallpox. Both girls were taken back to Mapledurham soon after the ceremony and missed the celebrations that followed. Pope tried to console them by writing a poem about a young woman taken away from the attractions of London and brought back to 'Old-fashion'd halls, dull aunts, and croaking rooks' and 'To morning walks, and pray'rs three hours a day.'

On the accession of the new King, the Oath of Allegiance was altered to include statements rejecting both the Pope and Prince James Edward Stuart. The oath could be demanded of anyone suspected of disloyalty. Failure to take it could lead to sequestration of two thirds of the refuser's estates.

John Young was steward to Lady Elizabeth Bisshopp, a Catholic convert who lived at Culham near Abingdon. Shortly after the revised oath was introduced he ignored an order to take it at Wheatley. The following year William Wollascott V of Woolhampton was listed as a non-juror - someone who refused to take the oath. Also listed was Thomas Kimber of Holywell in Oxford and of Littlemore.

In the coronation year George Browne, great grandson of Sir George, sold Great Shefford manor to Sir William Trumbull, formerly William III's Secretary of State. Thus the manor passed out of Catholic hands.

The visitor to the ancient parish church of Swyncombe who lifts the carpet will see a memorial slab to Francis Fettiplace of Swyncombe House who died in 1671. The slab states that he was 'descended from the ancient family' of Fettiplace. His son Bartholomew was the last male Fettiplace to hold Swyncombe. He died in 1686 leaving a twenty-seven year old widow, his second wife Margaret.

As a young girl she had been educated at Paris and had stayed abroad to avoid the aftermath of the Oates Plot. Before her marriage she had rejected the idea of becoming a nun, but in widowhood her views changed. Eight years after her husband's death she became Sr Margaret Theresa, eventually becoming prioress of the Teresine convent at Lier near Antwerp.

Bartholomew Fettiplace left financial provision for his widow and this caught the attention of the authorities. When in 1715 Sr Margaret returned to Flanders from a visit to England she was followed by government agents. Presumably they were concerned that she might be giving financial aid to the Jacobites. However, the nuns had support from an unexpected quarter. The Duke of Marlborough, hero of the recent war against France, had earlier helped obtain a pardon for William Stonor for his Jacobite activities. Now the Duke was in Flanders and used his influence in support of the convent at Lier.

Shirburn Castle had passed to Joseph Gage, whose mother was the former Mary Chamberlain. Joseph Gage had a reputation for his excellent team of six coach horses. His son Thomas inherited from his father both the castle and a taste for fine horses.

In the summer of 1715 Thomas was staying in London. His own team of Flemish coach horses had recently been seized by the authorities. The sight of other people's fine horses passing by so upset him that, according to Alexander Pope, he rushed out, took the Oath of Abjuration and became an Anglican.

Thomas Gage's liking for thoroughbred horses led to a major Catholic dynasty abandoning the religious heritage it had fostered through a century and a half of trials and tribulations. This was just what the authorities wanted and the return of his horses was only the first of many worldly benefits that Thomas Gage gained by abandoning his religion.

One of his first moves was to dispose of Shirburn Castle, which for so many years had been a Catholic house. He sold it to the Lord Chief Justice, Baron Parker, for £25,695 8s. 5d. (= £1.3m today). Thomas Gage subsequently became Baron of Castlebar, Viscount of Castel Ireland, a Fellow of the Royal Society and a Verderer of the Forest of Dean. In later life he was Master of Household to the Prince of Wales. In 1744 he succeeded to the baronetcy and estate of Firle in Sussex, thus becoming head of the Gage dynasty.

Thomas Gage married Benedicta Hall, a woman with a strong a recusant background. Her father was Henry Benedict Hall, her mother the former Frances Fortescue. Benedicta's father had sold the Noke estate partly to provide a marriage portion for her. The male line of the Halls had failed and she was the sole heir to their main estate, High Meadow, Gloucestershire, which passed to her husband on their marriage. Benedicta's Christian name perpetuated the link with Benedict Winchcombe, the Catholic Sheriff of Oxfordshire, who left his estates to his nephew Benedict Hall in 1623.

Before he died in 1754 Thomas Gage reverted to Catholicism. His portrait is on view at Firle. His younger brother Joseph's life was very different. In Paris he made and lost a paper fortune. His subsequent involvement in an unsuccessful Spanish mining venture was ridiculed by Alexander Pope.

In the spring of 1715 Pope paid his last visit to the family home at Binfield in Windsor Forest. Whitehill House, his parents' home, had been sold and a few weeks later they moved to Chiswick.

Pope's attitude to his religion was regarded by some Catholics as half-hearted. In his 'Essay on Man' he wrote:

'For modes of faith let graceless zealots fight,

His can't be wrong whose life is in the right.

In Faith and Hope the world will disagree,

But all Mankind's concern is Charity.'

When Pope's father died the Anglican Bishop of Rochester suggested that Alexander might as well join the Church of England. He replied that he did not wish to, because it would upset his mother. He summed up his own position by stating:

'I am not a Papist, for I renounce the temporal invasions of the Papal power ... I am a Catholic in the strictest sense of the word.'

Twixt Fifteen and Forty-five

(1715 - 1745)

The government's fears of a rebellion came true in September 1715 when the Scottish Jacobites rose. However, fifteen weeks were to pass before Prince James Edward Stuart landed in Scotland. By that time his supporters had suffered significant defeats.

The Pretender proved a poor and uninspiring leader. After six weeks he deserted the remnants of his army and sailed back to France.

As ever, the folly of those who sought to reimpose a Catholic monarch by force rebounded on the English Catholics. In the summer of 1716 Catholics were again ordered to leave London and stay at least ten miles from the City.

The Catholics of the Thames Valley area gave little or no active support to the Jacobites. However, one of those executed at Liverpool for taking part in the rising was George Collingwood, brother of a Jesuit priest based at Sandford-on-Thames. Fr Charles Collingwood had come to Oxfordshire in 1701 and stayed at Sandford until his death three years after the rebellion. He was buried in the Sandford parish church.

In 1716, as an aid to the collection of taxes, the government began registering land owned by Catholics. All Catholics were obliged to register their names and holdings. Among those in the Thames Valley area who did was a London Catholic, Roboaldo Fieschi, who with his step-sister held a small estate at Chinnor (4 miles SE of Thame).

At Paris in the same year John Talbot Stonor was consecrated titular Bishop of Thespiae by the Papal Nuncio. He returned to England as Vicar Apostolic of the Midland District with temporary jurisdiction also over the London District. His responsibilities therefore initially included the whole Thames Valley area.

Although the Vicar Apostolic's mere presence in England was punishable by death, Bishop Stonor was a supporter of the Hanoverian monarchy. George I showed his appreciation by persuading the Holy Roman Emperor to make the Bishop Abbot and Baron of Lieu Dieu de Jard. So, despite the anti-Catholic legislation, Bishop Stonor was able to travel relatively freely throughout his extensive territory. He spent much of his time visiting the small Catholic communities based around the country houses of the gentry. In between he often stayed at

---

Stonor House, Watlington Park or Heythrop, near Chipping Norton.

In 1718 Charles Eyston of East Hendred wrote his will. He was the son of George Eyston, the restorer of St Amand's chapel. Known as the Antiquary, he was a great friend of the Oxford diarist Thomas Hearne. Shortly after the Antiquary's death Hearne described Eyston as:

'a Gentleman of eminent virtues and my great friend and acquaintance. He was a Roman Catholic, and so charitable to the poor that he is lamented by all that knew anything of him ... He was a man of sweet tempers and was an excellent scholar, but so modest that he did not care to have it at any time mentioned.'

The Antiquary possessed a large library and many rare volumes and manuscripts. He wrote a number of books, mostly on church history and religion, including a history of Glastonbury Abbey. He died in 1721 at the age of fifty-four 'after he was seized with a Diabetes'.

Charles Eyston fathered eleven children by his wife Winefred Fitzherbert, who survived him by thirty-two years. He was buried in the Eystons' aisle in East Hendred parish church, where there is a monument to him and his wife. His will reveals his loyalty to the Catholic Church, because he describes himself as 'Being by God's grace steadfast and certain in the integrity of that faith which my ancestors have received and learned from the holy Roman Catholic church, in obedience to the Apostolic See of Rome ...'

In his will he left a gold enamelled cross and two guineas (= £109 today) to each of his God-daughters, Mrs Dormer, Mrs Englefield and Mrs Belson. He left £5 (= £260 today) to the poor of East Hendred. But most interestingly of all he left to his eldest son and heir Charles 'Bishop Fisher's staff', as noted earlier in this book.

In the year that the Antiquary wrote his will the main East Ilsley line of Hildesleys (from whom the staff seems to have come) was all but extinct. That very year the spinster Emerita Hildesley sold the family's last interest in East Ilsley, the village from which they took their name.

The Hildesleys' principal residence in the seventeenth century had been Littlestoke in a Thameside finger of the parish of Checkendon. About the time that the Hildesleys died out another Catholic family, the Doughtys, moved into the parish. They were related by marriage to the Blounts of Mapledurham via the Tichbornes.

The Doughtys occupied Checkendon Court in the village of Checkendon and are also believed to have held Braziers Park near Ipsden, and Woodcote House at Woodcote. (The present Woodcote House was built c.1733 and remodelled in the early twentieth century. It is now The Oratory School, the Catholic public school founded by Cardinal Newman.) At some time during the first half of the eighteenth century the Doughtys are said to have had a small Catholic chapel in the grounds of Checkendon Court. Subsequently it was used as a chicken house and fell into ruin.

In September 1721, six weeks before his death, Charles Eyston the Antiquary dined at the Mitre Inn, Oxford with Thomas Hearne and Mr Kimber of Holywell, one of the staunchest recusants in the city. Three years later Thomas Kimber of Holywell, who may have been Mr Kimber's son, was ordained. Fr Kimber worked in Wales and died at Powis Castle near Welshpool in 1742. The Earls of Powis had until recently been Catholic and still treated Catholic priests favourably. Like Thomas Gage, they had conformed to Anglicanism for materialistic rather than theological reasons.

The year after the Antiquary's death, 1722, his friend Thomas Hearne noted that a Catholic named Richard Hudson was operating a small school at Kidlington for several sons of the gentry. Hudson had settled at Kidlington three years earlier. His family stayed in the village until 1779. He had previously taught the young Lord Leinster and was rated a good grammarian but not much of a scholar. Hearne, who was sympathetic to Catholics, supplied Hudson with books.

Although the Pope family had moved away from Binfield, Alexander Pope maintained his contact with Berkshire and Oxfordshire. In 1718 he stayed at Stanton Harcourt (5 miles W. of Oxford). His refuge was the half-ruined Harcourt Manor. It belonged to Viscount Harcourt, some of whose ancestors had been recusants.

The Viscount had a modern house at Cokethorpe (2½ miles W. of Stanton Harcourt) but Pope seems to have preferred the old manor as a place in which to work. He ensconced himself in what is now called Pope's Tower, formerly part of the Harcourts' private chapel. There he completed the fifth volume of his translation of the works of the ancient Greek writer Homer.

Pope also visited Stonor and wrote of its then 'gloomy verdure' of damp yew trees. He penned a cryptic poem about a pig and a wig, which may have referred to Bishop John Talbot Stonor!

Henry Englefield of Whiteknights died in 1720, which was the last year in which the Prince family of Clifton Hampden were recorded as recusants. It was also the year in which Francis Hyde IV and his brother John sold Hyde Hall, Purley. Francis Hyde IV lived at St James, Westminster. He and his brother were great great grandsons of Francis Hyde I who built the hall. They sold it to Francis Hawes, a director of the South Sea Company, who gave the house its present name, Purley Hall. Shortly afterwards Hawes was financially ruined when the 'South Sea Bubble' burst and his company collapsed.

In 1723 the Oath of Allegiance was administered and lists made of those refusing it. About this time the Stonors were paying £240 a year (= £12,500 today) in recusancy fines. Their once vast land holdings now consisted of just the fields and woods between Stonor and Watlington, a couple of woods between Turville and Ibstone, and another between Fawley and Hambleden.

In the summer of 1726 Charles Eyston, son of the Antiquary, married Mary Hawkins, a relative of the Cursons of Waterperry. Thomas Hearne took a great interest in the son of his old friend. He described Mary as 'a very agreeable pretty young woman of about Mr Eyston's age, viz. little more than twenty ...'

Charles, Mary and Charles's mother lived together at Hendred House. Hearne noted that the bride's fortune was no more than £1,000 (= £52,000 today), an important point as Charles had 'many brothers and sisters that are to be considered out of his estate'.

At the time of the wedding in 1726, Hearne wrote in his diary of 'forty acres of land at East Hendred never ploughed, because the land belonged to the Chaplain of Hendred, a Carthusian'. This referred to land that, before the suppression of the religious houses, had belonged to Sheen Abbey, Surrey. This was a rare example of respect for former church lands, especially nearly two centuries after the dissolution of the monasteries. In most cases Catholic gentry in the Thames Valley area had shown little reluctance to exploit the spoils seized from the abbeys and convents, presumably taking the view that 'if someone is going to get them, it might as well be us'.

The year after Charles Eyston's marriage, Sir Edward Simeon was busily enclosing the land adjoining his crumbling manor house at Britwell Salome near Watlington. A legal agreement was drawn up between Sir Edward and twenty-one commoners. He agreed to make a one-off payment of 30s. (= £80 today) to the poor of the parish and to give them a 10s. (= £27 today) every Michaelmas. In return the commoners gave up their rights over more than eighteen acres of land near the ancient Icknield Way on which they had grown crops.

Sir Edward Simeon demolished the old manor house and built the present small but elegant mansion in the Italian classical style. In the autumn of the 1729 the first chaplain of the new house arrived, Fr William Brown. He and his successors are thought to have lived at the nearby West End Villa, now called The Priest's House. This was probably built at about the same time as Britwell House.

The mansion was probably designed by Edward Trubshawe. He had worked on Sir Edward's other house at Aston-by-Stone in Staffordshire. In 1790 single storey wings were added. In the early twentieth century a second storey was added to these wings. In 1960 the designer David Hicks restored the house as near as possible to its original state. He described the fireplace in the entrance hall as 'surely a very great example of English baroque architectural detail'.

The pressure to conform to Anglicanism was not confined to the gentry and nobility. In 1727 at Woolhampton, where there was a comparatively large Catholic community, an illiterate country woman, Winefrid Owen, formally submitted to the Church of England. Her submission occupies a full page in the parish register. It states that she had offended God by not acknowledging the King's lawful authority and not attending Anglican services. It adds that the Pope has, and should not have, any authority over the King.

Three years later a similar submission was made by another Woolhampton woman, Anne Arnett who had 'lived for several years in communion with the Church of Rome'. She copied out the submission in her own handwriting. Anne Arnett may later have been reconciled to Catholicism, because fourteen years later someone with a similar name was a member of the nearby Catholic congregation at Ufton.

Indeed, reconciliation to the Catholic Church was by no means unknown. In 1730, the year that Anne Arnett became an Anglican, John Willcott of Britwell and Mrs Haskey of Stonor were reconciled by Fr Monox Hervey at Watlington Park.

In 1727 George II became King. Apart from the Double Land Tax, most anti-Catholic legislation was no longer rigorously enforced. In the year of the coronation Sir Francis Curson succeeded his father Sir John at Waterperry. Until then he had been living two miles to the south at Great Milton. By his first wife, Elizabeth Knollys, he had a son who died at the age of fifteen while a student at the Jesuit school at St Omer in Picardy. His second marriage, to Winifred Powell, produced no heir.

Also in this coronation year Willoughby Bertie (pronounced Bartie), later third Earl of Abingdon, married Anna Maria Collins, the Catholic daughter of Sir John Collins. The wedding took place in Florence and the couple's daughters were raised as Catholics.

1728 saw the start of a public quarrel between Sir Richard Moore of Fawley, Berkshire and his wife Lady Anastasia. They had been married for twenty-one years and had fourteen children. The argument hinged around the sacrament of penance (confession). Lady Anastasia and one of her daughters preferred a secular confessor from Woolhampton, an ordinary priest who was not a member of a religious order. Sir Richard, whose brother John was at one time a Benedictine, insisted on the family using Fawley's resident Benedictine chaplain.

Lady Anastasia enlisted the support of the Vicar Apostolic of the London District, Bishop Bonaventure Giffard and his assistant Bishop Benjamin Petre. They recommended that

Sir Richard and Lady Anastasia separate, but this was not acceptable to Sir Richard.

At Christmas 1728 Lady Anastasia therefore fled from Fawley. She settled in Paris where she became involved with the Blue nuns. Her husband never forgave her for disobeying him. By the time Sir Richard died one of their sons, Benedict James Moore, had himself become a Benedictine at St Gregory's, Douai. He later became prior.

Lady Anastasia only succeeded in ridding Fawley of the Benedictines after her death in 1742. She left £200 (= £10,600 today) to maintain a secular chaplain, who was to be approved by the Vicar Apostolic or his assistant. Consequently in 1745, three years after Lady Anastasia's death, Fr James Angel became chaplain at Fawley. Thus ended the only significant Benedictine mission base in Berkshire during the seventeenth and eighteenth centuries. But perhaps the Benedictine presence was not entirely eliminated: Fawley is said to be haunted by the ghost of a monk.

The Fawley chaplain served a ten mile long strip of the Berkshire Downs which included Lockinge near Wantage in the north and the Lambourn Valley in the south.

In 1731 Fr John Capistran Eyston became Franciscan Provincial, that is, head of the order in England. He died in that post during the following summer, having worked on the English mission for more than a quarter of a century. His baptismal name was Charles Eyston but he does not appear in the pedigree of the Eystons of East Hendred. Nonetheless he lived at Hendred for two or three years from about 1725, possibly as chaplain to Hendred House. At the time he was Procurator-Definitor of the Franciscan Province, one of a number of high offices he held in the order.

As Fr Eyston was becoming Franciscan Provincial in 1731, the sixth Thomas Stonor came of age. He had inherited the family estates at the age of fourteen and now married Mary Biddulph, heiress of the baronies of Camoys and Vaux. The following year the diarist Thomas Hearne noted that the Bishop of Oxford had accused Thomas Stonor of using charity to bribe people to become Catholics, a charge that was strongly denied. Hearne described the Anglican bishop as 'stingy'.

Swyncombe House, situated in a fold of the Chiltern Hills beside the Ridgeway, had passed by marriage from the Fettiplaces to the Dormers of Peterley and Wing. The Dormers were absentee landlords, but it is said that some of the villagers still gathered round the Catholic chapel at the house. Also the Catholic mission at Britwell House was only a mile and a half away, and the Britwell Catholic register lists the death of James Price of Swyncombe.

Charles, the fifth Lord Dormer, who married Katherine Fettiplace, died in 1728. His eldest son, also Charles, succeeded him as sixth Baron. However, as he was a priest he had no need for the house. He therefore sold it in 1732 for £13,966 16s. 0d. (= £740,000 today). The Elizabethan manor house was subsequently destroyed by fire in the first half of the nineteenth century. The present house is a 1980s replacement.

In 1733, twenty-two year old Basil Eyston was a Benedictine Professor at Douai. He was the second son of Charles Eyston the Antiquary. Two years later Basil Eyston's younger brother William joined the Jesuits at Watten in Flanders, but he seems to have left after only a short while.

Whiteknights near Reading was held by Sir Henry Englefield, who inherited it in 1720 from his father, the Henry Englefield with whom Alexander Pope had fallen out. Sir Henry had inherited the Englefield baronetcy from his distant cousin, Sir Charles Englefield.

Sir Henry's Franciscan chaplain, Fr Clifton, died at Whiteknights in 1734. He left his 'bridle, saddle, whip, boots, spurs and spatterdashes' to his successor, 'if a brother of the Province'; in other words, provided that he was another Franciscan. Fr Clifton was probably succeeded by Sir Henry's Franciscan brother Charles, whose religious name was Fr Felix Englefield.

In 1736 Francis Perkins IV died, leaving £52 10s. 0d. (= £2,800 today) to support his wife Bell Perkins, the former Arabella Fermor. He left his landed property to his eldest son Francis. It was held in trust by Sir Henry Englefield of Whiteknights, William Wollascott V of Woolhampton, John Hyde of Hyde End, Brimpton and the Ufton estate's bailiff, John Berrington.

Francis Perkins left £100 each for his other sons (= £5,300 today) so that they could be placed as apprentices to some trade or profession. This bequest highlights the financial and social predicament of Catholic gentry in the eighteenth century. The sons of the star of 'The Rape of the Lock' were destined to go into trade.

The following year Bell Perkins herself died. Some of her books are preserved by the Benedictines of Douai Abbey, Woolhampton.

An indication of how anti-Catholicism was on the decline at this time can be seen in the response to the recusant returns for 1736. Less than a third of the Oxfordshire parishes bothered to submit returns, and those that did often failed to report Catholics. None was reported in Dorchester, Stonor, Haseley or Waterperry. Perhaps such glaring omissions caught the attention of the Anglican authorities. Two years later no less than twenty-five were reported by Pyrton, the parish that included Stonor.

Fr Peter Ingleby, a Jesuit priest, was living at Culham near Abingdon at that time. He probably lodged with Robert Gainsford, steward to Lady Elizabeth Bisshopp. She seems to have been responsible for a minor resurgence of Catholicism in the Culham district in the first half of the eighteenth century.

About 1740 the gardens at Mapledurham House were laid out in the style championed by Alexander Pope. The house had recently been inherited by Michael Blount II, nephew of Pope's friends Teresa and Martha. An uninterrupted view was created from the east-facing front of the house by constructing a ha-ha, a concealed ditch, to separate the parkland from the drive. An elegant low wall, surmounted by railings, separated the carriage turning circle from the court in front of the house.

The gardens to the north of the house, known as the Pleasure Ground, were intended to be as naturalistic as possible. A cedar of Lebanon was planted which still stands, now a great tree.

Despite these works of fashionable improvement, the Blounts were far from financially secure. They frequently let the house to tenants. About the time that the landscaping was carried out Michael Blount had to sell the family's fine collection of armour. His father, Michael Blount I, had overspent his income by £2,500 (= £133,000 today) during his twenty-nine year ownership of Mapledurham.

An account book for the various estates of Sir Henry Englefield during the early 1740s has survived and is kept at Reading University's site at Whiteknights. It shows that the Whiteknights estate had twenty-seven tenants, including six esquires, one of whom was William Wollascott V. The total annual income from Whiteknights was about £736 (= £39,000 today).

Sir Henry had four tenants at Kingston Winslow, only a mile from Compton Beauchamp where the wife of the exiled Sir Francis Englefield ended her days. These four tenants provided Sir Henry with about £239 a year (= £12,700 today).

At Englefield itself Sir Henry received nineteen free farm rents and had a tenant who provided him with £30 a year (= £1,600 today). One of the free farms was called Ilsleys; interesting because Ilsley is a version of the name Hildesley. Sir Henry rented the poor's land at Englefield for £6 a year (= £318 today).

There were differing opinions at this time as to whether Catholics could legally sell interests in their lands. This is shown by a surviving letter written in the summer of 1744 to Sir Henry Englefield about problems he was having 'taking up money' on the Englefield estate.

In 1741 John Moore died in the debtors' jail at Coventry. He was the brother of Sir Richard Moore of Fawley, Berkshire and had lived a most unusual life. Forty-three years earlier he had become a Benedictine monk at St Edmund's, Paris where his uncle was prior. As a monk John Moore had taken the name Francis. He lived a strange double life as a senior Benedictine and a financially independent Jacobite agent.

In 1701 ill health had forced him to return to England. He subsequently married and may well have been a factor adding to the friction between his brother and sister-in-law over the Benedictine chaplaincy at Fawley.

Richard Challoner was the Sussex-born son of a Nonconformist father who died while he was a boy. Richard's widowed mother went to work as a servant for the Catholic Sir John Gage of Firle in Sussex. About 1704 the thirteen year old Richard Challoner became a Catholic.

At about that time he and his mother moved to another Catholic house, at Warkworth near Banbury. There Richard Challoner was tutored by Fr John Gother, a former Presbyterian and a notable controversialist. Fr Gother arranged for the boy to be educated at Douai, commencing in the summer of 1705.

Thirty-six years later, in 1741, Richard Challoner was consecrated Bishop of Debra, at the headquarters of the Vicar Apostolic of the London District, a convent in Hammersmith. Bishop Challoner became auxiliary to the Vicar Apostolic, whose territory included Berkshire.

By this time Richard Challoner had written a number of books on religion, including his classic 'The Garden of the Soul'; a spiritual handbook, containing prayers, devotions and a summary of Catholic doctrine.

In the year of his consecration Bishop Challoner published 'The Memoirs of Missionary Priests', stories of the martyred and persecuted Catholic priests of post-Reformation England. He also made a visitation of Berkshire.

During this journey Bishop Challoner went to Whiteknights where the Franciscan chaplain at the time was Fr Jerome Beveridge. The Bishop noted a 'large congregation of 300 Catholics in the neighbourhood of Reading', although it is not clear how he defined that area. He then visited John Perkins of Ufton Court, his chaplain Fr Macarthy and William Wollascott V of Woolhampton. Bishop Challoner found a congregation of about eighty at Woolhampton. He administered Confirmation there and at Mr Doughty's house at Beenham. (Presumably Mr Doughty was related to the Catholic family associated with Checkendon Court.) The Bishop also visited East Hendred, where Charles Eyston was his host, and Fawley, where he found a congregation of sixty Catholics.

Christopher Stonor was ordained in 1743. He spent the next four years based at Stonor with his uncle, Bishop John Talbot Stonor. After that he was appointed English agent in Rome to the Vicars Apostolic. He held this post for nearly half a century until his death in 1795 at the age of eighty. He was also chaplain to Cardinal Henry Benedict Stuart, Duke of York and his niece, the Countess of Albany.

At first Monsignor Stonor lived in the household of the Cardinal Duke of York. Later he had his own quarters in the Vatican and lodgings in the papal palace at Monte Cavallo. He is buried in his own chapel at the church of Santa Caterina di Rota, opposite the English College in Rome.

Alexander Pope died in 1744. He had continued to correspond with Martha Blount of Mapledurham and had dedicated his 'Epistle on Women' to her. In his will he left her about £3,000 (= £160,000 today), sixty books of her choice, his household goods and plate, the furniture of his grotto at Twickenham and the urns that stand by the garden door at Mapledurham. These were designed by William Kent, that most revered landscape architect. A few of Pope's books are still at Mapledurham.

Alexander Pope's poetry is still enjoyed today. A modern writer has said: 'If it's neat, it rhymes and you've heard it before, it's Pope!'

Thirty years after his father's unsuccessful attempt to seize the throne, Prince Charles Edward Stuart, the Young Pretender, made his own bid. He landed in Scotland in the summer of 1745 and by early autumn most of Scotland was in Jacobite hands. But, instead of consolidating his position, he moved south into England. By early December he had reached Derby, only 120 miles from London. The Young Pretender expected a spontaneous rising of English Jacobites to support him, but was sadly out of touch with reality. His Scottish supporters, discovering the lack of English or French support, retreated.

This was the turning point of his campaign. The following April the half-starved Jacobite Highlanders were defeated at Culloden. Five months later 'Bonnie Prince Charlie' escaped back to France. His was the last armed attempt to restore the Stuart monarchy.

L o w   E b b

(1745 - 1770)

The quarter century that followed the rebellion of 1745 can be viewed as the low ebb of English Catholicism. Any hopes of the reinstatement of the Catholic Stuart monarchy had all but faded; the Jacobites were no longer a real threat to the Hanoverian succession. Yet the Protestant establishment made little effort to reintegrate Catholics into the mainstream of English society.

As with the Fifteen, there is little evidence of active support for the Forty-five Rebellion from Thames Valley Catholics. Most would have preferred the Stuart monarchy, but few were prepared to support armed rebellion. However, in 1746 a priest was arrested at Stokenchurch for trying to enlist support for the Jacobites. Naturally such incidents alarmed the authorities, and orders were given to the clerks of the peace to compile lists of Catholics and their estates.

Two years after the flight of the Young Pretender, Fr Thomas Martin became the first recorded resident priest at the Wollascotts' Woolhampton estate. He was a secular priest, in keeping with the Wollascotts' preference, and had been chaplain to a community of English Benedictine nuns at Brussels. Fr Martin stayed at Woolhampton for thirty years until his death.

Francis Perkins V died in 1751. He was the last of that name to hold Ufton Court. Unmarried and only thirty-four years old, he was succeeded by his brother James. The year before he died Francis Perkins V let Ufton Court for three years to the Protestant Lord Kingston. Both men belonged to the Aldermaston bowling club which met fortnightly during the summer at the Hind's Head Inn. Most of the members were local gentry or clergy, which suggests that there was little religious animosity towards Catholics.

In 1752 Sir Francis Curson of Waterperry died, also childless. The Curson baronetcy passed to his brother Peter, a Jesuit priest. Sir Francis's widow retained the estate until her death in 1764. The baronetcy became extinct the following year when Fr Peter Curson died.

Prince Charles Edward Stuart made a secret trip to London in 1752. It was rumoured that, while there, he renounced Catholicism and joined the Church of England to further his chances of becoming King. The Prince's father, the Old Pretender, did not hear the rumours for some nine years. He was horrified and wrote asking him 'what will avail to you all the

---

kingdoms of the world for all eternity, if you lose your soul...?' The Prince, who had not visited his father for seventeen years, did not reply.

By 1750 Bishop John Talbot Stonor was seventy-two and no longer able to travel. He therefore stayed at Stonor and managed the estate while his nephew Thomas and Thomas's wife spent three years at Cambrai. Their two daughters were at a school run by English Benedictine nuns in the town.

In February 1752, in the chapel at Stonor House, Bishop Stonor consecrated Dr John Hornyold as his auxiliary. Bishop Hornyold went to live at Longbirch in Staffordshire from where he administered the northern part of the Midland District. The consecration was illegal, and the first in England of a Catholic bishop since the time of Mary Tudor. However, Bishop Stonor was so highly regarded by the authorities that he could act with impunity.

Bishop Stonor's opposite number in the London District, Bishop Richard Challoner, visited Fawley, Berkshire in 1752, where he confirmed twenty people. Two years earlier Bishop Challoner had published his revised and annotated edition of the Douai Bible which, until the early 1960s, was the standard Catholic English translation.

Although Marlborough, Wiltshire is outside the main area covered by this book, it is only fourteen miles over the Downs from Fawley. In 1753, the year after Bishop Challoner administered confirmation at Fawley, the Vicar Apostolic of the Western District confirmed seven people at the Marlborough home of John Hyde. His father, also John Hyde, was co-vendor of Hyde Hall, Purley in 1720.

The modern Calendar, devised by Pope Gregory XIII, was finally adopted in England in 1752. The old Julian calendar was ten days behind the Gregorian which had been adopted by most other European countries, including Scotland. The Rector of East Hendred, writing in January 1753, noted newspaper reports that some people had shown great aversion to the new calendar: 'the common people don't like it, because it has something of popery in it they say; I wish we had no other reason but such as this to find fault with the Church of Rome ...' The Rector, however, did not object to the new calendar and wrote: 'it is evident enough, that upon the true principles of astronomy, we have been wrong for some two hundred years ...'

He noted that some of his parishioners had given their servants and cattle a holiday on the old Christmas Day. He also reported that gullible country folk had been tricked by a man at nearby Milton. The legendary Glastonbury Thorn was supposed to bloom only on Christmas Day. The trickster claimed to have a plant 'of the same nature' and charged people a penny each to see it open early on the morning of the old Christmas Day, thus confirming their prejudiced view that the old calendar was correct. In reality ne had controlled the growth by raising the plant under a beehive!

In 1753 a papal ruling known as 'Apostolicum Ministerium' clearly establisned the jurisdiction of the Vicars Apostolic. This ended the longstanding bickering between regular clergy (members of religious orders) and secular priests. Bishops Challoner and Stonor played a major role in obtaining this clarification. It was followed in 1754 by the Bull 'Regula Missionis', which gave the Vicars Apostolic greater control over private chaplains.

The Hardwick Marriage Act of 1753 made it compulsory to perform all marriages, other than those of Jews or Quakers, in an Anglican church. Any non-Anglican clergy officiating at a wedding service could be transported for fourteen years. In response the Vicars Apostolic decided that, as long as Catholic couples did not actively take part in the Anglican service by kneeling or joining in the prayers, they could go through both Anglican and Catholic ceremonies.

A hundred years earlier, in 1653, the Commonwealth had introduced a system of civil marriage and registration. The Catholic Chapter of Clergy had accepted this procedure provided that the couple consulted their priest first and received his blessing afterwards. The civil system had been abolished after the Restoration and, from then until the Hardwick Act, Catholics had effectively been free to marry according to their own rite.

In October 1753 Winefred Eyston, eighty-one year old widow of the Antiquary, died at Hendred House of 'chronical distemper'. The Rector was away visiting the Bishop of Salisbury but had written to Winefred's son Thomas that he would be willing to return to bury her. Accordingly Thomas sent a message to the Rector, wno cut short his visit and returned to East Hendred to conduct the funeral. For this he was paid a guinea (= £50 today).

The Rector wrote that, as soon as old Mrs Eyston was dead, all the Catholics of the village were summoned together and went to the chapel at Hendred House to celebrate Mass for her soul. The funeral at the Anglican church was very private. The coffin was carried by six of her tenants, followed by her eldest son and daughter, then the servants and remaining tenants.

There was evidently frequent friendly contact between the Eystons and the Rector's household, and they sometimes dined at each others' residences.

Prince Charles Edward Stuart made another clandestine visit to England in 1754. On such visits he used a number of pseudonyms, including 'Mr Stonor'. According to two sources quoted in 1892 by Mary Sharp, the Prince visited Ufton Court. She wrote:

'The Prince while travelling about the country would naturally stay at the houses of such Roman Catholic gentlemen as he thought might be favourable to his cause, and that Ufton Court contained hiding places and secret ways of escape in case of surprise might also be in its favour as a temporary halting-place.'

One wonders what the Perkins family would have made of this visit, if indeed it took place.

In 1755 Sir John Moore sold Maidencourt in the Lambourn Valley, which had long been Catholic property. Sir John was the second of three sons of Sir Richard Moore who succeeded in turn to the Moore estates. The same year as the Maidencourt sale his Benedictine brother, Fr James Augustine Moore, became prior of St Gregory's, Douai. He held the position for twenty years, a record at the time.

The Franciscan Fr Edward Madew became chaplain to the Blounts of Mapledurham in 1756. He had previously been chaplain to the Perkins of Beenham. (In 1748 he baptised baby Philip White of Beenham who became a priest and died aged 30 at the English College, Lisbon.) After two years with the Blounts Fr Madew spent three years with the Dormers at Grove Park, Warwickshire before returning to the Thames Valley.

Bishop John Talbot Stonor died in the spring of 1756. Among his last visitors was his nephew William Plowden, who brought his two sons. William's father was the Jacobite soldier from Shiplake who fought at the Boyne and married Bishop Stonor's sister. About that time William's son Edmund came to live on the edge of the Stonor estate at Ibstone, Buckinghamshire.

William Wollascott V died in 1757 and was buried in the family vault in Woolhampton churchyard. He was the last male Wollascott of the Woolhampton line. Two years earlier his daughter Henrietta Maria had married Arthur James Plunkett, the seventh Earl of Fingall. This Irish nobleman was of the same family as Archbishop Oliver Plunkett of Armagh, who was martyred in the aftermath of the Titus Oates Plot, beatified in 1920 and subsequently canonised. On the death of William Wollascott the Woolhampton estate became the Earl of Fingall's.

In 1757 Sir Robert Throckmorton transferred his attentions from his Buckinghamshire residence Weston Underwood to his Berkshire estate at Buckland. He decided to build a new mansion, Buckland House, and had it designed and built by John Wood the younger of Bath.

The classical new house consisted of a large stone-faced rectangular block, three storeys high, with lower wings, each terminating in an octagonal room. The west wing was a Catholic chapel. No expense was spared and the house was filled with art treasures and fine furniture. Pevsner considered that the house as originally built 'was the most splendid of smaller Georgian houses' in Berkshire.

Sir Robert proudly erected his coat of arms on the front of the house and on the gateway. He also carried out alterations to

BUCKLAND HOUSE

the old Buckland Manor House, the former Yate residence. A row of stables with a Gothick facade being formed at the rear. The parish church was altered to match by adding battlements to the roof and tower. The land in front of the new mansion was landscaped: a lake was formed and various follys were built, including grottoes and temples.

Buckland House was intended as a residence for Sir Robert and his eldest son George, who married in the year construction started. However, the project took ten years, and George Throckmorton died before its completion.

The year work started on Buckland House the Rector of Newbury dutifully submitted his list of parish papists. In 1757 there were fifteen. In every case the breadwinners were self-employed craftsmen. Thomas Walsh, his son John and John Wells were wigmakers, while William Casemore and his two sons were blacksmiths.

The first known resident priest at Ufton Court was the Franciscan Fr Price who was there in 1758. That year Fr Joseph Strickland, a secular priest and relative of the Stonors, became chaplain at Stonor House, a post he was to hold for thirty-two years. Also in 1758 the Stonors sold Watlington Park for £1,500 (= £69,000 today) to John Tilson, son of the Under Secretary of State, to raise funds to repair Stonor House.

Little is known of how, if at all, the Catholics of Reading town were served by their clergy during the first half of the eighteenth century. A Franciscan, Fr Grimstone, hired a room in Reading for use as a chapel about 1690, but it is not known for how long it was used.

About 1760 Anna Maria Smart rented a room in Minster Street for the same purpose. It had a side door opening discreetly onto a yard. About two years later Mrs Smart became proprietor of the only Berkshire county newspaper, the Reading Mercury. It had been founded thirty-nine years earlier and her father had once owned it.

Mrs Smart (nee Carnan) was the wife of the poet Christopher Smart, whom she had secretly married in 1752. When it became known that he had married a Catholic he was forced to resign from the Fellowship of Pembroke Hall, Cambridge. Thereafter he scraped a living in London as a contributor to literary and satirical magazines. In this he was helped by Dr Samuel Johnson and the actor David Garrick. Smart became increasingly subject to bouts of insanity, and consequently was separated from his wife and daughters. He spent most of his later years in an asylum and died before reaching the age of fifty.

The last Powells of Sandford-on-Thames were two heiresses, one of whom, Winifred, married Sir Francis Curson of Waterperry. By 1760 Sir Francis was dead and Lady Curson sold the Manor. Another Catholic male line had failed and another old mission base had been sold.

In September the following year the Franciscan Fr Edward Madew returned to Berkshire to become resident chaplain at Ufton Court. No doubt he already knew the place from his time as a chaplain to the Perkins of Beenham. Fr Madew was a keen diarist and kept good records. Hence we know that it cost him £1 7s. 6d. (= £67 today) to move himself and his goods to Ufton. We also know that in February 1762 he paid a Mr Ingram £1 0s. 7d. (= £49 today) for candles and breads, presumably communion wafers.

Fr Madew compiled some historical information on Ufton, including a list of the whole Catholic congregation as it had been in 1749, when it totalled ninety-eight. He also noted that Bishop Challoner twice administered confirmation at Ufton Court. Fr Madew remained at Ufton Court for twenty-one years until his death.

In 1761, the year Fr Madew moved to Ufton, confirmation was administered at another Franciscan mission, Whiteknights, by Bishop Talbot. He was Bishop Challoner's auxiliary and a kinsman of the Stonors. Five people were confirmed, their ages ranging from nine to eighty.

In view of the reduction during this period in the number of Catholic manor houses, it is interesting to note an addition. Milton Manor was bought by the Catholic convert Bryant Barrett in 1764. This was the house in an isolated hamlet near Abingdon where William of Orange heard of James II's flight to France. Completed in 1663, it is thought to have been designed by Inigo Jones or Thomas Archer. Barrett paid £10,600 for it (= £455,000 today).

Bryant Barrett was a lace-maker and embroiderer who lived in London's Strand. Three years earlier he had been given the Royal Warrant and hence was 'lace-man' to George III. The royal lace-maker was a convert to Catholicism through the influence of his friend Bishop Richard Challoner. He may also have been influenced by his French mother who may well have been a Catholic. Despite being the King's lace-maker, Barrett was a Jacobite and at one time a secret financial supporter of the Young Pretender.

Barrett's first wife was Mary Belson, who died after eighteen childless years of marriage. His second wife Winefred Eyston bore him six sons and two daughters. Winefred was born at Marcham (2½ miles WSW of Abingdon). Her father was the Thomas Eyston whose cordial relations with the Rector of East Hendred were noted above.

Shortly after moving into Milton Manor, Bryant Barrett began repairing and rebuilding the badly neglected house. He started a fortnight before Christmas 1764. Apart from the refurbishment, two wings housing a bakery and a brewery were added to the house. The project took seven years during which 700,000 bricks were used. Barrett employed many highly skilled craftsmen from London and used the services of the architect Stephen Wright.

Barrett was also keenly interested in the grounds and kept detailed records of the trees and bushes he planted. Thus he created a Georgian gem which has been used in recent times by film makers as the Scarlet Pimpernel's house and as a setting for television commercials.

Milton Manor contains a first floor chapel in Gothick style. The London carver Richard Lawrence was involved in its design. Two fine medieval stained-glass windows for the chapel's altar were bought from nearby Steventon parish church for £7 (= £300 today). Some later Flemish stained-glass was incorporated into the side windows.

The chapel furnishings are not conspicuously Catholic and the panelling to the upper part of the rear of the chapel folds away, so that the second floor bedroom behind can become a gallery. If a raid were suspected the congregation could gather for Mass in the bedroom gallery. Should a raid take place the celebrant could slip away through an exit near the altar and the gallery's folding panels could be closed. The search party would find an empty, ostensibly Anglican, chapel.

Barrett's friend Bishop Challoner often celebrated Mass in the chapel and, indeed, was the first to do so. His vestments, chalice and missal are still there. The chapel was always private and was never a mission centre. To this day only direct descendants of Bryant Barrett may marry there.

At Britwell House in 1764 Sir Edward Simeon built a monument to his parents. In front of the mansion he erected a remarkable column topped with an urn in the shape of a pineapple. The memorial offsets the pastoral view towards the Icknield Way, the Ridgeway and the Chiltern Hills beyond.

'James III', the Old Pretender, died the following year, 1765. The Pope withdrew his support for the Stuart claim to the throne and prayers for George II were immediately incorporated into the Mass. Paradoxically, that same year a press campaign attempted to revive the prosecution of Catholics by publicising the rewards available to informers and bounty hunters. The 1699 legislation still offered £100 (= £4,200) for the conviction of a Catholic priest. This was probably the reason why in 1767 the Archbishops of Canterbury and York ordered their Bishops to hold a census of Catholics, properly referred to as the Returns of Papists, 1767.

Berkshire was covered by the returns from the Diocese of Salisbury or, in the case of a few parishes such as Hurst and Sonning, the Peculiars of the Dean and Chapter of Salisbury. Oxfordshire was covered by the returns of the Diocese of Oxford. These did not list names but gave sex, age, occupation, family relationship and number of years resident in the parish.

MILTON MANOR

The census appears to be reasonably accurate and clearly shows the parishes where there was a significant Catholic presence.

In southern Oxfordshire these included Pyrton (including Stonor) with 82, Waterperry with 32, Mapledurham 29, Oxford (six parishes) 23, Dorchester 19, Watlington 18 and Haseley 11.

Old Catholic centres based around a Catholic gentry family that had died out generally had few, if any, papists. At Sandford, for example, the only Catholics were the old wife of a labourer and her two daughters, while at Shirburn there were just a middle-aged farmer, his four offspring and an elderly widow. No Catholics at all were reported in Checkendon or Swyncombe parishes, now that the recusant branches of the Hildesleys and Fettiplaces had died out.

In Berkshire Woolhampton had 84 Catholics, Ufton 43, Buckland 42, East Hendred 32, Bucklebury 30, Brimpton 29, Reading (two parishes) 28, Binfield 25, Sonning (which included Whiteknights) 21 and Padworth 20. In all 587 Catholics were listed for Berkshire and 317 for the area of southern Oxfordshire covered by this book.

The census noted that there were a dozen Catholics in the parish of Fawley, Berkshire. A neighbouring rector stated that his colleague at Fawley did not keep a proper baptismal register because 'during the residence of Sir John Moore and his Ancestors time immemorial, a Popish Priest had been maintained and connived at'. But two years before the census, in 1765, Sir John Moore had sold Fawley to Arthur Vansittart of Shottesbrooke. Sir John died childless and was succeeded as baronet by his brother Thomas. Sir Thomas died in Hampshire in 1807, also without issue. Thus the male line of another old Catholic family came to an end.

In 1765 Charles Stonor married a Blount of Mapledurham. Although the Blounts and Stonors lived less than nine miles apart, this was the only marriage. Charles Stonor had by then been running the Stonor estate for four years, although his father was still alive. His bride Mary Eugenia Blount was twenty years old. Her mother Mary was the daughter of Mannock Strickland, a solicitor. Her father Michael was the first Blount to marry into the professional classes and it appears that he also practised as a solicitor, despite the legal impediments.

According to local tradition, recusancy existed at Thame Park in the early seventeenth century when the then Lady Wenman was a Catholic. In 1766 a marriage took place which brought the return of Catholicism to Thame Park. Philip Wenman, seventh Viscount, married Eleanor Bertie, one of the Catholic daughters of Willoughby Bertie, third Earl of Abingdon. Lord Wenman allowed his wife to maintain a Catholic chaplaincy at Thame Park for the thirty-eight years of their married life.

Tne 1767 census of Catholics shows that the Catholic population of Thame consisted of Lady Wenman, her sisters, her two servants and a hatter's widow. The Jesuit Fr Bernard Cassidy (alias Stafford), Superior of the Oxford District, later lived at Thame Park and was buried in the small medieval chapel in 1788. The chapel was demolished in the nineteenth century and only a few traces remain.

The parish of Hampstead Norreys on the Berkshire Downs had contained a residence of the Catholic Dancastle family in the seventeenth century. In 1676 there had been twenty-one Catholics in the parish but the 1767 Returns of Papists list none. However, by that time a marriage had taken place that was to lead to a modest return of Catholicism to the area; Lady Elizabeth Bertie had married Giovanni Andrea Battista Gallini.

Gallini was born in Florence in 1728, five months after tne third Earl of Abingdon married there. Twenty-five years later ne arrived destitute in England and became the Earl's dancing master. By 1766 he had married one of the Earl's Catholic daughters, a sister of Lady Eleanor Wenman of Thame. One wonders whether Gallini was perhaps the Earl of Abingdon's illegitimate son.

The Italian made his name and a considerable fortune, not only as a fashionable dancing master, but also at the London Opera House where he rose to become stage manager. He even danced before the Pope who made him a Knight of the Golden Spurs. Thereafter he was usually referred to as Sir John.

His fortune enabled him to buy the manors of Hampstead Norreys and nearby Yattendon from his father-in-law. In 1789 the London Opera House burned down and Gallini thereby lost £400,000 (= £14m today). Yet he was still able to put up £300,000 (= £10.5m today) towards the rebuilding costs.

He spent most of his time away from his Berkshire estates and died at his residence in Hanover Square, London in 1805, aged seventy-seven. He and his wife had separated, but only after sne had borne him at least six children. There is a mural tablet to Sir John and his wife in Yattendon parish church.

Tne Hampstead Norreys and Yattendon estates passed to Sir John's eldest son, John Andrea Gallini. He died relatively young but Yattendon was still held by the Gallinis well into the nineteenth century. Hampstead Norreys passed to the Eystons in 1834.

In the first half of the eighteenth century John Wolfe, a Catholic, married Elizabeth Boulter of Haseley and thereby acquired Haseley Court which, throughout the previous century, had been a Catholic house.

The Wolfes were an Essex Catholic family and were related to the famous General James Wolfe who died capturing Quebec. John Wolfe of Haseley Court was the grandson of Thomas Wolfe, an eminent physician, who had left £10,000 (= £500,000 today) to

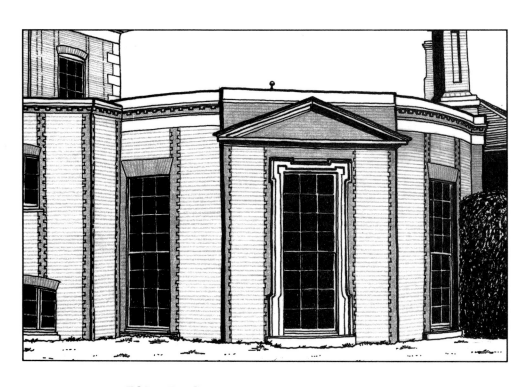

FORMER CHAPEL AT BRITWELL HOUSE

Catholic charities. John's brother was a popular lawyer whose
Protestant clients had been most supportive when he was barred
from practising by William III's anti-Catholic legislation.

John Wolfe became head of the family in 1739. His three sons
all died unmarried. The last to die was young Charles Wolfe,
who passed away at Brussels in 1768 in the company of his
tutor, Fr Joseph Strickland. Charles Wolfe's guardian and
executor was Thomas Stonor. Wolfe was a close friend of Michael
Blount of Mapledurham, to whom he left his belongings and some
land at Chalgrove.

The remaining Catholics of Haseley then seem to have turned to
Britwell as their Mass centre. Shortly before the death of
Charles Wolfe there were eleven Catholics in the parish of
Haseley, including a sixty-five year old priest who had been
there about twenty years.

Two days before Christmas 1768 Sir Edward Simeon died after a
nine day illness. He was eighty-six and with him the Simeon
baronetcy expired. Sir Edward was buried in a specially built
mausoleum near his other residence at Aston-by-Stone,
Staffordshire.

At the end of March the previous year he had started building a
new chapel at Britwell House. This was not yet complete and the
1767 Returns of Papists indicate that he and his retinue had
removed to nearby Newington, presumably so that the builders
could get on with the job unimpeded.

Sir Edward Simeon was succeeded at Britwell by his nephew
Thomas Weld, a member of the notable recusant family of
Lulworth Castle, Dorset. To perpetuate the Simeon link with
Britwell, the new owner styled himself Thomas Simeon Weld.
Thomas Weld's wife had died the previous year and he followed
her soon after inheriting the Britwell estate. He was succeeded
by his nephew, also known as Thomas Simeon Weld, who was said
to be the second largest landowner in England.

In 1769 the new chapel at Britwell House was completed at a
total cost of at least £1,000 (= £39,000 today). Sir Edward
Simeon is said to have designed it himself, but he may have
been assisted by his architect Edward Trubshawe. It is an
unusual design, being of oval plan, and is attached to the rear
of the south wing of the house.

The ceiling was finished in ornamental plasterwork of the
highest quality by Italian craftsmen. It incorporated
depictions of the Host (the consecrated Communion wafer), the
Sacred Heart of Jesus and the Greek-derived abbreviation of the
name Jesus, IHS. After Britwell House passed out of Catholic
hands the chapel was used as a dining and billiard room. The
altar was replaced with a fireplace and the IHS motif removed
from the ceiling.

Fr George Bruning, the Jesuit chaplain who had been at Britwell
since the summer of 1765 stayed on after Sir Edward Simeon's

death. He compiled a register of the Britwell mission, including retrospective notes. From these we learn that, in the year the chapel opened, Fr Bruning had a congregation of sixty-four living within six miles of Britwell. His parishioners lived at Chinnor, Shirburn, Watlington, Ewelme, Ipsden, Wallingford, Burcot, Overy, Dorchester and Britwell itself. The largest group comprised the parishioners from the Dorchester area, and included the old Catholic yeoman families of Day and Davey.

Fr Gilbert Wells, a Jesuit, had lived with the Daveys from 1752 to 1758. Fr Bruning wrote in his register: 'The Catholics in and about Dorchester had formerly a Missioner residing among 'em; but as they have no longer that help, and would otherwise be destitute, Charity can't consider 'em but as part of this Congregation.' He noted that at Overy they had all the necessary 'Altar-Furniture' which had 'been made use of regularly seven times throughout the year; i.e. some week day during each Indulgence Term, or thereabouts'.

In 1770 confirmation was administered at Britwell House and also at Stonor, where thirty-two candidates were confirmed.

A strange feature of Britwell House is an underground circular vault situated among trees to the right of the front of the house. It is linked by a tunnel to the wine cellar. The tunnel is small but could have been used by someone crouching. It has been blocked by subsidence for at least sixty years. In 1930 the then owner of the house opened the vault from above and allegedly found a round room with a stone bench around the walls. Local historian Biddy O'Sullivan was shown the room nearly forty years later and saw no sign of the bench. She concluded that the entrance from the collapsed tunnel had been sealed up.

There are many fanciful stories about secret escape routes from old Catholic houses. It is just possible that this might have formed a very late example. It could even have been retained from the earlier Britwell House. However, Biddy O'Sullivan suggested that the underground chamber was an ice house and this is almost certainly the case.

In 1769 John Perkins, youngest son of Bell and Francis Perkins V, died. He had inherited the Ufton estates nine years earlier. His brothers Francis, James and Charles had each held Ufton Court before him, and all had died childless. James had sold the family's Buscot property. Their Great Bathampton, Langford and Wylie estates were sold after Charles' death to pay his debts.

John Perkins was a childless widower, but had two step-daughters to whom he left £1,000 (= £39,000 today) each when they achieved their majority. He left £20 (= £780 today) to his housekeeper. The rest of his personal effects went to his land agent Henry Deane of Reading and Francis Prior, a Catholic neighbour who held a life interest in Pam Hall, Padworth. (This was a large house belonging to the Perkins family which was demolished in the nineteenth century.)

When Charles Perkins left Ufton Court to his brother John, he provided for the eventuality of John having no heirs. If this happened the estate would go to their cousin Katherine Jones or her heirs. If she had none it would pass to Sir Henry Englefield of Whiteknights. So, even as the Perkins's male line died out, they maintained the link with the Englefields that had been forged in the time of Mary Tudor.

In reality Ufton passed to Katherine Jones's son, John Jones of Llanarth, Monmouthshire. Jones preferred to stay in Wales and never lived at Ufton Court, which consequently became increasingly ruinous. But Fr Madew stayed on. He had persuaded the dying John Perkins to leave the 'church stuff' in trust for the benefit of the congregation. The ailing Perkins repeated over again 'I think it is the best way.'

Fr Madew stayed at Ufton Court until his death in the spring of 1782. He had been a priest for more than fifty years. His successor was Fr George Baynham, another Franciscan, who was also the chaplain to Whiteknights. Fr Baynham continued to minister to the Ufton Catholics from the increasingly ramshackle former Perkins residence.

When Bryant Barrett moved to Milton Manor, the Rector of the parish church (which is just outside the manor house gates) did not relish the presence of papists on his doorstep. Although Barrett played down the outward signs of Catholicism at his house and stressed its links with William of Orange, the Rector probably knew the true identity of Barrett's friend and frequent visitor Richard Challoner.

Bryant Barrett wanted to build a family vault onto the Anglican church, but the Rector refused to allow it. Barrett therefore threatened to charge the rector and his congregation for use of the road to the church. This piece of polite blackmail did the trick and in 1769 Barrett got his way.

By this time enforcement of the penal laws against Catholics had almost ceased. A quarter of a century had passed since the Forty-five Rebellion, and there were now signs of hope for the Catholics of the Thames Valley. Yet during those twenty-five years many of the old gentry families that had kept an ember of Catholicism glowing in Berkshire and southern Oxfordshire had died out or left the area. The Perkins, Wolfes, Simeons, Cursons, Moores, Powells and Wollascotts had all gone. As for the homes of those who remained, John Henry Newman wrote of the typical 'old-fashioned house of gloomy appearance, closed in with high walls, with an iron gate and yews, and the report attaching to it that "Roman Catholics" lived there.'

A Little Relief

(1770 - 1792)

By the early 1770s the enforcement of the penal laws against Catholics had all but ceased. In 1774 the Quebec Act gave official recognition to the rights of the Catholic Church in Lower Canada and this added to the impetus for Catholic emancipation in Britain. Later in the decade the struggle for civil rights was to come to the fore, but the 1770s started quietly and seemed a good time to start a family.

The second Thomas Simeon Weld did just that, marrying in 1772. He and his wife lived at Britwell House where their first three children were born. However, in 1775 Weld succeeded to his family's Lulworth Castle estate in Dorset. He therefore left Britwell and leased it to Joseph Blount, who was to die near Lyons during the French Revolution.

The Blount family seat, Mapledurham House, served as a mission centre in the same way as Britwell. In the year Joseph Blount leased Britwell House, the daughter of Thomas and Theresia Smith was baptised at Mapledurham, having been 'brought over the water from Tilehurst Common'. A dozen years earlier the Blounts' chaplain had received into the Church a Tilehurst woman and an Anglican clergyman.

In 1776 Sir Henry Englefield's son Francis went to Vienna as a member of an English regiment serving the Holy Roman Emperor. The following winter Sir Henry received a good report of Francis's behaviour 'both as an officer and a gentleman'. According to the report Francis had spent four months in Vienna in good company, gaining esteem by modesty and propriety of behaviour.

Francis Englefield seems to have spent the rest of his life in Vienna. He died there in 1791 after a painful illness. By then his modesty and propriety had evidently slipped a little. He left wills 'for the use of his most Intimate Friend' Mrs Rosina von Stockel of Gerburg and for the education of their child Francisca Seraphim Rosina. Thus the last Francis of the main Englefield line died abroad, as did his Elizabethan namesake.

In 1778 the first Catholic Relief Act was passed. This followed negotiations by the government with a group of Catholic nobility and gentry headed by Lord Petre. The group had drawn up a new oath, endorsed by Bishop Challoner, that denounced Stuart claims to the throne, denied the civil jurisdiction of the Pope, and stated that Catholics could not be released from the oath by the Pope. The Act put a formal end to the prosecution of Catholic priests by informers. It also enabled

Catholics who took the new oath to purchase and inherit land legally.

An immediate repercussion of the Catholic Relief Act was a Protestant backlash. Although many Anglicans and others favoured toleration, there was still a strong element of anti-Catholicism in England. Early in 1780, for instance, John Wesley, Anglican clergyman and founder of Methodism, published a pamphlet attacking the advance of Rome's 'purple power'.

Lord George Gordon's Protestant Association then petitioned for the repeal of the Act. This led to the Gordon Riots of 1780 which, in London, caused damage or destruction to a dozen public buildings, and over a hundred other properties. More than 450 people were killed or injured while regular soldiers and militia attempted to restore order in the capital.

At Bath the Catholic chapel was burned down. With it were destroyed the archives of the Western District, and the books and papers of Bishop Walmesley, the Vicar Apostolic. Charles and Mary Eugenia Stonor, who were living in the city, had to flee their house by night and return to the safety of Stonor.

The following year they moved to Gravelines on the Normandy coast. There Molly Stonor, daughter of the Jacobite colonel William Stonor, had been a Poor Clare nun for nearly half a century. After only three months in France, Charles Stonor died and was buried in the convent chapel. Within the year his widow married an impoverished Catholic lawyer called Charles Canning. As Charles Stonor had not left a will, she sold all the furniture and paintings from Stonor.

One of the London buildings demolished during the Gordon Riots was the Old Ship Tavern, where Bishop Challoner regularly celebrated Mass. The old Bishop was greatly upset by the riots and died the following January, 1771. His friend Bryant Barrett took the Bishop's body back to Milton Manor, which had also been attacked by an anti-Catholic mob.

Bishop Challoner was buried in the Barrett family vault in the parish church. The parish register describes Richard Challoner as 'a Popish Priest and Titular Bishop of London and Salisbury, a very pious and good man, of great learning and extensive abilities.'

In his forty years as a bishop he had confirmed some ten thousand Catholics. In 1946, despite some local opposition, his remains were moved to Westminster Cathedral. The Catholic church authorities considered this to be a more fitting resting place for the greatest of the Vicars Apostolic.

Sir Henry Englefield died in 1780. He was succeeded by his eldest son, Henry Charles Englefield, who became the seventh and last baronet. Sir Henry Charles was an eminent scientist and antiquarian. Already a Fellow of the Royal Society, he subsequently became President of the Society of Antiquarians.

Sir Henry Charles Englefield settled in Hanover Square, Middlesex (now London) which was conveniently situated for someone with his scientific and historical interests. Because of this and 'the offensive prejudices of the neighbouring gentry' he decided to dispose of Whiteknights. Therefore Lord Cadogan, the surviving trustee of old Sir Henry's will, sold the estate via an indenture dated May 1783, to which Sir Henry Charles, his mother and others were party.

The purchaser was William Byam Martin of Marylebone who had made a fortune in India. He paid £13,400 (= £523,000 today). The estate's timber was sold separately through the same indenture for £2,448 (= £95,500 today). Martin subsequently conveyed the manor to the Marquis of Blandford. The chaplaincy continued to operate until 1794 when Fr George Baynham retired to Ufton Court.

Sir Henry Charles Englefield died in London in 1822, the last male of his line. Three years earlier the contents of Whiteknights had been sold by the Marquis of Blandford, whose extravagance had caused his financial ruin. After protracted litigation Sir Henry's nephew, Sir Francis Cholmely, successfully claimed the estate. (His mother Teresa Ann Englefield was named in the 1783 indenture.) The Cholmelys mortgaged the estate in 1839 and the old Englefield mansion was demolished the following year. Thus ended the Englefields' claimed thousand year connection with the Reading area.

In 1786 confirmations were again held in Oxfordshire. At Stonor no less than fifty-two people were confirmed, at Mapledurham twenty-three. That year the seventh Thomas Stonor, son of the widowed Mary Eugenia, set out from Douai on the Grand Tour. He was twenty years old and travelled with Fr Gregory Stapleton, who later became Vicar Apostolic of the Midland District.

The seventh Earl of Fingall sold the Woolhampton estate in 1786 to John Crewe, who was not a Catholic. Two years later Bishop Challoner's successor, Bishop James Talbot, administered confirmation at Woolhampton. Although there were fifteen candidates, he expressed concern for the future of the congregation in the absence of a Catholic lord of the manor.

In fact, the Earl of Fingall had done his best to minimise this problem by leaving his chaplain, Fr William Anstead, at Woolhampton, and endowing him with seven acres (where the present Catholic church and parts of Douai School now stand). On this plot were cottages which provided rent income, and a chapel in the form of a room in Woolhampton Lodge 'floored with brick tiles like a labourer's cottage'. The Earl may even have left an altar-piece, a copy of Guercino's painting 'Madonna and Child', now in the refectory of Douai Abbey, Woolhampton.

When the Moores left Fawley, Berkshire in 1765, Catholicism in the western part of the Berkshire Downs continued through the Youngs. They lived at Whatcombe, a small hamlet a mile and a half to the south, which was the site of a 'lost' medieval village. The Youngs, like the Hydes, had been a family with many branches in Berkshire. A Franciscan, Fr Anthony Young, was one of the priests who officiated at the reopening of St Amand's chapel at Hendred House in 1687.

In 1788 Elizabeth Young died and it seems that thereby another old Berkshire Catholic family became extinct. Whatcombe was inherited by the Hydes of Marlborough who maintained a Franciscan chaplain at the manor house. The principal tenants were the Dearloves, a Catholic family whose members had been baptised at Fawley Manor before the departure of the Moores. The mission at Whatcombe continued until 1820.

As mentioned earlier, the last baronet Curson of Waterperry was Fr Peter Curson, a Jesuit. The estate subsequently passed to a niece, then to John Barnwell, the son of another niece. He took the name John Barnwell Curson and died in 1787. He was succeeded by his half-cousin, Francis Henry Roper, a Catholic but not a descendant of the Cursons. The following year, by royal licence and in accordance with Sir Francis Curson's will, he too adopted the surname Curson and the Curson arms.

Although traditionally a Jesuit mission, the rapid change of ownership during this period was reflected in the type of chaplains at Waterperry. They were successively Franciscan, Benedictine, secular and Jesuit.

About the time Francis Henry Roper succeeded to the Waterperry estate, its mission absorbed that of Britwell. The last entry in the Britwell register records the baptism in 1788 of John Davey of Overy. Two years later the main thrust of the Waterperry mission was transferred to the St Clement's district of Oxford by Fr Charles Leslie. He was a Jesuit and a younger son of the twenty-first Baron of Balquhain. Sir Francis Curson and his widow had left a bequest stipulating that Mass should be said on alternate Sundays at Waterperry and Oxford.

Fr Leslie bought a house in St Clement's and moved there. For the next three years he continued to celebrate Mass at Waterperry but by 1793 there were only six Catholics in the village. A quarter of a century earlier there had been thirty-two. On the other hand the number in Oxford had grown to sixty or more. It was a classic example of how urban Catholicism was growing while rural Catholicism declined.

At St Clement's in 1793 Fr Leslie built the chapel of St Ignatius on land provided by the Boulter family, who at one time held Haseley Court. The chapel was partly funded by subscription throughout Oxfordshire, and partly by a bequest of £1,000 (= £28,000 today). In 1799 Fr Leslie was joined by a fellow Jesuit, Fr William Hothersoll, the former chaplain at Thame Park.

In 1787 the Catholic Committee was re-formed. It had been established five years earlier by leading laymen keen to achieve Catholic emancipation. Its secretary was Charles

Butler, whose wife Mary Eyston was a granddaughter of Charles Eyston, the Antiquary. Other leading members included Sir Henry Charles Englefield, lately of Whiteknights, and Sir John Throckmorton of Buckland. In 1788 the Protesting Catholic Dissenters, a group within the Catholic Committee, produced a 'Protestation' denying that the Pope had any temporal powers. Three of the Vicars Apostolic and 240 priests signed it. However, the following year the Vicars Apostolic, fearing unacceptable compromise, condemned an oath proposed by the same group.

Sir John Throckmorton of Buckland published three tracts in 1790 arguing for a lay voice in the appointment of Catholic bishops. Sir John, then thirty-seven, was quite prepared to take the existing Oath of Supremacy, and contended that nominations of Catholic bishops in England were invalid unless acclaimed by the priests and laity. The following year he inherited Buckland House on the death of his grandfather Sir Robert, who had held it for seventy years.

Sir John and his wife Maria (nee Giffard) were friends of William Cowper, the religious poet. From 1786 to 1795 Cowper lived at Weston Underwood, where the Throckmortons owned Weston Park (now demolished). Cowper, a Protestant nonconformist, wrote that the Throckmortons were 'Papists, but much more aimable than many Protestants'. Of Sir John he wrote 'I have not found his equal' as far as a well-informed, expressive gentleman goes.

In 1792 Fr Joseph Berington, a member of an old Catholic family, became chaplain to the Throckmortons. He was based at Buckland until his death thirty-five years later. Fr Berington wrote many books, particularly on church history. He had met Sir John Throckmorton through the Catholic Committee. He had been unfacultied by the Vicar Apostolic shortly before moving to Buckland and consequently Fr Addis of East Hendred had to journey twelve miles to hear confessions at Buckland. Fr Berington's priestly faculties were not restored until 1797. Two years later they were again withdrawn because of letters published by Fr Berington in the Gentleman's Magazine.

Of his education abroad Fr Berington wrote: 'when eleven years old, I was sent to a foreign land for education and did not return till after almost twenty years of miserable exile'. He added: 'Catholic is an old family name which we have never forfeited ... I am no Papist, nor is my religion Popery'. This attitude, while not endearing him to the Vicars Apostolic, enabled him to get on unusually well with Protestant clergy. John Wesley, no great friend of Catholic emancipation, congratulated him on his 'mildness and good humour'. The Vicar of Buckland, writing after Berington's death, called him a 'truly venerable man', 'sincere, pious, just and true' who 'discharged his sacred functions in so even and upright manner as to merit and secure the affections of those over whom he had charge, and at the same time to avoid giving offence to his

Protestant brethren: to all he was equally kind, benevolent and bountiful.'

Fr Berington was a keen supporter of Catholic emancipation and integration. He noted that Catholic squires tended to avoid socialising and to be reserved, traits which some of their descendants were to exhibit even in the first half of the twentieth century. He saw his fellow Catholic clergy as 'upright ... but narrowed by a bad education'. He said they were 'rough and unsociable' and 'bred up in the persuasion that on coming to England they are to meet with racks and persecution'.

The Catholic Relief Act of 1791 re-opened the professions to Catholics, although they were still barred from certain universities, including Oxford. The act also gave legal existence to registered Catholic places of worship, provided that the officiating clergy took an oath of allegiance.

Among the first applicants for registration was Fr Isaac Bellass, the new priest at Woolhampton, who had previously served the Portuguese embassy chapel in Westminster. (Bellass may be a variant of the recusant surname Bellasis.) Fr Bellass's successful Quarter Sessions application for registration of the Catholic chapel at Woolhampton is dated 10 January 1792. It certified that Woolhampton Lodge was now a 'chapel or place of religious worship for persons professing the Roman Catholic religion' and that 'Isaac Bellass doth officiate there as Minister'. Fr George Baynham registered the chapel of nearby Ufton Court the very same day.

The newly legalised Catholic chapels were not allowed to have steeples or bells for fear of confusion with Anglican churches. They were not registered for marriages for civil purposes. Catholic burials were forbidden in their grounds, as in all other churchyards. And - a sign of continuing distrust - they were not to be 'locked, barred or bolted'.

The French Exiled Clergy

(1790 - 1808)

The French Revolution broke out in 1789. In England it caused 'a wave of vague sentiment towards every form of Christianity'. This undoubtedly helped the progress towards Catholic emancipation. But even more beneficial was an influx of French Catholic priests.

In the summer of 1790 the French revolutionary government introduced its Civil Constitution of the Clergy. Papal influence was to be minimised and clergy were to become salaried civil servants, bound to the state by an oath of loyalty. Most French bishops and many priests rejected the new legislation. In the following spring so did the Pope.

By the time of the 1791 Catholic Relief Act a few French priests had already sought refuge in England. These were mainly clergy from aristocratic backgrounds and therefore most at risk.

Meanwhile the French revolutionary government retaliated to the Church's rejection of the Civil Constitution; after August 1792 a priest not taking the oath faced deportation. A mass exodus of clergy followed. They went to the Low Countries, Germany, Russia, Portugal, Spain, Italy, and Protestant Britain.

By September 1792 there were 1,500 French priests in England and in little more than a year the number rose to about 5,000.

Initially the British Government used the King's House at Winchester as a hostel for some of these priests. It could house more than 600 at a time, although conditions were fairly poor. When in 1796 the government feared a French invasion, it converted the King's House into a barracks, dispersing many of the priests to two locations in the Thames Valley. Norman clergy were sent to Reading, Bretons to Thame.

Anna Maria Smart's Reading Mercury put the case for the exiles in its edition of 15 October 1792 under the heading 'Distressed French Clergy':

'They have been driven from a country where no one is safe ... to seek shelter among Englishmen and Christians. The glory of our national character is generous compassion and they surely have the strongest claims on us who suffer persecution for conscience sake.'

Many Protestant clergy contributed to funds for the French exiles. But Fr Charles Leslie, struggling to pay for the new chapel of St Ignatius at St Clement's, Oxford, found the

---

appeals for the French clergy detrimental to his own fundraising.

The good treatment given to the exiles resulted in greatly improved relations between the Vatican and the British government. Furthermore, the government could not long maintain the curious anomaly whereby French Catholics enjoyed greater freedom in England than their English co-religionists.

Early in 1794 double land tax was abolished. Perhaps this was the spur to Thomas Stonor who, that same year and with parliamentary sanction, negotiated the return of the beech and yew woods surrounding Stonor House. These had been given to the Canons of Windsor 280 years earlier by the Protector Somerset as a result of the Chantries Act. Regaining the woods necessitated an exchange involving loss of other Stonor woodland.

The yew trees around Stonor House are said to have made it a very damp residence. Thomas Stonor therefore had many of them felled. He also completed the Gothicisation of the chapel of the Holy Trinity, which his father had begun in the 1750s.

Thomas Stonor employed one of the French exiles, Fr Jean-Baptiste Mortuaire of Rouen, as his chaplain. One of Fr Mortuaire's duties was the spiritual care of the exiled Marshal of France Dumouriez, who lived at Turville Park on the eastern edge of the Stonor estate. Fr Mortuaire celebrated Dumouriez's Requiem Mass and officiated at his funeral. The Marshal was buried in Henley-on-Thames parish church.

Fr Mortuaire served Stonor until his death in 1830. He was interred at nearby Pishill and his gravestone was incorporated into the paving of the Stonor aisle of the Anglican church.

By the time the French exiled clergy started arriving in England, the room Mrs Smart had rented in Reading's Minster Street could no longer be used as a Catholic chapel. Soon after the French Revolution broke out the landlord had asked her to stop using it, claiming that it would bring bad luck to his pregnant wife. Mrs Smart ignored his request and Mass was subsequently interrupted by 'vessels being emptied with accompaniment of offensive smells'. Never again was the room used for Mass.

Mrs Smart's younger daughter Elizabeth had been educated at a convent in Boulogne. In 1792, through friends in France, she learned of four priests waiting at Dover for the government to find them a refuge. She decided to invite them to Reading.

Using funds from a legacy Elizabeth Smart bought a tenement in Finch's Buildings. This had been built as a dower house for Lady Vachell, whose husband's uncle was the Elizabethan recusant, Thomas Vachell of Ipsden. The tenement stood on the south side of Hosier Lane (now Hosier Street) which runs westwards from St Mary's Butts and which was then on the quiet western outskirts of Reading.

On a winter's evening late in 1792 the four priests, all from the Rouen diocese, arrived at the Reading Mercury office, 'looking like a party of smugglers'. Under cover of darkness they were taken to Finch's Buildings. Elizabeth Smart put her knowledge of French to good use, as none of the priests spoke English.

Soon another Rouen priest joined them. In an airy room on the second floor a chapel was established, which seems to have been open to the public. Vestments and church fittings were obtained from the Englefield's recently vacated Whiteknights chapel.

With the closure of the King's House at Winchester in 1796, the government requisitioned the King's Arms in Castle Street, Reading, as a hostel for French clergy. The King's Arms, now four houses numbering 154 to 160 Castle Hill, was a large coaching hotel serving the Bath road. It was transformed into a hostel for more than 340 Norman priests.

On Sundays and Holydays there were Masses from five in the morning until noon. Benediction was celebrated every evening. The hotel's assembly room was used as the chapel and is said to have been capable of accommodating up to 400 worshippers.

The priests' superior was Abbé Noël Martin, formerly head of the seminary at Liseux, who had been their superior at Winchester. They lived to an almost monastic regime and had little contact with the townspeople. However, in the front garden the priests created floral tributes for all to see in gratitude to George III. These incorporated slogans used such as 'God Save the King' and 'You Could Not Have Guided Us Better'.

At Thame the government requisitioned the Mansion House in the High Street. This became home to a hundred Breton priests under Abbé Louis Despons, former principal at the college of Saint-Brieuc. There too, a near monastic regime applied. The Mansion House is believed to have become the Thame Girls' Grammar School, subsequently demolished.

The Thame hostel received additional support from local well-wishers, including the Marquis of Buckingham and the vicar's father-in-law. The latter gave them £250 a year for four years (= £5,000 a year today).

Two priests died at Thame and were buried in the parish churchyard. The rest returned to France in 1802, after a public service of thanksgiving at which the vicar preached the sermon.

As has been mentioned, not all refugee clergy lived in the large government-sponsored hostels. Monsignor Michel Thoumin des Valpons, an archdeacon and the Vicar-General of Dol in Normandy, stayed with William Davey at Overy, near Dorchester. This saved the Daveys the inconvenience of having to travel to

THE FORMER KINGS ARMS HOTEL, READING

Mass: the Dorchester congregation having been absorbed into Britwell, which had been absorbed into Waterperry, which had been relocated to St Clement's, Oxford!

Archdeacon Thoumin des Valpons died in the spring of 1798 at Overy Manor. He was buried with honour in Dorchester Abbey, at the expense of the Warden of New College, Oxford. There is a memorial slab to him in front of the altar of Dorchester parish church (the south-west aisle of Dorchester Abbey). By 1801 his place at Overy Manor had been taken by Fr Julien Triquet of the diocese of Le Mans.

While the French clergy settled into their new homes, Michael Blount III of Mapledurham took advantage of the second Catholic Relief Act to build a chapel onto the back of Mapledurham House. It is believed to be the first legal, purpose-built, Catholic chapel in England since the Reformation. It faces the parish church but is separated from it by a courtyard and a high wall. As at Milton Manor and Stonor House, the Mapledurham chapel was built in Gothick style. It was dedicated in 1797 and designed to seat about fifty people. It soon had to cope with almost twice that number.

During the French Revolution twenty-one of the twenty-three English convents in France found it preferable to risk returning home. The Poor Clares of Aire in Picardy had been established in 1629 as an offshoot of the convent at Gravelines. Mary, the sister of Thomas Simeon Weld II, was a nun at Aire, where she was known as Sister Euphrasia.

For some years the revolutionaries imprisoned the nuns in the convent, but in 1799 the sisters obtained passports and were allowed to travel to England. Thomas Simeon Weld gave them the use of Britwell House as a temporary convent; they stayed there for fifteen years. During that time four new sisters were received into the order, and one nun died.

The nuns' cells are said to have been in the servants' wing, and to have consisted of small interconnected bedrooms with peep-holes in the doors. Apartments were kept aside for Thomas Simeon Weld to stay when he visited with John Palmer, his valet (who later became first abbot of St Bernard's Abbey, Leicestershire). The nuns were also visited by Thomas's relative Cardinal Weld, who gave them an organ.

Unlike the French exiled clergy, the English religious communities received no help from the British government. Indeed, there was something of a backlash against them. Catholics still had no representation in Parliament and the House of Commons gave a large majority to a bill reinstituting restraints on Catholic education and monasticism. Fortunately the House of Lords rejected the bill and communities such as the Poor Clares of Britwell wisely adopted a low public profile.

The year 1800 saw further reconciliation between the English Catholic community and the Crown. In January George III requested that Cardinal Henry Stuart, impoverished by the Napoleonic regime, be granted a pension of £4,000 a year for life (= £80,000 today). The Cardinal, known to Jacobites as Henry IX, was the last Stuart claimant to the English throne. However, the claim did not have the support of the Catholic Church and Henry Stuart did not press for its recognition.

In 1800 Fr Thomas Webster took charge of the Woolhampton mission. In little more than two years he baptised eighty children. He was based at Woolhampton for twenty-eight years and travelled widely, substituting for clergy up to fifteen miles away.

Henry Addington, later Viscount Sidmouth, was invited to form a government in 1801. He was a firm opponent of Catholic emancipation but that year sold his estate at Woodley to James Wheble, a prosperous Catholic businessman. Wheble made Woodley Lodge, later known as Bulmershe Court, a Catholic mission.

Woodley Lodge (2 miles E. of Reading) had been built by the Whebles in 1777. After James Wheble repurchased the house, the family stayed there for more than a hundred years. The estate was former Reading Abbey land. James Wheble was fascinated by the abbey's history and largely financed the excavation of its ruins.

The parish boundary between Earley and Woodley ran through Woodley Lodge, the main rooms being in Earley. The house was demolished in 1963 to make way for a teacher training college now affiliated to Reading University.

Fr Pierre Miard de la Blardière of Liseux became James Wheble's chaplain at Woodley Lodge. He was the fifth Norman priest housed by Miss Smart at Finch's Buildings, Reading. Hitherto he had supported himself, like many other French exiled clergy, by giving French lessons.

Fr Miard de la Blardière ministered from Woodley Lodge for thirty-one years before retiring to France in 1833. He celebrated Mass daily and his congregation consisted of nearly two dozen Catholics, most of whom were members of the Wheble household. He lived in a very small cottage on the east side of Church Road, Earley (considerably extended early in the twentieth century). As recently as the mid 1950s it was known as Maisonette, French for little house. However, it seems that later occupiers considered the name too down-market and it is now called Bulmershe Cottage.

In June 1802 Fr George Bruning died at Isleworth. In the Middle Ages the Eystons had moved from Isleworth to East Hendred. Now Fr Bruning's body made the same journey. As brother-in-law of Thomas Eyston (who died six years earlier) he was buried in the Eyston aisle of East Hendred parish church. Fr Bruning had been chaplain at Britwell House for nearly a quarter of a century from 1765, and had also been chaplain at Milton Manor and East Hendred.

Fr George Baynham, the old Franciscan chaplain, lived on alone at tne deserted and crumbling Ufton Court until his death in the spring of 1803. The previous year John Jones of Llanarth, who had inherited the estate, sold it to Mr Congreve, the squire of Aldermaston.

Congreve stripped out much of Ufton Court's oak panelling. Some was reused in Aldermaston parish church. However, there is still original panelling at Ufton Court, including fascinating painted panels in the priest's oratory (place of prayer). There are also painted panels in a bedroom, which bear the monogram MR for Maria Regina, Latin for Queen Mary. These are said by some to refer to Mary Tudor but are more likely to show devotion to the Virgin Mary, Queen of Heaven.

Ufton Court was sold again in 1837, at which time it was considered unfit to be a gentleman's residence. The new purchaser was Richard Benyon de Beauvoir of Englefield, who refurbished it as estate workers' tenements. His successor, William Benyon of Englefield, leases the property to Berkshire County Council which uses it as a residential centre for schoolchildren. The property has been greatly restored and is open to the public one day a year.

In the summer of 1805 twenty-one people were confirmed at Mapledurham. One of these was Mary Ilsley whose younger brother Joseph was born five days before Christmas that year. It seems that their father was a servant at Mapledurham House.

Ilsley is one of the commonest variants of the name Hildesley. It is possible that downwardly mobile branches of the Catholic main line of the Hildesleys may have become known as Ilsleys or Illsleys. A will was written in 1633 by a ploughmaker called Griffin Illsley of South Stoke. This is only a mile south of Littlestoke Manor, a principal residence of the Hildesleys, whose heraldic badge incorporated a griffin.

Although most downwardly mobile branches of recusant families tended to conform to Anglicanism, it is an intriguing possibility that perhaps one or two branches of the Ilsleys had maintained Catholic continuity with the recusant Hildesleys. This would not have been too difficult if they had entered the service of Catholic gentry. And after all, the Blounts of Mapledurham were only ten miles downstream from Littlestoke.

Michael Blount was Joseph Ilsley's godfather. Up to the age of thirteen Joseph was taught by Fr Antoine Le Febvre of Rouen. This French priest became chaplain at Mapledurham in 1798, shortly after dedication of the new chapel, and stayed with the Blounts for twenty-four years.

At the age of thirteen Joseph Ilsley went to the English College at Lisbon, where he spent most of the rest of his life. Fr Le Febvre's former pupil achieved great distinction, becoming a priest, professor and eventually president of the college. He was even dubbed a knight of the Order of the Immaculate Conception by the King of Portugal.

In his late fifties Dr Ilsley returned to England because of ill health. He spent his last five years as a parish priest near Garstang in Lancashire and was buried under the porch of his church in 1868.

COTTAGE IN EARLEY
the original half timbered part was the home of the Whebles' French chaplain

Emancipation

(1808 - 1829)

In 1808 the Catholic Board was established to press the Catholic case for emancipation. Founder members among the Thames Valley gentry included Michael Blount of Mapledurham, his son Michael Henry Blount, Thomas Stonor, and James Weld, who soon afterwards inherited Britwell House.

All four Vicars Apostolic were members. The Vicar Apostolic of the Midland District, whose territory included Oxfordshire, was Bishop John Milner. He was opposed to lay committees and their aristocratic nationalistic members. Even the Pope described him as 'a firebrand', but he had a strong following among the rising Catholic middle class. He was twice a baptismal sponsor for the Whebles of Woodley Lodge, in 1820 and 1824.

In 1810 the Catholic Board approved the principle of a state veto of candidates for Catholic bishoprics much to Bishop Milner's disgust. Three years later he was expelled from the board because of his refusal to compromise on the grounds for emancipation.

The year the Catholic Board was established the parson of Britwell Salome noted the winter evening activities of a Catholic labourer. The man, whose name was Campbell, taught 'writing and accounts' to about thirteen local pupils, but never interfered 'with the religious principles of his Scholars'.

About two years later a room in the Hermitage at Clewer Green, Windsor was in use as a Catholic chapel, thus laying the foundation for the present Catholic parish of St Edward. The house belonged to John Riley whose French chaplain lived at the Hope Inn in Frogmore Road. This was probably Fr Noel Duclos of Evreux, who taught French at Eton College from 1802 until 1826 or later.

Not far away at Warfield (5 miles SW of Windsor) another French priest, Fr François Dubois of Laon had administered baptism in 1800 and 1801. There had been a Catholic mission or chaplaincy at Warfield for at least eight years from 1776, and Catholics are said to have had their own burial ground at Wick Hill. Little else is known and it seems that Mass was no longer being said regularly at Warfield by this time.

Sir John Throckmorton, keen though he was on putting the lay case for Catholic emancipation, had other interests. As a proud sheep farmer he wagered 1,000 guineas (= £20,000 today) that, by sunset of the longest day, he would wear a coat made from wool which until that sunrise had been on his sheep.

The wager was accepted and on 25 June 1811 the task began. At 5 o'clock in the morning Sir John handed two Southdown sheep to Mr Coxeter, the miller at Greenham Mills near Newbury. The sheep were then shorn, the wool sorted and spun, and the yarn spooled, warped, loomed and woven. The resultant cloth was then burred, milled, rowed, dyed, dried, sheared and pressed to produce a hunting Kersey in 'the admired dark Wellington colour'; a shade of brown which, today at least, has a somewhat stripy appearance.

Production of the cloth took eleven hours. It was then passed to Isaac White the tailor. He and his team completed the coat in two hours and twenty minutes, with plenty of time in hand.

An estimated 5,000 people witnessed the event. They were sustained with 120 gallons of strong beer and two roasted sheep, the donors of the wool used for the coat.

That evening Sir John Throckmorton wore the coat at the Pelican Inn, Speenhamland (1 mile W. of Newbury). About forty gentlemen dined with him on a meal provided by the miller. The record stood for more than a century. Forty years later the Throckmorton Coat was displayed at the Great Exhibition. Today it is at the Throckmortons' Warwickshire residence, Coughton Court, near Alcester.

The family sold Buckland House in 1908 to the Wellesley family. In 1963 it became an independent college called University Hall. Plans were afoot in 1991 to convert it into a hotel.

Lady Mary Mannock lived at Badgemore near Henley-on-Thames from about 1812 to 1814. She was born Mary Brownlow-Doughty and was presumably related to the Catholic Doughtys who had lived at Checkendon and Beenham. She employed as her chaplain Fr François d'Allard of Bayeaux, who lived seven miles away at Fingest House on the eastern edge of the Stonor estate.

Lady Mannock died at Windsor in the spring of 1814. The poor priest had great difficulty recovering his salary and travelling expenses from her solicitors. She left £800 (= £15,000 today) to help fund the mission at Poole, Dorset. This was also supported by a legacy from Thomas Simeon Weld, owner of Britwell House, who had died fourteen years earlier.

Meanwhile Finch's Buildings in Hosier Street, Reading continued to serve as a mission centre and presbytery (priests' house) for four or five French priests from the dioceses of Rouen and Seez. Their leader was Fr Jean Baptiste Longuet, a farmer's son from Ussy. His elder brother Louis was martyred in the French Revolution.

Fr Longuet was ordained in England and was working in Reading by the autumn of 1802. Over the next nine years he and his colleagues saved £300 (= £5,600 today) which they earned by giving French lessons. With this money a plot of land was bought in Vastern Road, behind the old site of Reading School. There Fr Longuet built the first Catholic church in Reading since the Reformation, aptly named the chapel of the Resurrection.

The church stood on the site now occupied by the Rising Sun public house. The project was completed little more than a year after it was approved by Bishop William Poynter, the Vicar Apostolic of the London District. He consecrated the chapel in 1812.

Once again the church furniture from Whiteknights was reused, despite a quarrel over the issue with Elizabeth Smart and her sister. The new chapel soon served a congregation of more than 170, consisting of Reading's few native Catholics, recent converts, French emigrés and Italian traders.

Thomas Simeon Weld the younger died in 1810 at Stonyhurst, Lancashire. His death induced the Poor Clares of Britwell House to look around for a more permanent home. Three years later the abbess, chaplain and a few nuns moved to Coxside near Portsmouth, where they were later joined by the rest of the community. They later returned to France then moved to Scorton in Yorkshire before settling in Darlington, County Durham. It was there that the last of the Britwell nuns died in 1892, aged ninety-seven.

James Weld, seventh son of Thomas Simeon Weld, inherited Britwell House. After the nuns left he made it his home. He lived at Britwell for nineteen years and several of his children were born there. In 1832 the Welds sold the house and it passed out of Catholic ownership.

In 1814 twenty-three year old Maria Teresa Metcalfe of Bath married Charles Eyston, a year her senior, at St Mary's Catholic chapel, Queen's Square, Bath. Maria's mother was a Throckmorton and her paternal grandmother was Bridget More, a descendant of Sir Thomas More. Through Maria Metcalfe the Eystons of East Hendred derive their descent from Sir Thomas More. It was also through her that they acquired his timber and silver tankard, which is kept at Hendred House.

Charles and Maria Eyston's son Charles married Agnes Mary Blount of Mapledurham. The male line of the Blounts of Mapledurham became extinct in 1943 and Mapledurham thereby became an Eyston property. The present owner of Mapledurham House, John Joseph Eyston, is Charles and Maria Eyston's great great grandson.

One afternoon in February 1817, six years after completion of Reading's the chapel of the Resurrection, Fr Longuet left a house at Wallingford. He had been teaching French to the children and had just been paid several months' tuition fees. After visiting friends at Pangbourne he rode through the evening along the Oxford Road towards Reading. It seems that someone in the darkness ahead of him knew about the money. Near where the road meets Norcot Hill, Fr Longuet was robbed and murdered. He was only two and a half miles from home.

At that time Norcot Junction was in the country. Fr Longuet's horribly gashed body was not found until the postman passed along the road the following morning. The priest's horse was nearby, grazing by the Thames.

This murder caused great embarrassment to the authorities because the French exiled priests were in England under the Prince Regent's protection. The government therefore offered a large reward for the capture of the murderer. But, even though a Bow Street detective was sent from London to help the local constabulary, their efforts were in vain. The murderer, the 'son of a good family', confessed shortly before his death.

Fr Longuet was buried in the chapel of the Resurrection. His remains were transferred to St James's church in the ruins of Reading Abbey when it replaced the chapel in 1841. There is a small brass plate to his memory in the altar step of the church. His body is buried at the entrance to the sanctuary.

Fr Longuet was not the only French priest to suffer a violent death in the Reading area. Nineteen years earlier, in 1798, Fr Pierre Nourry of Coutance was found dead in the mill stream near Caversham Lock. He was probably the 'poor emigré priest' thrown into the Thames by three young men. The drowning priest is said to have asked God for the conversion of his assailants, one of whom became a Catholic on his deathbed.

After Fr Longuet's death Fr Webster of Mapledurham helped the two remaining French priests at the chapel of the Resurrection. Fr Jean Godquin of Rouen died the following year, but his colleague from the same diocese, Fr Jean Gondré, who had earlier served the Catholics of East Hendred, lived for another nine years.

Although it was no longer necessary to travel to the Continent for a good Catholic secondary education, Catholics were still prevented from attending Oxford University (and remained so until the late nineteenth century). In 1817 therefore, twenty year old Thomas Stonor went to the English Seminary at Paris to study for a degree. While there he hunted with a party that included Arthur Wellesley, the Duke of Wellington. The Iron Duke was an Anglo-Irish Protestant who had been given £600,000 (= £12m today) by the state for his role in the defeat of Napoleon. With part of this reward the Duke had recently bought Stratfield Saye House (7 miles S. of Reading). He was to become a crucial figure in the struggle for Catholic emancipation.

In 1819 Fr Pierre Senechal died at Oxford. He and Fr Pierre Bertin, both of Amiens, taught French in Oxford for many years, though neither was formally attached to the University. Fr Senechal also taught Latin and Italian. Although by this time there were some Catholic graveyards, their use was technically illegal until the Burial Act of 1852. Fr Senechal was therefore buried at the Anglican church of St Clement, Oxford. At that time the church stood to the east of Magdalen Bridge. It was rebuilt in Marston Road in 1828, at which time John Henry Newman was the curate.

Fr Charles Leslie, the Jesuit founder of the chapel of St Ignatius in the St Clement's district of Oxford, had died in 1806, greatly respected by many at the University. He is said to have been the inspiration for the character Mr Keith in J. G. Lockhart's 1823 novel 'Reginald Dalton'. By 1818 the priest at St Ignatius was Fr Robert Newsham, another Jesuit. He established a school in the presbytery for the sons of gentlemen, and in 1849 transferred it to Dorchester-on-Thames.

The chapel of St Ignatius was the only Catholic church in Oxford until 1873 when St Aloysius's in the Woodstock Road opened. It was there in 1845 that Newman attended his first public Mass after converting to Catholicism. St Ignatius's, 'a solemn and handsome edifice decorated in a style of elegant simplicity', closed in 1911. It was replaced by the church of SS Edmund & Frideswide in Iffley Road. However, the former chapel still exists and is now used as offices.

The Prince Regent became George IV in 1820. That year Fr Francis Bowland was appointed to replace the murdered Fr Longuet. Fr Bowland is said to have been Reading's first English secular priest since the Reformation. In the recent past he had worked at Stonor. He was to serve the Catholics of Reading for seventeen years.

In 1821 William Davey of Dorchester, then sixty-one years old, was presented with a 'handsome inscribed goblet' by the Oxfordshire Agricultural Society, of which he was a founder. He farmed 320 acres and kept 600 sheep. His agricultural techniques were so advanced that George III ('Farmer George') is supposed to have inspected the Davey holdings in person.

Arthur Young's book 'Agriculture in Oxfordshire' had described William Davey's ploughing as 'the neatest and truest ... I anywhere viewed'. Young described William Davey as 'one of the most intelligent farmers in the county'. William Davey obviously took after his father, who had been regarded as one of the most painstaking and progressive farmers in Oxfordshire.

William Davey's wife was Sarah Haskey whose family were stewards to the Stonors for two or three generations. In 1811 William had laid the first stone of the present Dorchester Bridge, an indication of the esteem in which his family was held.

When William Davey died in 1831 one of his five sons, George, continued the farming tradition. In 1849 another son, John, paid for the building of St Birinus's Catholic church, opposite Dorchester Abbey.

In 1821 the eighth Earl of Fingall put forward legislation for Catholic emancipation. This included a veto for the government on nominees for Catholic bishoprics and a modification to the Oath of Supremacy. Bishop Milner, Vicar Apostolic of the Midland District, (who had been a baptismal sponsor to the Whebles at Woodley Lodge the previous year) opposed the bill. However, the Vatican and Bishop Poynter of the London District supported it with reservations. The bill was subsequently passed by the House of Commons but rejected by the Lords.

Two years later, in 1823, the clergy-dominated middle class Catholic Association was established. Its purpose was to counter the influence of the old Catholic gentry and nobility.

In 1825 another emancipation bill was proposed, this time by Sir Francis Burdett. It had been drawn up by the Irish lawyer Daniel O'Connell without consulting English Catholics. Again, Bishop Milner opposed it, Bishop Poynter supported it with reservations, the Commons passed it and the Lords threw it out. Bishop Milner died the following year.

In 1828 the Test Act and the Corporation Act were repealed, to the benefit of all non-Anglicans. The same year Daniel O'Connell was elected Member of Parliament for County Clare. Thomas Stonor was one of his proposers. But as a Catholic, O'Connell could not take his seat in Parliament.

The Duke of Wellington was now Prime Minister. He and Home Secretary Robert Peel feared that civil war might break out in Ireland if Catholic emancipation were further delayed. Until then the King had opposed the restoration of Catholic civil rights. He now changed his mind and allowed a new bill to proceed. It was introduced in January 1829.

The resultant Catholic Emancipation Act prescribed a new parliamentary oath denying the Pope any non-spiritual jurisdiction and undertaking not to subvert the position of the Anglican Church. Catholic priests were forbidden to be Members of Parliament. Catholic bishops were not to use titles adopted since the Reformation by Anglican bishops. Catholic clergy were not to officiate except in Catholic places of worship. But there was to be no state veto on nominations for Catholic bishoprics.

Catholics could now belong to corporations. Most public office was open to them, apart from that of Lord Chancellor, Keeper of the Great Seal, Lord Lieutenant of Ireland and High Commissioner of the Church of Scotland. These restrictions still apply and the Royal Marriage Act continues to forbid the Royal Family to marry Catholics, a proscription that applies to no other religious denomination.

The new legislation was passed quickly, without consultation or negotiation with the English Catholics. Nonetheless, all four Vicars Apostolic approved the new parliamentary oath. Many anti-Catholic laws remained, but they were ineffective and no serious attempt was made to enforce them.

During the previous twenty years there had been few demonstrations against the campaign for Catholic emancipation. But at least two Anglican parishes in Oxford petitioned against the 1829 act, as did Oxford city council.

Two weeks after the act was passed Daniel O'Connell, 'the Liberator' became godfather to James Wheble's youngest son at Woodley Lodge.

The leading Catholic families of the Thames Valley rapidly moved back into the public life from which they had so long been barred. Sir Robert Throckmorton of Buckland became Member of Parliament for Berkshire in 1831 and Sheriff of the county for 1843. Charles Eyston of East Hendred became Sheriff of Berkshire for 1831, and the following year Michael Henry Blount of Mapledurham became High Sheriff of Oxfordshire. In 1833 Thomas Stonor was elected Member of Parliament for Oxford and three years later he became High Sheriff of Oxfordshire. He was a friend of Lord Gladstone and a founder of the Henley Royal Regatta. He also instigated an annual meeting of the Royal Buckhounds at Stonor, became the third Lord Camoys and was Lord-in-Waiting to Queen Victoria under five Liberal administrations.

Although the Earl of Fingall's family had left Berkshire in the previous century, in 1831 the eighth earl became Baron Woolhampton of Woolhampton Lodge. Six years later James Wheble became Sheriff of Berkshire. In 1841 Charles Scott-Murray of Medmenham became Member of Parliament for Buckinghamshire and eleven years later he was High Sheriff of the county.

Thereafter there was a slow but steady growth of Catholicism, bolstered by immigration from Ireland and by conversions from the Anglican Oxford Movement. That growth continued well into the twentieth century and today about one in ten of Thames Valley people are baptised Catholics.

Appendix A

Acknowledgements

The author gratefully acknowledges the assistance provided in ways great and small by the following people:

The Hon. Georgina Stonor, President of the Catholic Family History Society.
Mr Leslie Brooks, Founder President of the Catholic Family History Society.
Mr Michael Walcot, Founder Vice-President of the Catholic Family History Society.
Miss Rosemary Rendel, Honorary Secretary of the Catholic Record Society.
Mr Michael Hodgetts, General Editor of the Catholic Record Society.
Mrs Christine Kelly, historian.
Mr J. C. H. Aveling, historian.
Dr Alan Davidson, historian.
Mrs Mary Howarth, local historian.
Mr Leslie North, local historian.
Mr John Chapman, local historian.
Mrs Mary McInally, family historian.
Mr Walter Pease, family historian.
Mr Ron Hildersley, family historian.
Lady Sara Grayson.
The late Mrs Marjorie Mockler of Milton Manor House.
Mr Anthony Mockler of Milton Manor House.
The Baroness von Twickell.
The Hon. Mrs Douglas Woodruff.
Mrs J. J. Dingwall of Lyford Grange.
Mrs Julia Skinner of Ipsden House.
Mrs Mary Newton of Fawley Manor.
Mrs Carolyn Saunders of Waterperry House.
Ms Ann Duncan of Tidmarsh Grange.
Mr John Joseph Eyston of Mapledurham House.
Mr Thomas More Eyston of Hendred House.
Mr Peter Ducker of Littlestoke Manor.
Mr Christopher Tucker of Bere Court.
Mr Lance Wright, formerly of Bere Court.
The Hon. William Benyon, MP, of Englefield House.
Mr Thomas Kressner of Britwell House.
Mr Joseph Robinson, Master of the Temple.
Mrs J. E. Edgell, Librarian & Keeper of Records, Honourable Society of the Middle Temple.
Mr Peter Keepax, Headteacher, Ufton Court Residential Centre.
Mr Howard Bush, formerly of Ufton Court.
Mr H. E. Wells-Furby, Second Master, Shiplake College.
Mr M. Dalton, Director of Bryant Homes Southern Limited, Popes Manor, Binfield.

Mr Brian S. Folley, Director of the Harleyford Estate Limited.
Mr A. J. Herbert, Manager, Finance and Administration, and
Mr Chris Stammers, Photographer, Johnson Matthey Technology
Centre, Blount's Court.
Sr Marguerite Kuhn-Regnier, Honorary Secretary, The Catholic
Archives Society.
Sr Anne of the Visitation Convent, Caversham.
Dom Geoffrey Scott, Headmaster of Douai School, Upper
Woolhampton.
Dom Aidan Bellenger of Downside Abbey.
Dom A. J. Stacpoole of Ampleforth Abbey.
Right Revd Maurice Wood, Resident Priest of Englefield.
Very Revd Anthony Griffiths, Parish Priest of Marlow.
Revd John Garvey, formerly Parish Priest of Dorchester-on-
Thames.
Revd T. G. Holt, Archivist, Department of Historiography and
Archives, English Province of the Society of Jesus.
Revd Ian Brayley, former Vice-Master, and
Revd Joseph T. Munitiz, Master, Campion Hall, Oxford.
Revd Francis Isherwood, Information Officer, Diocese of
Portsmouth.
Revd Peter Dennison, Diocesan Archivist, Archdiocese of
Birmingham.
Revd David Wood-Robinson, Rector of Holton, Albury, Waterperry
and Waterstock.
Revd J. Donald Shepherd, Rector of Checkendon.
Revd A. J. H. Salmon, Vicar of Chobham.
Revd Jack Lewis, Rector of Compton.
Revd Richard B. Miller, Vicar of Aldermaston with Wasing and
Brimpton.
Revd R. D. Ind, Vicar of Hurley and Stubbings.
Mr T. N. Rosser, Churchwarden, Shiplake Parish Church.
Mr C. Payne, Assistant Archivist of Berkshire County Council.
Mrs Margaret Smith, Senior Librarian, Local Studies Section of
Reading Central Library.
Mr M. Bott, Keeper of Archives and Manuscripts, University of
Reading.
Mr Paul Cannon, Assistant Curator, Newbury District Museum.
Mr Arthur MacGregor, Assistant Keeper, Department of
Antiquities, Ashmolean Museum, Oxford.
Mrs Georgina Strauss, Superintendent, Old Library Reading
Rooms, Bodleian Library.
Miss S. J. Barnes, County Archivist, Oxfordshire County
Council.
Mr L. White, County Librarian, Oxford Central Library.
Dr Malcolm Graham, Principal Librarian of the Centre for
Oxfordshire Studies, Oxford Central Library.
Ms Sheila Weatherhead, Centre for Oxfordshire Studies, Oxford
Central Library.
Ms Christine Nelson, Acting Records Assistant, Hampshire County
Museums Service.
Mrs Avril Hart, Victoria & Albert Museum.
Mr Hugh Carter, Keeper of Natural History, Reading Museum.

Appendix A - Acknowledgements

Mr Leslie Cram, Principal Keeper, Reading Museum.
Mr Dorrien Belson.
Dr Francis Andrews.
Dr David Chappell of James R Knowles & Company.
Mr Andrew Cope, Economics Division, Bank of England.
Mr Ian Stewart of Savills plc.
Mr Les Bowerman.
Mrs Vivienne Beaumont.

A p p e n d i x   B

B i b l i o g r a p h y

The following list contains virtually all written sources
consulted during the writing of this book. They vary from
unpublished notes, through leaflets, magazine articles and
booklets, to hefty tomes. Their relevance ranges from crucial
to marginal.

Suggestions for further reading are given in Appendix C.

Abridgement of all the Statutes in Force and Use, HM Printers,
1725.

Adair, J., They Saw It Happen, booklet, Hampshire County
Council, 1981.

Aspects of the Catholic History of the Caversham Area,
typescript notes, Visitation Convent, Caversham, 1983.

Amann, Prof.(trans. Raybould), The Church of the Early
Centuries, Sands, 1930.

Anderton Webster, L. & V., 'The Packingtons of Harvington',
Recusant History, Vol.12., No.5, Catholic Record Society.

Anstruther, G., The Seminary Priests, Vol.1, St Edmund's
College, Ware/Ushaw College, Durham, 1968.

Anstruther, G., The Seminary Priests, Vol.2, Mayhew-McCrimmon,
1975.

Antheunis, L., The Rt. Rev. George Chamberlain, Bishop of Ypres
(1576-1634), Biographical Studies No.2, Catholic Record
Society, 1953.

Aveling, J.C.H., The Handle and the Axe, Blond & Briggs, 1976.

Aveling, J.C.H., Catholic Recusants in Berkshire, unpublished
notes for lecture given at Oxford University External Studies
day-school, 1990.

Babbage, T., Tylehurst Described, booklet, Reading Libraries,
1976.

Baker, J.H., The Ipsden Country, William Smith, 1959.

Beckinsale, R.P., Companion into Berkshire, Spurbooks, 1972.

Bede, The Venerable (ed. Colgrave and Mynors), The
Ecclesiastical History of tne English People, Oxford University
Press, 1969.

Bellenger, D.T.J., The French Exiled Clergy, Downside Abbey,
1986.

Bellenger, D.T.J., 'The French Exiled Clergy in Reading', South Western Catholic History, No.2, 1984.

Bere Court, unpublished historical research commissioned by Tucker, C., owner of Bere Court.

Berkshire Federation of Women's Institutes, The New Berkshire Village Book, Countryside Books, 1985.

Bettenson, H. (ed.), Documents of the Christian Church, 2nd edition, Oxford University Press, 1963.

Bindoff, S.T., Tudor England, Pelican, 1950.

Blackburn, I.,'Our Catholic Ancestors', Catholic Ancestor, Vol.2, No.8, 1989.

Boardman, B.M., The Life of Thomas More, booklet, Catholic Truth Society, 1978.

Bossy, J., The English Catholic Community, 1570-1850, Darton, Longman & Todd, 1975.

Bowler, H., 'Recusant Roll No.2 (1593-94)', Records Series, No.57, Catholic Record Society.

Britannia, Vol.20, p.319, 1989.

Brooks, L., various unpublished notes on Catholic history.

Brooks, L., 'Family at the Manor', series of articles in Catholic Women's League Journal, dates unknown.

Brooks, L., 'Households of the Faith', series of articles in Catholic Women's League Journal, dates unknown.

Brown, J.H. & Guest, W., History of Thame, 1935.

Burden, V., Discovering the Ridgeway, booklet, Shire Publications, 1976/81.

Burfit, D., The Church of St Mary the Virgin, Hurley, booklet, Hurley Parochial Church Council.

Burke, J., An Illustrated History of England, BCA, 1974.

Bush, H., 'Ufton Court', ECA Journal, spring 1988.

Caraman, P., Saint Nicholas Owen - Maker of Hiding Holes, booklet, Catholic Truth Society, 1980.

Chadwick, H.,The Early Church, Pelican, 1967.

Challoner, R. (revd. Pollen), Memoirs of Missionary Priests, Burns Oates & Washbourne, 1924.

Chapman, H.W., The Last Tudor King, Jonathan Cape, 1958, republished by New Portway.

Chapman, J., A History of the Parish Church of St Mary the Virgin, Purley-on-Thames, Berkshire, booklet, St Mary's Parish, 1988.

Chapman, J., various unpublished notes on the Hydes of Hyde Hall, Purley, 1989.

Chaucer, G. (ed. Hieatt, A. & C.), The Canterbury Tales, Bantam, 1964.

Church of St Swithun, Compton Beauchamp, parish leaflet.

Clancy, T.H., 'Priestly Perseverance in the Old Society of Jesus, Recusant History, Vol.19, No.3.

Clifton, M., Three English Martyrs Knights of St John, booklet, privately published, 1989.

Climenson, E.J., A Brief Guide to Henley-on-Thames, Sidney H Higgins, 1896.

Climenson, E.J., The History of Shiplake, Eyre & Spottiswoode, 1894.

Colwell, S., The Family History Book, Phaidon, 1980.

Coward, B., The Stuart Age, Longman, 1980.

Cram, L., Reading Abbey, booklet, Reading Museum & Art Gallery, 1988.

Cross, C., Church and People, 1450-1660, Fontana, 1976.

Davey, E.C., Memoirs of an Oxfordshire Old Catholic Family and its connections from 1566 to 1897, Vail, c.1897.

Davidson, A., 'An Oxford Family: A footnote to the life of John Donne', Recusant History, Vol.13,No.4, Catholic Record Society.

Davidson, A., Roman Catholicism in Oxfordshire from the late Elizabethan Period to the Civil War (c.1580-c.1640), Thesis, Bristol University, 1970.

Dickens, A.G., The English Reformation, Batsford/Fontana, 1964/67.

Dictionary of National Biography

Doble, D., A History of the Parish of Shinfield, Berkshire, booklet, privately published, 1961.

Dorchester Abbey, booklet, Dorchester Abbey, 1985.

Duchesne, Abbe, The Early History of the Church, Vol.3, John Murray, 1924.

Eagle, D. & Carnell, H., The Oxford Illustrated Literary Guide to Great Britain and Ireland, Oxford University Press, 1981.

Elvins, M., Old Catholic England, booklet, Catholic Truth Society, 1978.

Encyclopaedia Britannica

Englefield Family Archives, University of Reading.

Eppstein, J., History of the Faith in an English Town, privately published, 1926.

Erickson, C., Bloody Mary, BCA/Dent, 1978.

Eyston, C.J., Pedigree of Eyston of East Hendred in the County of Berkshire, privately published, 1875.

Farmer, D. H.(ed.), Benedict's Disciples, Fowler Wright, 1980.

Finucane, R.C., Miracles and Pilgrims - Popular Beliefs in Medieval England, BCA/Dent, 1977.

Foley, H.(ed.), Records of the English Province of the Society of Jesus,, 1877-83.

Forster, J., Forsters of Aldermaston History, typescript notes, 1983 or earlier.

Fox, G.E. (rev. Stephenson), Short Guide to the Silchester Collection, 5th edition, booklet, Reading Public Museum & Art Gallery, 1912.

Fraser, A., Cromwell - Our Chief of Men, BCA/Weidenfeld & Nicholson, 1974.

Fraser, A., King James VI of Scotland, I of England, Weidenfeld & Nicholson, 1974.

Fulford, M., Calleva Atrebatum - A Guide to the Roman Town at Silchester, booklet, Calleva Museum, 1987.

Gaffney, W.J., Notes on the Marlow Relic, unpublished?, Catholic Rectory, Marlow.

Garlick, V.F.M., The Newberry Scrapbook, 1970.

Geere, J., Index to Oxfordshire Hearth Tax, 1665, booklet, Oxfordshire Family History Society, 1985.

Gibbs, V.(ed.), The Complete Peerage, St Catherine's Press, 1916, republished Alan Sutton, 1982.

Gibson, D.(ed.), A Parson in the Vale of White Horse, Alan Sutton, 1982.

Gillow, J. (ed.), 'The Common-place Book of Edmund Napper of Holywell, Oxon', Records Series, Vol.1, Catholic Record Society, 1904.

Gillow, J., Bibliographical Dictionary of the English Catholics.

Green, B., The English Benedictine Congregation, booklet, Catholic Truth Society.

Guiney, L.I., Blessed Edmund Campion, R & T Washbourne, 1914.

Hansom, J.S., 'List of Convicted Recusants in the Reign of Charles II', Records Series, Vol.6, Catholic Record Society, 1909.

Harris, C.G., Oxfordshire Parish Registers and Bishops Transcripts, 2nd edition, booklet, Oxfordshire Family History Society, 1984.

Harris J. & Higgott, G., Inigo Jones, The Drawing Center, New York, 1989.

Hervey-Bathurst, P. and Taylor, J., Catholic Wayside Guide to the West Country & Wales, booklet, Catholic Wayside Guide, 1964.

Heyworth, P., The Oxford Guide to Oxford, Oxford University Press, 1981.

Higham, R., Berkshire and the Vale of White Horse, Batsford, 1977.

Hill, C., Milton and the English Revolution, Faber & Faber, 1977.

Hishon, R., College of Saints and Martyrs, booklet, Catholic Truth Society, 1989.

History of St Mark's, Englefield, parish leaflet.

Hodgetts, M., 'Loca Secretiora in 1581', Recusant History, Vol.19, No.4, Catholic Record Society.

Hodgetts, M., Midlands Catholic Buildings, Archdiocese of Birmingham Historical Commission, 1990.

Hodgetts, M., 'Elizabethan Priest-Holes II', Recusant History, Vol.12, No.3, Catholic Record Society.

Hodgetts, M., Secret Hiding Places, Veritas Publications, 1989.

Holmes, P., Resistance and Compromise, Cambridge University Press, 1982.

Howkins, C., Discovering Church Furniture, 2nd edition, booklet, Shire Publications, 1980.

Humphreys, A.L., Bucklebury, A Berkshire Parish, privately published, 1932.

Humphreys, A.L., East Hendred - A Berkshire Parish Historically Treated, Hatchards, 1923.

Hunt, W, The English Church - From its Foundation to the Norman Conquest (597-1066), Macmillan, 1899.

Hurry, J.B., Reading Abbey, Elliot Stock, 1901.

Hyde End House - Historical Notes, uncredited, undated, unidentified magazine article in Berkshire Libraries' Cuttings Collection.

Hutton, E., The Franciscans in England, Mayflower Press, 1926.

Jebb, L., Englefield, booklet, Englefield Estate.

Jennett, S (ed.), Oxford and District, Darton, Longman & Todd, 1965.

Kelly, C., Blessed Thomas Belson - His Life and Times, Colin Smythe, 1987.

Kemp, B.R., Reading Abbey 2 - An Introduction to the History of the Abbey, booklet, Reading Museum & Art Gallery, 1968.

Kemp, B.R., 'The Miracles of the Hand of St James', Berkshire Archaeological Journal, Vol.65.

Kemp, B. & Slade, C., Guide to Reading Abbey, booklet, Friends of Reading Abbey, 1988.

Kift, M., Life in Old Caversham, privately published, 1980.

Knowles, D., Bare Ruined Choirs, Cambridge University Press, 1959/76.

Lamb, C., Discovering Berkshire, booklet, Shire Publications, 1968.

Lethbridge, R., Oxfordshire and Berkshire, Michael Joseph, 1988.

Livingstone, E.A.(ed.), The Concise Oxford Dictionary of the Christian Church, Oxford University Press, 1977.

Lyon, W., Chronicles of Finchampstead, Longmans, Green & Co., 1895.

Marius, R., Thomas More, Dent/Fount, 1985/6.

Mathew, D., Catholicism in England, 1535-1935, Longmans, Green & Co., 1936.

McFarlane, K.B., John Wycliffe and the Beginnings of English Nonconformity, The English Universities Press, 1952.

Milliken, E.K., English Monasticism, Yesterday and Today, Harrap, 1967.

McLynn, F., The Jacobites, Routledge & Kegan Paul, 1985.

Mockler, S., Milton Manor, booklet, Milton Manor Estate.

Money, W., A Guide to Donnington Castle, 1888.

Money, W., John Winchcombe, manuscript notes in the Walter Money Collection, ref.B/D, Acc.No.10,919, Reading Central Library.

Money, W., Letter in Newbury Weekly News, 22nd November 1877.

Money, W., The History of Newbury, 1887.

Morey, A., The Catholic Subjects of Elizabeth I, George Allen & Unwin, 1978.

Moule, A.W.H., History of Woolhampton, 1955.

Mullaney, J., St James's Catholic Church and School in the Abbey Ruins, Reading, booklet, Caversham Bookshop/St James, 1987.

Neill, S., Anglicanism, Penguin, 1958.

Noel-Perkins, P., Tidmarsh Grange - Notes of (conjectural) History, unpublished typescript, 1990.

Norman, E., Roman Catholicism in England, Opus, Oxford University Press, 1986.

O'Sullivan, B., The Two Britwells, privately published, 1969.

Parkinson, C.N., Gunpowder, Treason and Plot, Weidenfeld & Nicholson, 1976.

Parmiter, G. de C., Edmund Plowden, Catholic Record Society, 1986.

Parmiter, G. de C., 'Plowden, Englefield and Sandford: I 1558-1585 & II 1585-1609', Recusant History, Vol.13, No.3 & Vol.14, No.1, Catholic Record Society.

Parmiter, G. de C., 'Elizabethan Popish Recusancy in the Inns of Court', Bulletin of the Institute of Historical Research, Special Supplement No.11, 1976.

Pevsner, N., Berkshire, Penguin, 1966.

Philip, K., Reflected in Wantage, part 2, privately published, 1970.

Phillips, D., The Story of Reading, Countryside Books, Newbury, 1980.

Plowden, A., Danger to Elizabeth, Macmillan, 1973.

Pollen, J.H., The English Catholics in the Reign of Queen Elizabeth, Longmans, Green & Co, 1920.

Pontifex, D., The Fires of Smithfield, booklet, Catholic Truth Society, 1955.

Preston Guardian, article on funeral of Father Joseph Ilsley, 5th September 1868.

Quennel, P., Alexander Pope - The Education of Genius, 1688-1728, Weidenfeld & Nicholson, 1968.

Reade, C., A Record of the Redes of Barton Court, Berkshire, 1899.

'Berkshire Residences', Reading Mercury, date unknown.

Reed, M., The Georgian Triumph, 1700-1830, Routledge & Kegan Paul, 1983.

Rendell, E.W., A History of Blount's Court, Oxfordshire, 1974.

Rose-Troupe, F., The Western Rebellion of 1549, Smith, Elder & Co, 1913.

Rude, G., 'The Gordon Riots', History Today, July 1955, reprinted in Catholic Ancestor, Vol.3, No.3, November 1990.

Rumbold, V., 'Alexander Pope and the Religious Tradition of the Turners', Recusant History, Vol.17, No.1, Catholic Record Society.

St Peter & St Paul, Checkendon, parish leaflet, 1978.

<u>Saint Edmund Campion</u>, leaflet, British Library Board, 1981.

Scantlebury, R.E., 'The Catholic Registers of Reading 1780-1840 and Woodley Lodge 1802-1869', <u>Records Series</u>, Vol.32, Catholic Record Society, 1932.

Scarisbrick, J.J., <u>Henry VIII</u>, Eyre & Spottiswoode, 1968.

Scarisbrick, J.J., <u>The Reformation and the English People</u>, Blackwell, 1984.

Scott, A.F., <u>Every One a Witness - the Stuart Age</u>, White Lion, 1974.

Scott, G., <u>St Mary's Church, Woolhampton</u>, booklet, Douai Abbey, 1975.

Scott, G., 'A Berkshire Benedictine Mission in the Eighteenth Century', <u>South Western Catholic History</u>, No.1, 1983.

Sharp, A.M., <u>The History of Ufton Court</u>, Elliot Stock, 1892.

Sharratt, M. (ed.) <u>Lisbon College Register 1628-1813</u>, Catholic Record Society, 1991.

Sherwood, J. and Pevsner, N., <u>Oxfordshire</u>, Penguin, 1974.

Simpson, R., <u>Edmund Campion</u>, John Hodges, 1896.

Smith, D.J., <u>The Horse on the Cut</u>, Patrick Stephens, 1982.

Smith, E., <u>A History of Whiteknights</u>, University of Reading, 1957.

Stainer-Rice, Hilary, <u>Country Churches of the Chilterns</u>, booklet, Corinthian, 1983.

Stapleton, B., <u>A History of the Post-Reformation Catholic Missions in Oxfordshire</u>, Henry Froude, 1906.

Stapleton, B., 'Catholic Registers of Waterperry, Oxon, 1700-1793', <u>Records Series</u>, Vol.7, Catholic Records Society, c.1910.

Stark, A., <u>Bishop Richard Challoner - His Life and Times</u>, booklet, Guild of Our Lady of Ransom, c.1982.

Stonor, R.J., <u>Stonor</u>, R H Johns, 1951.

<u>Stonor</u>, booklet, Stonor Enterprises.

Surtees, R., <u>The History and Antiquities of the County Palatine of Durham</u>, Vol.2, 1820.

Tapp, M., <u>Walks in East Berkshire</u>, booklet, Countryside Books, 1984.

<u>The Four Visitations of Berkshire</u>, Vol.1, Harleian Society, 1907.

<u>The History of St Mary's Church, East Ilsley</u>, booklet, St Mary's Parish.

<u>The Martyrs of England and Wales, 1535-1680</u>, booklet, Catholic Truth Society, 1985.

The Shrine of Our Lady of Caversham, leaflet, Our Lady & St Anne, Caversham, c.1990.

Thompson, J.A.F., The Later Lollards, Oxford University Press, 1965.

Todd, J., Waterperry Church, booklet, Waterperry Parish, 1955.

Trappes-Lomax, T.B., 'The Englefields and their Contribution to the Survival of the Faith in Berkshire, Wiltshire, Hampshire and Leicestershire', Biographical Studies, Vol.1, No.2, Catholic Record Society, 1951.

Trimble, W.R., The Catholic Laity in Elizabethan England, Bellknap Press (Harvard), 1964.

Transactions of the Newbury & District Field Club, Vol.4, 1886-95.

Turner, W.H.(ed.), The Visitations of the County of Oxford, Harleian Society, 1871.

Wantage - The Official Guide, booklet, Wantage UDC & RDC, c.1969.

Waterton, E., Pietas Mariana Britannica, St Joseph's Catholic Library, 1879.

Watkins, J., 'Haseley Court Gardens', The Garden, October 1990.

Waugh, E., Edmund Campion, Longmans, Green & Co., 1935.

Wilcox, A., 'Berkshire Catholic Missions and Their Registers', Catholic Ancestor, Vol.3, No.4, 1991.

Williams, R., The Bardolf Aisle, booklet, Mapledurham Estate, 1977.

Williams, R., Mapledurham House, booklet, Mapledurham Estate, 1977.

Wilson, D., England in the Age of Thomas More, BCA/Granada, 1978.

Wilson, D.G., The Making of the Middle Thames, Spurbooks, 1977.

Victoria County Histories, Berkshire, Oxfordshire, Buckinghamshire and Durham.

Woolley, A.R., The Clarendon Guide to Oxford, Oxford University Press, 1983.

Worrall, E.S.(ed.), Returns of Papists 1767, Vol.2, Catholic Record Society, 1989.

Wright, A.S.N., The History of Buckland, privately published, 1966.

Van der Zee, H. & B., 1688: Revolution in the Family, Viking, 1988.

Yarrow, I., Berkshire, Robert Hale, 1952/74.

Youings, J., <u>The Dissolution of the Monasteries</u>, George Allen and Unwin, 1971.

Young, P. & Emberton, W., <u>Sieges of the Great Civil War</u>, Bell & Hyman, 1978.

Appendix C

Suggestions For Further Reading

This appendix lists a small selection of books which may be of interest to the general reader. For details of publishers see Appendix B, where the authors are listed alphabetically.

Background Reading
(Not specific to the Thames Valley)

John Bossy's 'The English Catholic Community, 1570-1850' is the most comprehensive sociological survey of the community from the Elizabethan Settlement until the re-establishment of a formal Catholic hierarchy in England.

J. C. H. Aveling's 'The Handle and the Axe' is a comprehensive history of Catholicism in England during the recusant period.

Edward Norman's 'Roman Catholicism in England' is a concise history covering the period from the Elizabethan Settlement to the Second Vatican Council.

A. Morey's 'The Catholic Subjects of Elizabeth I' and Alison Plowden's 'Danger to Elizabeth' both contain much about Catholics during the reign of the last Tudor monarch.

Prof. Scarisbrick's 'The Reformation and the English People' describes the long and erratic process of the English Reformation, and the responses to it by ordinary men and women.

Fr Godfrey Anstruther's two volumes on 'The Seminary Priests' contains biographies of the Catholic secular clergy of the Elizabethan and early Stuart periods.

Michael Hodgetts's 'Secret Hiding Places' is the definitive book on priest-holes and gives good coverage to Ufton Court and Nicholas Owen.

Dom Aidan Bellenger's 'The French Exiled Clergy' tells the story of the French clergy who sought refuge in England during the French Revolution.

Catholicism in the Thames Valley
(Many of these books should be held by the local studies sections of the Reading or Oxford central libraries)

'The Victoria County Histories' contain much on ecclesiastical, monastical and parish history. The Oxfordshire volumes are not yet complete. However, unlike the much older Berkshire volumes, they clearly identify recusant history for each parish.

Mrs Bryan Stapleton's 1906 book 'A History of the Post-Reformation Catholic Missions in Oxfordshire' is a major source of information.

John Eppstein's 'History of the Faith in an English Town', written in the 1920s, tells the story of Catholicism in Reading.

Dom Geoffrey Scott's booklet 'St Mary's Church, Woolhampton' contains much information on the survival of Catholicism in the Kennet Valley.

R. J. Stonor's 'Stonor' comprehensively recounts the story of the Stonor family and its associates.

Emily Climenson's 'The History of Shiplake' is nearly a hundred years old and contains much about the Plowdens of Shiplake Court.

Mary Sharp lived at Ufton Court during the late nineteenth century. Her book 'The History of Ufton Court' contains much on the Perkins and their connections.

E. C. Davey's 'Memoirs of an Oxfordshire Old Catholic Family etc.' is another late nineteenth century book and covers the Davey family of Dorchester and area.

Christine Kelly's 'Blessed Thomas Belson' is full of information on his life and times. It was published to coincide with his beatification in 1987 and was the main source for the chapter on Thomas Belson.

A. L. Humphreys 'East Hendred', written in the 1920s, contains much interesting information about the Eystons and their associates.

Volume two of Kathleen Philip's 'Reflected in Wantage' has a chapter on the survival of Catholicism in the Wantage area. It deals particularly with Lyford and East Hendred.

A. S. N. Wright's 'History of Buckland' contains much about the Yates and their successors, the Throckmortons.

Part of Biddy O'Sullivan's 'The Two Britwells' covers Britwell House and its Catholic history.

Michael Hodgett's recent and well illustrated 'Midlands Catholic Buildings' is a glove box sized 'Popish Pevsner' with details of about a hundred sites in the Archdiocese of Birmingham. More than a dozen of them are in southern Oxfordshire.

A p p e n d i x   D

U s e f u l   A d d r e s s e s

This list includes relevant societies, local studies centres and old Catholic houses regularly open to the public. A number of other houses mentioned in this book may welcome visitors from time to time, for instance, under the National Gardens Scheme.

Mapledurham House
Mapledurham
Reading
RG4 7TR
(Open to the public from spring to autumn)

Stonor House
Stonor Park
Henley-on-Thames
Oxfordshire
RG9 6HF
(Open to the public from spring to autumn)

Milton Manor House
Milton
Near Abingdon
Oxfordshire
OX14 4EN
(Open to the public from spring to autumn)

Basing House
Redbridge Lane
Basing
Basingstoke
RG24 0HB
(Open to the public from April to September, not Mondays or Tuesdays)

Ufton Court Residential Centre
Green Lane
Ufton Nervet
Reading
RG7 4HA
(Open to the public on one day of the year only)

Englefield House
Englefield
Near Reading
RG7 5EN
(Open to the public at certain times)

Waterperry Horticultural Centre
Waterperry
Near Wheatley
Oxfordshire
OX9 1JZ
(The horticultural centre is in the grounds of
Waterperry House which are open to the public)

The Catholic Record Society
Membership Officer
Dr L Gooch, MA
12 Melbourne Place
Wolsingham
Co. Durham
DL13 3EH
(Founded in 1904 to make available material necessary
for the study of English & Welsh Catholic history
since the Reformation)

William Dawson & Sons Ltd
Back Issues Department
Cannon House
Park Road
Folkestone
Kent
CT19 5EE
(Suppliers of Catholic Record Society publications)

The Catholic Family History Society
The General Secretary
Mrs Barbara Murray
2 Winscombe Crescent
Ealing
London
W5 1AZ
(Publishers of Catholic Ancestor magazine)

Oxford Central Library
Westgate
Oxford
OX1 1DJ
(Includes a local studies section)

Reading Central Library
Abbey Square
Reading
RG1 3BQ
(Includes a local studies section)

I n d e x

of people and buildings

Blount, Mary Eugenia, 137
Blount, Michael, (d. 1649), 93
Blount, Michael Henry, 155
Blount, Michael Henry, 161
Blount, Michael I, 127
Blount, Michael II, 127, 139
Blount, Michael III, 151, 153, 155
Blount, Philippa (nee Benlowes), 93
Blount, Sir Charles, 80, 88, 89
Blount, Sir Christopher, 63, 68
Blount, Sir Michael, 60, 75
Blount, Sir Richard, 60, 61, 80, 93
Blount, Teresa, 115, 117
Blount, Walter, 93, 100
Blount's Court, Rotherfield Peppard, 17, 39, 83, 89, 97, 101,
    105, 107, 113
Bluet, Fr Thomas, 64, 65
Blunden, Andrew, 43, 66
Bold, Richard, 43, 44
Bolingbroke, Lord, 116
Boulter, Elizabeth, 138
Bourne, Sir John, 66
Bowyer, Ludovic, 84
Bray, see Lowbrook Manor
Braybrooke, James, 28, 35, 59, 95
Braybrooke, Margaret, 95
Braybrooke, Martha, 59
Braybrooke, Richard, 95
Braziers Park, Ipsden, 121
Breedons of Bere Court, 13
Bridges, alias of Fr Edward Grately, 53
Bridges, Anthony, 41, 60
Bridges, Eleanor, 41
Brightwell Baldwin church, 10
Brightwell Park, 9
Brimpton Manor (Farm), 45, 59
Brimpton parish church, 84, 117
Brimpton, St Leonard's chapel, 45
Brimpton, see also Hyde Hall, Hyde End
Brinkley, Stephen, 38, 40
Britwell House, 123, 125, 139, 140, 142, 145, 151, 153, 155,
    157
Britwell Salome, see Priest's House,
Brome family of Boarstall, 51
Brome, George, 44
Brooks, Bishop James of Gloucester, 18, 23
Brown, Fr William, 123
Browne family of Caversham, 69
Browne, Eleanor (nee Bridges), 41
Browne, Elizabeth (nee Blount), 100
Browne, George great grandson of Sir George, 118
Browne, George, son of Sir George, 100
Browne, Joanna or Jane, 72
Browne, Mary (later Dancastle), 83

Dorchester, St Birinus's RC church, 116, 159
Dormer, Charles, 5th Lord, 125
Dormer, Fr Charles, 6th Lord, 126
Dormer, Lady Jane, Duchess of Feria, 73, 103
Dormer, Katherine (nee Fettiplace), 125
Dormer, Robert, 1st Earl of Caernarfon, 89
Dormer, Sir Michael, 75
Dormer, Sir Robert, 52, 72, 94
Dormer, W. of Caversham, 88
Douai Abbey, Woolhampton, 126, 144
Doughty family, 121, 122, 156
Doughty, Mr of Beenham, 128
Duclos, Fr Noël, 155
Dumouriez, Marshal, 149

Earley Whiteknights, see Whiteknights
East Court, Finchampstead, 73
East Hendred parish church, 9, 110, 115, 121, 152
East Hendred, Abbey Manor, 78, 79
East Hendred, see also Hendred House
East Ilsley parish church, 9, 71
East Ilsley, see Ilsley Farm and Ilsley Hall
East family of Bledlow, 51
East, Dorothy (later Fitzherbert), 51, 89
East, Richard, 42
Edmonds, Ambrose, 52
Edwards, Thomas, 41
Eliot, George (informer), 35, 37
Ellis, graduate of Magdalen College, 53
Emerson, Bro. Ralph, 34, 35
Englefield Farm, 58, 82
Englefield House, 16, 18, 45, 58, 63, 98
Englefield parish church, 82, 98
Englefield, see also Ilsley's Farm
Englefield family of Whiteknights, 150
Englefield, Anthony I, 82, 88, 97, 100
Englefield, Anthony II, 113, 115
Englefield, Fr Felix (Charles), 126
Englefield, Francis, son of Sir Henry 142
Englefield, Henry son of Anthony II, 116, 117, 122, 126
Englefield, Henry son of Francis II, 96
Englefield, John, 20, 42
Englefield, Lady Catherine (nee Fettiplace), 22, 32, 36, 127
Englefield, Margaret, 58
Englefield, Martha (later Blount), 115
Englefield, Sir Charles, 126
Englefield, Sir Francis I, 16-19, 22, 25-28, 37, 42-46, 48, 49, 58, 59, 127
Englefield, Sir Francis II, 42, 43, 52, 67, 71, 72, 82, 96
Englefield, Sir Henry, 126, 127, 141-144
Englefield, Sir Henry Charles, 143, 144, 146
Englefield, Sir Thomas, 100
Englefield, Teresa Ann (later Cholmely), 144
Englefield, William, 96

Garnet, Fr Henry, 43, 50, 61, 69, 70
Gayler (informer), 61
Gerard, Fr John, 52, 57, 59, 61
Gibbes, Dr William, 83
Giffard, Archbishop William, 29, 52
Giffard, Bishop Bonaventure, 124
Giffard, Jane (later Yate), 29
Ginacre, Catherine, 42
Gladstone, Lord, 161
Gloucester Hall, Oxford, 63
Godquin, Fr Jean, 158
Godstow Abbey, 11, 49
Gondré, Fr Jean, 158
Goodman, Dr Godfrey, 67, 78
Goring Priory, 11
Gother, Fr John, 128
Grange, The, Shaw, 83
Grately, Fr Edward, 53
Great Coxwell Manor, 32
Great Haseley Manor, see Horseman family and Lenthall family
Great Milton parish church, 75
Great Shefford Manor (Farm), 41, 60, 80, 100
Green, Charles, 87
Greenwood, John, 28
Greys Court, 17, 60, 81
Grimstone, Fr, 134
Grindal, Archbishop, 29
Grovelands, Shiplake, 109
Gunnes, Fr Gregory, 42

Hall Grove, Bagshot, 112
Hall family, 114
Hall, Benedict, 76, 95, 119
Hall, Benedicta (later Gage), 119
Hall, Frances (nee Fortescue), 119
Hall, Henry Benedict, 115, 119
Hampden, John, 94
Hampstead Norreys Manor, 138
Hanington, John, 24
Harcourt, Fr, 103
Harcourt, Mary (later Taverner), 47
Harcourt, Michael, 73
Harcourt, Robert, 73
Harleyford Manor, 43
Harman, Sr Julian, 40
Harpsden Court, 37
Hart Hall, Oxford, 63
Hartley, Fr William, 34, 38, 40
Haseley Court, 105, 138
Haskey, Mrs, 124
Haskey, Sarah (later Davey), 159
Hawes, Francis, 122
Hawkins, Anne (later Hildesley), 86
Hawkins, Mary (later Eyston), 123

Lingen, Fr George, 46
Lingham, George, 46
Little Coxwell Manor, 32
Little Haseley, see Haseley Court
Little Marlow Priory, 11
Littlecote House, 107
Littlestoke Manor, 30, 85, 105, 121, 153
Lloyd, Bishop William, 107
Lockhart, J. G., 159
Longuet, Fr Jean Baptiste, 156 et seq
Lovelace, Lord, 107
Lovell, Fr, 104
Lowbrook Manor, Bray, 96
Lowe, Sr Joan or Philippa, 40
Loyalty House, see Basing House
Lyford Grange, 34 et seq, 43, 86

Macarthy, Fr, 128
Madew, Fr Edward, 133, 135, 141
Magdalen College, Oxford, 53, 63, 101, 106
Mahew, Fr Edward, see Madew
Maidencourt Farm, 41, 111, 133
Maisonette, Earley, 152
Manfield, Sir Edward, 77
Mannock, Fr William, 112, 113
Mannock, Lady Mary (nee Brownlow-Doughty), 156
Manor Farm, Brimpton, see Brimpton Manor
Manor Farm, East Ilsley, see Ilsley Farm
Mapledurham House, 60, 88, 89, 115, 117, 127, 142, 144, 151, 153
Mapledurham parish church, 60, 84
Marlborough, Duke of, 114, 115, 118
Marlow, St Peter's RC church, 13
Marlston Manor, near Bucklebury, 95, 96
Martin, Abbé Noël, 150
Martin, Fr Thomas, 130
Martin, William Byam, 144
Martyn, Mary (nee Reade), 14
Marvyn, Lady, 37, 45, 95
Mary I, Queen, local connections with her regime, 17 et seq
Massey, John, 107
Meales Farm, Sulhamstead, 59
Medmenham Abbey, 11
Medmenham, see also Danesfield
Merton College, Oxford, 74
Metcalfe, Maria Teresa (later Eyston), 9, 157
Meysey, Thomas, 46
Miard de la Blardière, Fr Pierre, 152
Migheals, Burghfield, 59
Milner, Bishop John, 155, 160
Milton Manor, 105, 108, 135, 141, 143, 151, 153
Milton parish church, 143
Milton, Christopher, 88
Milton, John, 87, 88, 90, 94, 102

Perkins family of Beenham, 135, 141
Perkins family of Ilsley, 67
Perkins family of Ufton, 72-74, 133, 141
Perkins, Anna (nee Plowden), 45, 97
Perkins, Anne (nee Eyston), 99
Perkins, Anne of Beenham, 110
Perkins, Arabella (nee Fermor), 116, 126
Perkins, Catherine (later Tattersall), 74
Perkins, Charles, 140, 141
Perkins, Edward, 77
Perkins, Frances (nee Winchcombe), 77
Perkins, Francis I, 45, 46, 48, 49, 58, 62, 63, 71, 74, 77, 95, 97
Perkins, Francis (grandson of Francis Perkins I), 77
Perkins, Francis II, 78, 79, 95, 97
Perkins, Francis III, 110
Perkins, Francis IV, 115, 116, 126
Perkins, Francis of Padworth, cousin of Francis Perkins I, 46
Perkins, Francis V, 126, 130
Perkins, Francis VI, 140
Perkins, Henry of Ilsley, 46, 58
Perkins, James, 130, 140
Perkins, Jane (nee Winchcombe), 77
Perkins, John of Beenham, conformed c.1606, 71
Perkins, John of Beenham, conformed c.1660, 97
Perkins, John of Ufton, 128, 140, 141
Perkins, Margaret of Ilsley, 58
Perkins, Richard of Padworth, cousin of Francis Perkins I, 46
Perkins, Richard, uncle of Francis Perkins I, 48
Perkins, Richard of Beenham, cousin of Francis Perkins I, 58, 71
Perkins, Richard of Beenham, JP, 99, 110
Perkins, Thomas, 62
Perkins, William of Brimpton, 19, 20, 45
Persons, Fr Robert, 31 et seq, 34 et seq, 44, 49, 50, 55
Petre, Bishop Benjamin, 124
Petre, Fr Edward, 104
Petre, Lord Robert, 116
Phillipson, Dom John, 99
Phillipson, Dom William, 99
Phillipson, George, 99
Phillipson, Margaret (nee Eyston), 99
Pishill Anglican church, 84, 149
Pitts, Arthur, 31
Pitts, Fr Arthur, 34, 83
Pitts, Margaret, 31
Plowden family of Shiplake, 113
Plowden, Anna (later Perkins), 45, 97
Plowden, Anne (later Lake), 77
Plowden, Earl, see Edmund Plowden II
Plowden, Edmund I, 19, 20, 25, 27, 28, 30, 37, 42, 43, 46, 67, 77, 78
Plowden, Edmund II (Sir), 47, 100
Plowden, Edmund III, 100

Wollascott, William IV, 84, 97
Wollascott, William, son of William Wollascott IV, 97
Wollascott, William V, 117, 118, 126-128, 133
Wood, Anthony à, 89
Wood, John the Younger, 133
Woodcote House, 121
Woodley Lodge (later Bulmershe Court), 13, 152, 160
Woodstock Park, 17
Woolhampton Lodge & estate, 144, 147, 152
Woolhampton Lodge, Baron of, 161
Woolhampton parish church, 133
Woolhampton, St Mary's RC church, 144
Woolhampton, see also Douai Abbey
Wright, Fr Peter, 91
Wright, Stephen, 136
Wycherley, William, 113
Wycliffe, John, 4

Yate, Edward I of Buckland, 29, 52
Yate, Edward II of Buckland (Sir), 79
Yate, Francis of Lyford, 34
Yate, Jane (nee Giffard), 29
Yate, John of Buckland, 18, 27-29
Yate, John of Lyford, 31
Yate, John, son of Sir Charles, 103
Yate, John, Merchant of the Staple, 35
Yate, Lady Frances (nee Gage), 103
Yate, Lady Mary (nee Packington), 82, 96, 101, 102
Yate, Mary of Lyford (later Eyston), 74
Yate, Mrs (mother of Francis), 34 et seq
Yate, Sir Charles of Buckland, 103
Yate, Sir John I of Buckland, 82
Yate, Sir John I of Buckland, 96
Yate, Sir John I of Buckland, 101
Yate, Sir John II of Buckland, 110
Yattendon Manor, 138
Yaxley, Fr Richard, 53-55
Young family, 144, 145
Young, Arthur, 159
Young, Elizabeth (nee Hyde?), 145
Young, Fr Anthony, 145
Young, John, 118
Young, William, 95